THE WORLD WE MADE

When I started teaching in 2022, the world was in a much more troubled state than it is today - both economically and environmentally. 28 years on, it's a very, very different world, as you'll see - and most of the world's countries are both more stable and more content.

This project has one simple aim: to tell the story of how we got our world back from the brink of collapse to where we are now in 2050.

We're still hard pressed by the legacy of all those wasted decades, but there's a renewed sense of purpose as a family of nations, and we have confidence in our shared ability to make a better world for all those who come after us.

Alex McKay
31/12/2050

Contents

Here's a bit about me before we launch in.

My name is Alex McKay. I'm 50 years old, and I've been a history teacher for the last 28 years, 19 of them at Ashton Vale Community College. My family and I have lived in the same house, just a few hundred metres from the College, throughout that time.

But now we're moving. In January next year, I start a new job as Head Teacher at the other end of the country. This news prompted my senior year students – some of whom I've been teaching from the day they first arrived at Ashton Vale – to suggest that I should write a 'history' of the changes I've seen happen in the world – with them as my research assistants.

Somehow, I found it impossible to refuse. And they've certainly lived up to their side of the bargain, throwing themselves into the role of the Research Team for this project with real passion.

So that's what follows: 50 snapshots (writing one a week, throughout the year, was the only way we could keep it going) drawn somewhat randomly from things that have happened over the last 30 years or so.

What's really jumped out at us in doing the research for this project was a sense of impending doom in the 2010s. Everything that had made sense of people's lives since the end of the Second World War in 1945 had pretty much ground to a halt by then. Economic growth, globalization, consumerism, profit maximization – politicians kept dragging them out, like talismanic charms, but they'd lost all their power.

In fact, by 2018, most people in the 'rich world' (as it was known then) had seen a serious decline in their standard of living over the preceding decade. Unemployment in Europe was at an astonishing 15 per cent in 2018 – and worse for young people. And although the economies in countries like China, India and Brazil were doing much better, comparatively, most people there were confronting such horrendous social and environmental problems as to put at risk all their new-found economic success.

Much of the 'poor world', meanwhile, was still very poor indeed. In 2000 (the year I was born), the rich world had committed itself to a number of so-called Millennium Development Goals, to be achieved by 2015. Come 2016, the scorecard still looked pretty depressing. Rich-world countries clearly felt that they had a hard enough job looking after their own citizens at that time, let alone supporting those in far-flung countries where corruption was rife and life was cheap – or so it seemed to them.

Rich world, poor world, developed or emerging – it didn't really matter. Whatever their persuasion, politicians looked cornered, exhausted, incapable of addressing the world as it was, rather than the world as they still wanted it to be. They were weighed down by the legacy of mind-numbing levels of debt built up over the preceding 30 years, and were devoid of any compelling vision as to what should happen over the next 30 years. Fundamentalists of every description – political and religious – had begun to fill the space vacated by the mainstream.

Happily, that generation of politicians did not go unchallenged – even then. By 2015, there was a vast army of young people, NGOs (non-governmental organizations), business leaders, entrepreneurs and academics who had already called time on the old world view.

We're still very hard pressed by the legacy of all those wasted decades, but with a renewed sense of purpose as a family of nations, celebrating afresh the collective genius of what it is that makes the human species so special.

And we have confidence, once again, in our shared ability to make a better world for all those who come after us.

2014	• President Obama launches EarthCorps, a global initiative • 20th anniversary of Convention on Biological Diversity	
2015	• Pro-Poor Urban Alliance launched	
2016	• Emergency Report of the Intergovernmental Panel on Climate Change • China phases out all incandescent light bulbs • Grid parity for photovoltaics	
2017	• Water Riots in the Middle East • Peak oil moment • Cap and Prosper Act (launch of Rebuild America)	Death of my father
2018	• Enough! movement (demonstrations from July to October) • Papal Decree on contraception • World Bank report on wealth distribution in the twenty-first century • The USA imposes EU-style carbon standards for liquid fuels	Finished school Volunteered with EarthCorps in Kenya (Oct 2018 - March 2019)
2019	• Cyber-terrorist attacks on nuclear reactors in the USA & UK	First year of university
2020	• Houston Concord on Climate Change • Agreement on International Financial Transaction Tax • GM breakthrough on nitrogen fixing in wheat and rice • New EU Directives on Maximum Working Time	Second year abroad, studying at Tsinghua University, China
2021	• Hurricane Wilma devastates the USA • The Internet Wars (2021–2030) • Introduction of Universal Taxation Convention	Third year of university
2022	• Kiev Treaty on Nuclear Decommissioning • Lhasa Declaration • First Global Geoengineering Summit in Dhaka, Bangladesh • International Financial Transaction Tax comes into force • Vigo Declaration	Started teaching

2023
- Rimini Riots
- The War of Ages (2023–2038)
- Oil and gas prices hit highest point
- Agreement on Global Aviation Carbon Cap

Got married!

2024
- Shanghai Inundation
- Arrest of Luiz Hernandez in Mexico

Birth of our daughter, Marika

2025
- The Great Famine
- First EV car to do 500 miles between recharges
- Lithium-air batteries available
- International Court for the Environment established
- First commercial flights with 100% biofuels
- UK's last Trident submarine decommissioned
- National and Community Service Act introduced in the UK

2027
- Convention on Cyber and Bio-Aggression signed

Birth of our son, Ben

2028
- Oil blow out in the Kara Sea, Russian Arctic
- Launch of C2050 Airliner

2031
- InterJust campaign
- European SuperGrid completed
- Fourth Global Geoengineering Summit in Dhaka

Started teaching at Ashton Vale

2032
- Global food riots

2034
- 40th anniversary of Convention on Biological Diversity

2035
- RED Rocks Convention in Ecuador
- Final evacuation of New Orleans, USA

Attended Ecuador Summit on Biodiversity

2037
- Completion of new Thames Barrier, UK

2041
- Reconciliation between China and Tibet

Visited Tibet

2045
- Worst year on record for climate change disasters

Birth of Haruki, our first grandchild

2049
- Major report from American Civil Liberties Union on internet privacy

Ben moved to Los Angeles

07.01.2050

My World

This is where we've lived ever since I started teaching at Ashton Vale in 2031, in the two units closest to the road. Our son, Ben, and our daughter, Marika, grew up here. Marika has her own child now – Haruki, who was born in 2046 – and lives in Japan, but she is still here in a way, most days of the year, via the videowall. Ben prefers to keep himself to himself.

You can't actually see our solar array here, but it's hopelessly out of date anyway, which means we make almost nothing on the electricity we sell back to our local grid. But the house is brilliantly insulated (we invested in the new multi-glaze windows more than five years ago) so we still pay nothing for our energy.

I guess we kind of got stuck here. It's true that people move around much less these days than they used to, and we couldn't see any point in moving just for the sake of it – although it did make us think when Marika settled in Japan with her partner. And then Ben headed off to LA just last year.

Anyway, that's what our 2020s flat-pack house looks like from the outside. It's seen better days, but nothing ever seems to go wrong with it. They made homes to last back then.

And over the page is what you see, looking out from our bedroom window. Pretty much everything that we need is no more than a kilometre from the house, even though we're more or less in the middle of the city.

That's our Community Car Club to the right – a three-vehicle dock, which just about works for the 100 households who belong to the Club (I think they are now planning to upgrade anyway). Nearest to the house is part of our Community Farm (of which more later), and the tree that Marika planted when she was seven years old. Over on the left is Ashton Vale Community College, where I teach, and next to it (in a building that's more than 100 years old), the Fabrication Centre. And the big city beyond!

This is our media room, with two video walls. We use the wall on the left as our 'window on the world', and we change the background all the time to suit our mood. We can randomly connect with new places around the world – or (what I like to do) go back into the past to some amazingly sophisticated re-creations of different historical periods. The other screen is our comms wall, which we use for everything from films, mindshares, news and sport to arranging meetings and outings, as well as linking up with friends and family. It's been brilliant with Marika now living in Japan, and we talk most days, sometimes over breakfast or when I get back from the College. That's Haruki, top left!

We're online pretty much all the time. Household by household, we pick and choose what works for us personally in terms of available systems. For instance, we've long since rejected all the FoodWatch stuff, which monitors sell-by dates, orders the food and does everything short of actually cooking it. We like doing that ourselves. On the other hand, anything to do with energy efficiency, water recycling or waste has become so routine that we don't have to bother about any of that from one year to the next – whilst still saving a lot of money. Likewise, one of the things that works brilliantly for us is all the CommunityShare stuff – hiring bits of kit that you might only want occasionally, taking full advantage of our community TimeBank scheme, getting things made in the Fabrication Centre, taking part in impromptu musical events, pop-up cook-ins and so on.

Together with my Research Team at Ashton Vale, it's been really interesting mapping out how different things were. One of the main ideas at the beginning of the twenty-first century was 'consumerism' – emphasizing that each individual should aspire to own and consume as much as possible – and that's what kept the wheels of the economy spinning for 40 years or more. But then came the crash of 2008 and the Age of Austerity that followed, together with accelerating climate change and the collapse of political authority in many countries around the world.

By the early 2020s, that age of selfish consumerism was over, personal ownership became much less important, while renting, sharing, swapping and bartering became the new norm. New web businesses sprang up all the time, enabling direct peer-to-peer relationships that developed in every sector of the economy – and almost always in ways that saved us lots of money. It was referred to as 'collaborative consumption' back then.

Back in the 2020s, for instance, I was a keen user of a web-based company called Airbnb, which enabled people to rent out their homes and spare rooms to tourists and visitors – who got good, cheap accommodation without having to check into a hotel. It was a huge success, and since then this model has been copied by small companies everywhere providing peer-to-peer services on a completely local basis.

These innovations didn't just promote collaborative consumption: they provided the means for collaborative wealth creation. My favourite is a company called Kiva, which is still going strong 45 years on! This allows anybody in the world to lend money to entrepreneurs anywhere else in the world via peer-to-peer micro-financing. (By the way, the Team discovered that 'kiva' is the Swahili word for 'unity', which goes some way towards explaining how this kind of collaborative approach to finance pretty much killed off the old-fashioned idea of 'charity'.)

And that's more or less where we are with consumerism today – not just in the once-rich world, but throughout the global economy. All the ridiculous status seeking and ownership fetishism that dominated the second half of the twentieth century has all but disappeared. Happily, living standards are now relatively good in almost all countries – but only after a lot of pain.

For instance, we've spent a lot of time following developments in Japan over the last few years – not just because of Marika, but because Japan provides a really good example of what economists today call 'twenty-first century cooperative capitalism'.

It's been suggested that it was the sheer number of 'shocks to the system' endured by Japan earlier in the century that sowed the seeds of the economic revolution there: a decade of economic stagnation; the nuclear disaster at Fukushima and the first tsunami in 2011; the second tsunami in 2017; a more painful 'demographic time bomb' (in terms of the ratio of young and old) than in any other OECD country; chronic political instability throughout the 2020s following the currency collapse in 2023; and the continuing stand-off with China – amongst others.

But Japan is one resilient country: with each new crisis, the population increasingly fell back on their centuries-old tradition of cooperatives – in retailing, agriculture, forestry, small-scale manufacturing, house building and so on. There are now hundreds of thousands of thriving cooperatives all across Japan, and they seem to cohabit perfectly comfortably with the 20 or so large Japanese multinationals that still play a critical part in the global economy.

Again, it's all a question of balance: small is no more beautiful than big, and virtual no more exciting than bricks and mortar. And 'not-consuming' can be just as rewarding as consuming – even though that was once thought of as complete heresy by those twentieth-century economists whose sterile orthodoxies took such a long time to die out in this century.

13.01.2050

Solar Revolutions

The Economist, 6 March 2016.

Here's an interesting issue of 'The Economist' that we've dug up from 2016, with a huge feature on the development of solar power. By then, people had woken up to the fact that solar technology would be able to meet a huge chunk of the world's demand for electricity.

The key moment for solar power was when we reached 'grid parity' – the point at which a unit of electricity from solar energy cost no more than a unit of electricity from any other source, and often a lot less. This had a major psychological effect: solar was no longer seen as an irrelevant add-on, but as the main thing. Different countries reached grid parity at different dates (due to rather more sunshine in some countries than in others), anywhere between 2012 and 2018.

In the USA, for instance, grid parity helped redefine the American Dream, as it freed both individuals and the country as a whole from dependence on big foreign energy companies. Ironically, however, it was the Chinese that originally made all this possible.

PV panels are universal, and the less energy you use yourself, the more you sell. Once people got their heads around that business opportunity, energy efficiency wasn't such a hard nut to crack!

From a standing start at the turn of the twenty-first century, Chinese companies gained a greater and greater share of the total solar market over the following decades – with a good deal of help from the Chinese government. Forty years on, they still dominate the market.

Today, there are thousands of large-scale solar plants generating very low-carbon electricity all over the world. Some of the biggest are in the western and southern states of the USA, along the shores of the Mediterranean, and across the Middle East and Southeast Asia. The dream child for Europe's biggest solar venture was the Desertec project, launched in 2009. Twelve of the biggest European companies set out to turn a solar dream into reality – which required huge investments, not just in the solar farms themselves, but also in the high-voltage direct current transmission lines bringing the electricity directly from the farms in North Africa to Europe's emerging super-grid.

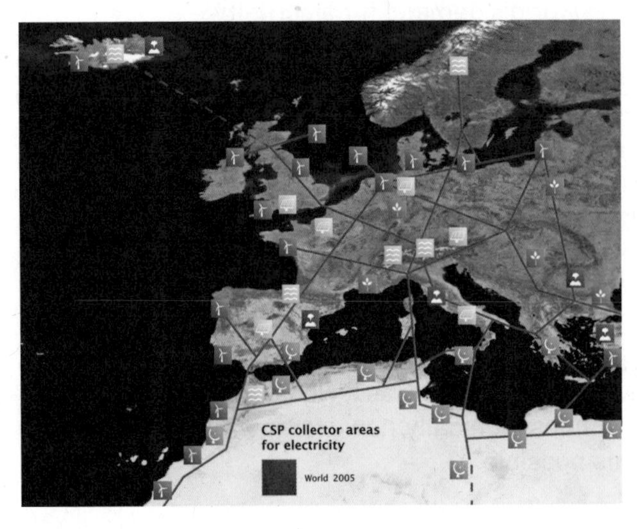

The world's deserts receive more energy from the sun in 6 hours than humans consume in a year. The red square in this DESERTEC map shows the theoretical area of desert that would be required to provide solar power for the entire world. Understandably, perceptions of the strategic significance of solar energy began to change around that time.

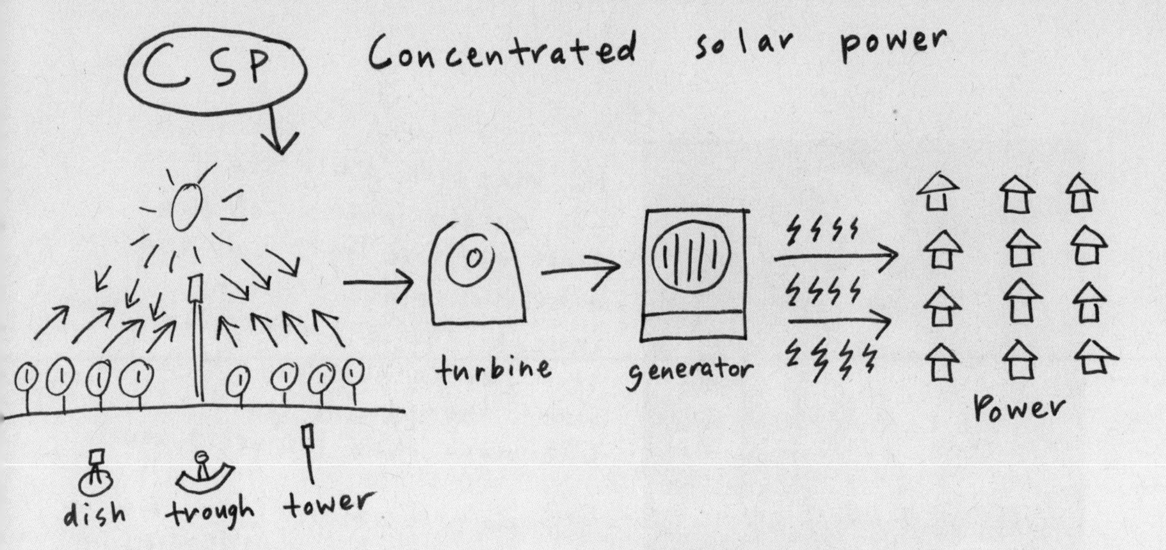

Variations of the two main solar technologies (photovoltaics (PV) and concentrated solar power) now dominate global energy markets as comprehensively as coal, oil and gas dominated those markets back in the twentieth century.

NEARLY 30% OF TOTAL ELECTRICITY DEMAND NOW COMES FROM SOLAR.

It's delivered through installations of every conceivable shape and size, some of them off-grid, and some of them connected to the grid; some on roofs or on the ground, and some embedded in windows, walls or roof tiles; some still using the old crystalline technologies, but most now using thin-film technologies of one kind or another.

And all competing furiously with each other!

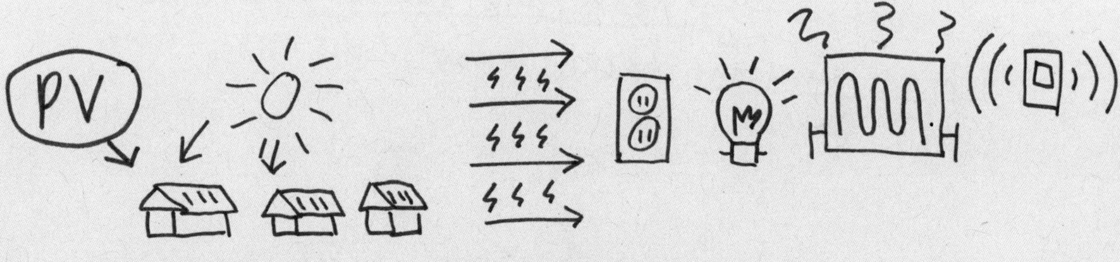

Photovoltaics

Thomas Edison
(1847 – 1931)

He may look a bit stuffy, but as the inventor of the first electric light bulb and a host of other brilliant innovations, engineers today still revere this guy. He saw what the future could be like more than 100 years ago:

'I'D PUT MY MONEY ON THE SUN AND SOLAR ENERGY. WHAT A SOURCE OF POWER! I HOPE WE DON'T HAVE TO WAIT UNTIL OIL AND COAL RUN OUT BEFORE WE TACKLE THAT.'

Unfortunately, with oil, coal and gas being so cheap throughout most of the 20th century, that's pretty much what happened!

We now know that solar power has been THE BIGGEST SINGLE GAME CHANGER OVER THE LAST 40 YEARS ~ substituting real time sunlight for the stored sunlight locked away in all those fossil fuels.

This has been a success by any standards. The prosperity and stability enjoyed today by countries like Morocco, Tunisia, Algeria and Egypt has a lot to do with the huge growth in solar power within those countries, and the same is true all around the world. Initially, there were lots of problems coping with high winds and dust (because of the desert conditions), but advanced cleaning systems using either water or compressed air soon sorted that out. There were also serious political problems, with radical political groups in North Africa protesting at the 'theft of Africa's solar birthright by the EU's mega-rich'. It wasn't until 2023 that the EU and the World Bank made the commitment to a second round of investment, to help power the rest of Africa as well as Europe.

Ground-mounted solar panels, just outside Timbuktu, Mali, 2019.

In 2015, there were still around one billion people who were not connected to any electricity grid, most of them in Africa. This contributed significantly to very high levels of poverty and hunger. But coming off the back of the mobile telephony revolution, cheap solar power and other renewable technologies that didn't need to be connected to the grid transformed the lives of hundreds of millions of Africans within the course of a single decade.

Many of the early solar technology investments look pretty clunky now, in light of all the amazing research work done since then in Germany, the USA and China, both in crystalline-silicon PV (with laser cutters dramatically reducing costs) and thin-film technologies. Germany led the world in terms of photovoltaic (PV) technology for two decades, after deciding to opt out of nuclear energy in 2011 and increase R&D investment in solar energy and other renewables. Even small refinements (such as self-cleaning coatings or special films to prevent the solar cells getting over-heated) made a big difference. The breakthroughs in nano-PV (using nanotechnology and smart semiconductors) produced by Germany's Fraunhofer Solar Institute led to PV cells becoming three times more efficient by the late 2020s. And since then, it's just got better and better.

A concentrated solar power (CSP) plant in a remote area of Riverside County, California. Commissioned in 2015, this was one of the early mega-plants, and it is still operating very successfully today.

20.01.2050

Water – A Matter of Life and Death

They called it the 'Arab Spring' back in 2011. There were years of chaos, followed by more or less stable democracies in Tunisia, Egypt and Libya, followed fairly soon after by Syria, Algeria, the Yemen and Bahrain. It took even longer (and three separate uprisings) in Iran to get rid of that country's authoritarian theocracy. And that was enough to make even Saudi Arabia start off on its own reform programme.

The 2017 Water Riots had a massive impact in many of those countries – out of the blue, some people said, although it's hard to imagine how they could have been so unaware of what was going on. 1.7 billion people at that time were living in conditions of extreme water stress.

As soon as people saw the images of the first riots in the West Bank, hundreds of equally hard-pressed communities suffering from one kind of water-related injustice or another (through the theft of their water or the sheer lack of it) seized that moment to try and put things right. There were thousands of protests, occupations, riots – and the death toll was grim. Most of the protests were in the Middle East and Africa. Big dam projects in Turkey and Syria (on the Tigris and Euphrates) had caused severe problems downstream in Iraq and Iran, while the Jordan river had been a flashpoint for decades. At that time, nine countries depended on the waters of the Nile, which was massively over-exploited even then.

Tragically, one common feature of nearly all those countries was population growth way above the global average, resulting in very large numbers of young men with little if any prospect of full-time employment. An explosive situation, with water the cause that lit the fuse.

Those were the stories that grabbed the headlines in those days, month after month. There was a real fear of 'water wars' – of countries who saw their national security directly threatened going to war with each other. Thankfully, those risks were largely averted: after the riots, the UN machine belatedly moved into action and many deals were done between countries, which in turn unlocked new investments.

Ataturk Dam on the Euphrates River, Turkey, 2027 – a source of constant tension throughout much of this century.

But there was a deeper injustice going on back then. It's hard to believe, but 750 million people still had no access to safe drinking water, and 1.4 billion had no proper sanitation or sewage treatment. And it was often the poorest who paid the most for their water at the hands of ruthless water traders. For the world not to have sorted out such basic entitlements by 2017 was a shocking indictment of political systems at that time. A lot of the deprivation caused by water scarcity could so easily have been avoided.

Although water isn't like oil – reserves of which are strictly finite – it is only available to us in a useable form if we manage it properly. My father, who was a water engineer, kept pointing this out, but until the riots happened people were just blind to the combined impact of rising population and increased demand. Something had to give.

But even then, around 2017, it wasn't a totally negative scene. Places like California and many parts of Europe were already very efficient in their use of water for irrigation. Rainwater harvesting systems had become commonplace in the USA, South Korea, Germany and other European countries, and Australian cities had achieved very good reductions in domestic water use, largely through simple things like spending less time in the shower, not washing the car, and choosing drought-resistant plants for their gardens.

Sana'a was once the capital city of the Yemen – and had been for centuries, drawing on supplies of scarce fossil water. (Some people say it provided the inspiration for the 'Dune' trilogy, Frank Herbert's science-fiction masterpiece.) But from 2015 onwards, those scarce resources began to run out, and water had to be tankered in, at great cost, from desalination plants on the coast.

The population exodus started, gathering momentum over the next 10 years as the port of Aden became Yemen's principal city. Sana'a is now completely deserted, providing an exotic destination for hardy travellers who can cope with its blistering temperatures.

Aerial view of farms drawing water from the Ogallala Aquifer, Great Plains, USA, 2010 and 2050. Trillions of gallons of fossil water drawn from the Ogallala Aquifer transformed more than a 100 million acres of marginal farming land in Texas and Oklahoma in the second half of the twentieth century. But in the dry southern half of the region there wasn't enough rainfall to recharge the aquifer. More efficient irrigation systems kept things going until around 2020, but we all know what happened in the end. Conflicts over water became commonplace, often causing serious violence.

At one level, all we've done since then is to build on the lessons we learned in the Ogallala (above) and elsewhere. Some things haven't changed much: for instance, we still use roughly 70 per cent of available water for agriculture. But we now produce nearly twice as much food as we did in 2017, for the same amount of water. And in terms of total global manufacturing, we make nearly three times as much stuff today as we did back in 2017, using half as much water! It was the small things that have made the biggest difference: grey water recycling; waterless toilets; hydroponic and aquaponic farming systems; drip feed irrigation – all of which I'll be revisiting a bit later.

In contrast, some of the big water diversion schemes in the USA, China and India (pumping vast amounts of water from water-rich areas to water-scarce areas) proved to be far too costly in terms of energy consumption – let alone emissions of CO_2.

But despite the successes, there are still large numbers of people living in water-stressed regions where accessing the bare essentials is a real struggle.

This has been a difficult topic for me to write about. My father was killed in the 2017 riots. He was working on a water efficiency project on the Palestinian West Bank, using his skills as an experienced engineer to help mediate between the Palestians and Israeli settlers. He mailed us the night before he died:

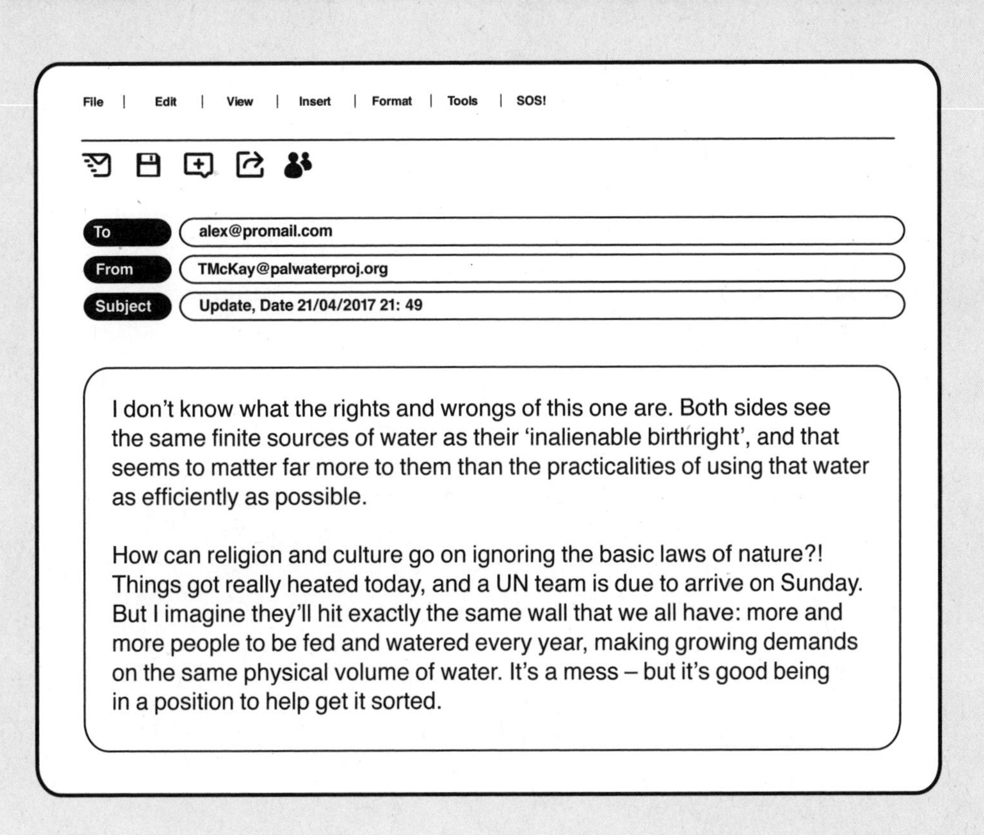

File | Edit | View | Insert | Format | Tools | SOS!

To: alex@promail.com

From: TMcKay@palwaterproj.org

Subject: Update, Date 21/04/2017 21: 49

I don't know what the rights and wrongs of this one are. Both sides see the same finite sources of water as their 'inalienable birthright', and that seems to matter far more to them than the practicalities of using that water as efficiently as possible.

How can religion and culture go on ignoring the basic laws of nature?! Things got really heated today, and a UN team is due to arrive on Sunday. But I imagine they'll hit exactly the same wall that we all have: more and more people to be fed and watered every year, making growing demands on the same physical volume of water. It's a mess – but it's good being in a position to help get it sorted.

That was not to be. Even as he was sending that mail, another confrontation just 20km away exploded into violent conflict. My Dad went to work the next day, where the same thing happened. He tried to intervene and got caught up in a firefight: nine people died.

Although I was only 17, I suppose that was my first personal brush with history.

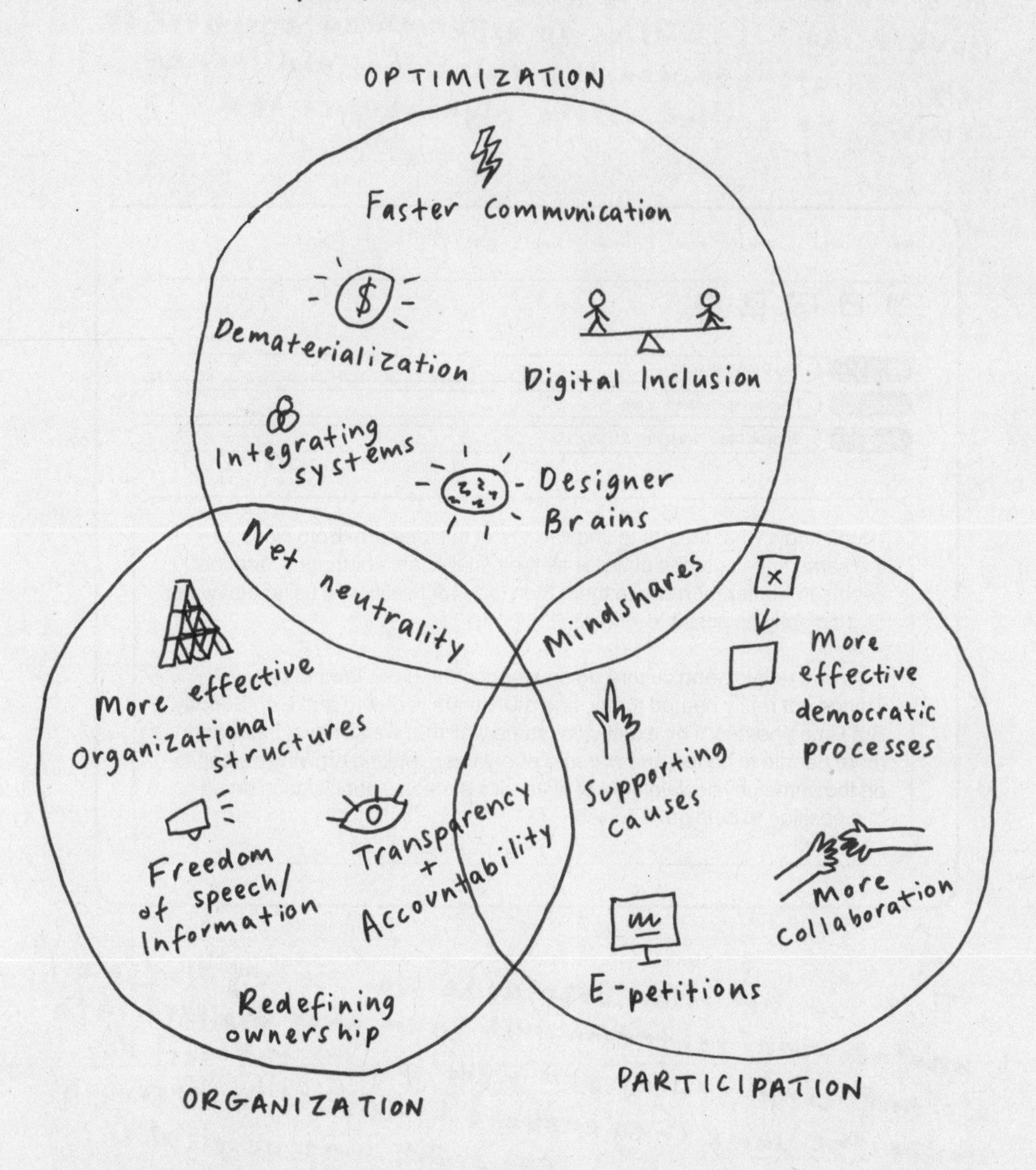

In 2015, the Cloud had just appeared on the horizon and the pace of IT-driven change was speeding up. Today, our standard IT devices are computing at the same rate as the human brain, and have indeed delivered a digitally ubiquitous world. Internet use just kept on growing year after year: 5 billion by 2020, 6.8 billion by 2035 and more than 8 billion today. That's around 97.5% of humankind!

28.01.2050

Internet Wars

'For Good or Ill: The Power of the Cloud' was the best-selling non-fiction book in 2015, providing a preview of some of the dramatic changes to follow.

The 'rolling IT revolution' of the last 40 years has shaped our lives more powerfully than any other advance. Without it, we simply wouldn't be living in the more or less sustainable world we have today. But it's been quite a struggle. The 'Internet Wars', which broke out in 2021 and went on for over a decade, proved to be at least as important as the technologies themselves in shaping our digital world.

There had always been a noisy minority of people who were deeply sceptical about the 'everything, everywhere' revolution, believing that the internet led to a narrowed view of the world, rather than a wider one, by becoming an echo chamber for all their prejudices and playing on their worst fears and instincts. Some of the most serious concerns were to do with privacy – with the creeping colonization of people's lives by corporate interests. The addictive nature of many online games, social media, apps and immersive experiences provided companies with a wealth of data – which they got better and better at manipulating to draw people deeper into increasingly pathological consumerism. But most people only started to care about this after 2021, when it became apparent just how much of this information was being used by governments all around the world in the name of 'national security'.

Ubiquity

The digital 'ubiquity' story ('everything, everywhere, for everyone') really began around 2015. It's hard to remember the excitement as everything migrated to the Cloud – leading to an explosion in innovation.

For instance, with IST (instantaneous simultaneous translation), the journey from slow, inaccurate and limited (with just two or three languages involved) to ultra-fast, word-perfect and comprehensive (covering around 50 of the world's most spoken languages) took no more than five or six years – and in the process pretty much put an end to the cultural dominance of the English language. Voice recognition software took a lot longer to perfect, but eventually unleashed a revolution in voice-activated technologies.

Now, of course, we've had more than 15 years of the MiMac revolution – comprising a host of mind-machine interface technologies that analyze our neuroelectrical impulses and convert them directly into digital signals.

It's now 40 years since a guy called Larry Page, one of the founders of a huge company at that time called Google, first speculated about search engines embedded in people's brains: 'When you think about something you know nothing about, you'll be able to instantly conjure up the relevant information'.

Of course, that's exactly what happened more than 15 years ago. A cascade of mindshare applications have transformed the way we now communicate with each other. Most of my generation are still very suspicious – memories of the 'Last Frontier' are hard to banish – but there is no such hesitation amongst the young.

Interestingly, in a way that is difficult to pin down, a sense of balance has somehow been achieved in our relationship with these technologies. We don't seem to be as obsessed about this 'ubiquity' story as people were earlier in the century. Just last week, for instance, I saw that no fewer than 85 per cent of people around the world are now subscribing to AdOut, a free service that completely blocks the constant stream of personalized adverts and digital litter sent directly into our devices or displayed all around us. Campaigners had fought for 20 years to have this kind of pervasive intrusion made illegal, but it now looks as if people are just doing it for themselves.

Ever since the 9/11 attacks on the Twin Towers in New York in 2001, the 'war on terror' had provided governments with a potent justification for intruding more and more into the lives of their citizens. Campaigners seeking to protect personal liberties on the internet (including the right to anonymity) were worn down in an unrelenting war of attrition with security forces – particularly in the USA, where the majority of citizens were subjected to constant surveillance and monitoring of every aspect of their lives, without the first idea that it was going on.

The full extent of just how far this had been taken, often against the law and without any due legal process, didn't become known until 2020, when a former head of the FBI called Henrik Lazarides blew the whistle on the whole sorry saga. Stricken with guilt at the way in which he'd personally betrayed the US Constitution, he killed himself the following year.

At exactly the same time, a court in Sweden compelled a number of the largest companies in the world to make full disclosure of what was

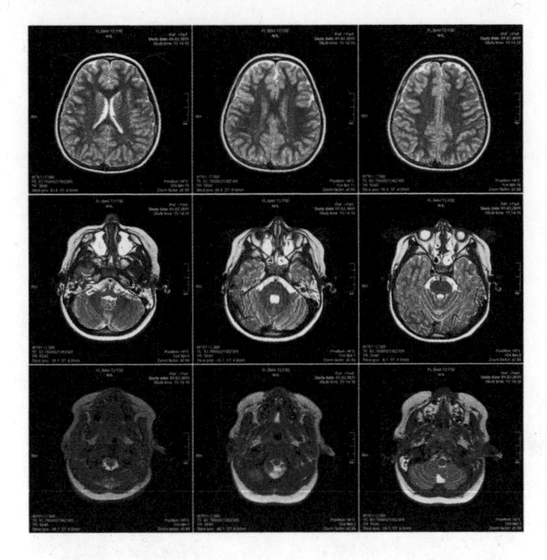

This was just one of the millions of brain scans seized by Swedish police investigating the Last Frontier project in 2020. It showed how easy it was to stimulate pleasure centres in the brain, via electronic signalling kits illegally embedded in people's smart devices, inducing intense feelgood sensations.

known as the Last Frontier – a covert project using all the research that had already been done on mapping the workings of the human brain (the twenty-first century equivalent of the Human Genome Project a couple of decades earlier) to manipulate responses to consumer messages. A series of experiments, conducted on people without their knowledge, proved it was possible to deliberately trigger every kind of addictive behaviour.

Those two things led directly to the Internet Wars – a 10-year running battle involving both legal campaigns (co-ordinated by the amazing Electronic Frontier Foundation) and completely illegal actions to restrain the power of both corporations and government. Activists set up shadow internet systems and peer-to-peer mesh networks (which operated independently of each other and of the internet), many of which still survive to this day. So, where there was one Cloud then, now we have more 'clouds' than on a rainy day in April!

There were no outright winners in the Internet Wars. But these days, we can (and do) decide for ourselves how important privacy is. We buy exactly as much Cloud time as we need, tailored to our own particular requirements, along a privacy spectrum with 'open to all' at one end and 'for me alone' at the other. As to restraining the power of governments, who knows? It's still a battleground. The impressive safeguards that many countries put in place back in the 2020s would appear to have worked well, as last year's report from the American Civil Liberties Union confirmed.

I still think that the internet has been an incredible force for good in promoting democracy. But there have been many places where the ability to manage information has crushed democracy, creating 'controlled environments' that have surpassed even the worst nightmares of George Orwell in his dystopian novel, '1984'.

03.02.2050

Enough!

Enough! protest, London, UK, 2018.

The decade between 2008 and 2018 was one of popular protests. Sometimes these were major tyrant-toppling events such as the Arab Spring; more often it was pretty low-key and haphazard, such as the Occupy anti-capitalism protests that kept exploding into life throughout the decade. There was growing anger with the lack of political leadership, but no one quite knew what any 'new order' would look like.

All protests were shaped and amplified by the use of social media, with new, ever-more versatile platforms to facilitiate sharing, networking, blogging – and stirring. Growing all the time, the activism operated in both spheres of reality – online and offline – combining forms of protest as old as human society with ways of organizing that were so entirely new as to leave the Establishment in country after country floundering in its technological ignorance. Culture jamming and protest art kept people laughing as well as protesting. The instantly networked

truth of what was happening on the ground trumped all the spin, lies and propaganda of those seeking to maintain the status quo. The courage shown by countless thousands of protestors was awe-inspiring. Defiant optimism became a political act in its own right.

Political leaders responded by summoning up apocalyptic images of what would happen if public order broke down any further, relying on the mainstream media to back them up with the same old exhausted clichés. So political life as we had known it since the middle of the twentieth century staggered on – until 2018.

That year marked the tenth anniversary of the collapse of the US bank Lehman Brothers in October 2008 – a financial disaster that had brought the global banking system close to collapse. This was followed by the transfer of staggering levels of debt from the banks, who had to be bailed out, to desperate governments – which simply took them to the verge of bankruptcy. Austerity became the defining feature of that decade, and for most people in Europe and the USA, with incomes falling and unemployment rising, the pain was both intense and prolonged.

The World Bank report that started it all off.

On 5 January 2018, the World Bank published its report 'Wealth Distribution in the 21st Century'. It was meant to be just another worthy contribution to the debate but it turned out to be pure dynamite, demonstrating as it did that, since 2008, the very rich had got even richer. At the turn of the century, the richest one per cent of the world's population had owned 35 per cent of global assets. By 2016, that had grown to just over 50 per cent. Below the top one per cent, the next five per cent had done pretty well too. But the incomes of most people in the rich world had declined, and in many parts of the poor world things were far worse.

Enough!
A Manifesto for Tomorrow

We accept that capitalism is the 'least worst economic system' we have. But we have to make it deliver for all of us. And for those who follow us.

1. Introduce the International Financial Transaction Tax within the next year.
We know we need efficient capital markets. But let them serve us, not the other way around.

2. Allocate a minimum of 10% of the International Financial Transaction Tax revenues to meeting the remaining Millennium Development Goals.
We all know it's wrong that more than two billion people still live in chronic poverty. So get it sorted.

3. Introduce a Carbon Tax (or a minimum price per tonne of CO_2) within the next two years.
We know it's tough coping with climate change. But do it now, before it's too late.

4. Make the system work for all people, not just for the rich.
We know that some will always be richer than others. But start reducing those gaps rather than letting them get wider all the time.

5. Strengthen the UN, pay off all dues that are owed and increase its budget.
We know the UN isn't perfect. So make it better.

6. Stop obsessing about economic growth and competitiveness. Make wellbeing your priority.
We all know that constant growth on a finite planet is a pathetic illustion. So just get over it.

7. Put an end to all further deforestation, over-fishing and economic development that damages biodiversity.
We all know that capitalism can't work without protecting natural capital. So stop talking about it and make it happen.

8. Get behind the EarthCorps initiative and fund it properly by introducing immediate and radical cuts in military expenditure.
We all know that today's challenges require unprecedented cooperation. So let young people work together, even if you can't.

No surprise then, that an old slogan, 'We are the 99 per cent', first used by the Occupy protestors in 2011, came back with a vengeance. Two other factors were already in play. First, youth unemployment figures in 2017 had reached all-time highs in many countries, affecting people right across the socioeconomic spectrum. Large numbers of graduates across Europe and in the USA were unable to find any paid work at all – let alone work that was commensurate with their qualifications. The old social contract ('get qualified; get a good job; get on in the world') was clearly dead and buried.

Second, in a way that politicians had assumed would never happen, young people suddenly realized the full implications of accelerating climate change. The 2016 Emergency Report of the Intergovernmental Panel on Climate Change (delayed by politicians from 2014 because its findings were so devastating) could not be ignored, and a sequence of horrendous, climate-induced disasters around that time had left no room for doubt.

And that was it. On 14 July 2018, the Enough! movement exploded into life in France, the USA, India and Russia, and then went global. Huge numbers of young people were mobilized by Avaaz (which was still the largest online campaigning community at that time) to fashion a collective rallying cry, enabling us to come together around a shared vision, which we expressed in the Enough! 'Manifesto for Tomorrow'. It had a massive impact, with young people occupying government buildings, parliaments, stock exchanges, newspapers and TV companies, banks, oil and mining companies, town halls and civic centres – an irresistible tide of shared fury and compassion for those who didn't even have what we had.

Even I got caught up in all this – though I'd never been involved in any radical politics before. It seemed hugely important, right there and then, to stand up and be counted before it was too late. I'd just finished my final school exams, and was about to head off to Kenya as an EarthCorps volunteer but that got a bit delayed (see p.189).

In the first couple of weeks, thousands were killed or injured in the riots that ensued, especially in China, Iran, Nigeria and Russia. But that just brought more young people onto the streets. Smart mobs materialized all over the place at the same time, making it impossible for the police (and military back-up) to respond effectively.

Chaos reigned for several months – at which point governments all around the world began to respond to our demands, pledging to introduce radical reforms, particularly on fair taxation, climate change and protection of the natural world. Some meant it, and were almost grateful for the fresh start. Most didn't – but it didn't matter. Too high a price had been paid; too many young people had been mobilized to let things slide back.

09.02.2050

The End of the Age of Oil

Here's an amazing statistic: oil production last year was down to around 4 million barrels a day – from a high of 76 million barrels a day in 2017. The Age of Oil is well and truly over – and, happily for all of us, civilization hasn't collapsed!

I was in my late teens in 2017, but I can still recall the almost apocalyptic tone in which people used to speculate about the so-called 'peak oil' moment – the year in which we took more crude oil out of the ground than in any other. The answer, it turned out, was 2017, and the amount was 76 million barrels a day. While the world did not grind to a halt after this, few countries were properly prepared for the profound changes that ending their dependence on oil entailed – despite having had decades to get themselves ready.

Oil's Last Gasp

The peak oil moment might have come a lot earlier were it not for the last-gasp efforts of the oil companies as they took advantage of very high oil prices to go after the oil that would otherwise have been way beyond their reach, geologically and economically – especially from reservoirs in very deep water or very harsh conditions in places like the Arctic.

There were also the 'unconventional' sources of oil and gas that added another 10 to 15 million barrels a day, such as tar sands – a kind of claggy, bituminous fuel that had to be heated up before it could be extracted. Billions of dollars were spent on developing Canada's tar sands between 2005 and 2018, despite endless warnings this was sheer madness: a barrel of oil from tar sands emitted at least 50 per cent more CO_2 than a conventional barrel – at a time when we were already trying to reduce CO_2 emissions per barrel.

Investors in the tar sands got horribly burned in 2018. After the Emergency Report in 2016 from the Intergovernmental Panel on Climate Change, the USA grudgingly agreed to follow Europe's example in setting very tough carbon standards for liquid fuels – which the oil extracted from the tar sands simply couldn't meet – primarily because of the impact of weather-related disasters on public opinion. The Canadian economy nosedived, so great was its dependence on oil exports to the USA, and it didn't properly recover for another five years.

There was no going back when, a year later, a disastrous release of waste water from one of the largest tar sands operations, contaminated with mercury, lead and other toxic elements, killed off almost every living creature along a 160-kilometre stretch of the Athabasca river. It's taken the Athabasca a full 30 years to recover.

Gothenburg, Sweden, 2036. Cities like Gothenburg really set the pace in terms of low-carbon, high quality urban living, and by 2016 Sweden was well on the way to reaching its goal of being the world's first 'oil-free economy'. In Denmark, Copenhagen became the first genuinely carbon-neutral city in 2022.

The next 30 years after the peak oil moment was a story of managed retreat away from oil. Of the 4 million barrels a day used in 2048, almost all was used in aviation, shipping and the production of high-value chemicals. In 2017, there were 708 oil refineries operating worldwide; today, there are just 11 – two in the USA, two in China, one each in Brazil, the Netherlands, Indonesia and India, and three in the Middle East (Abu Dhabi, Saudi Arabia and Iraq).

We shouldn't beat ourselves up too much here. Oil was cheap and easy to get (until the turn of the century) and it was energy-dense, delivering a lot of energy for not much volume. It was also incredibly versatile, providing not just liquid fuels but also the basic feedstock for the entire chemical industry, from plastics to pharmaceuticals – even though no more than five per cent of the oil was used for those purposes. So it was highly addictive – as a former US president, George W. Bush, once acknowledged.

Today's algae-based materials are now so cheap and useful that they've displaced almost all of the oil we once used for plastics, pharmaceuticals, paints, lubricants and so on. They still can't quite provide everything we need – hence the continuing requirement for small amounts of high-quality crude oil. Although for how much longer, I've no idea. As my daily GreenStream bulletins from the 'New Scientist' keep reminding me, the pace of innovation is as intense today as it's ever been. Give us another 20 years and I suspect we'll be down to a few hundred thousand barrels a day from those super-efficient oil wells in Iraq. And that will be it.

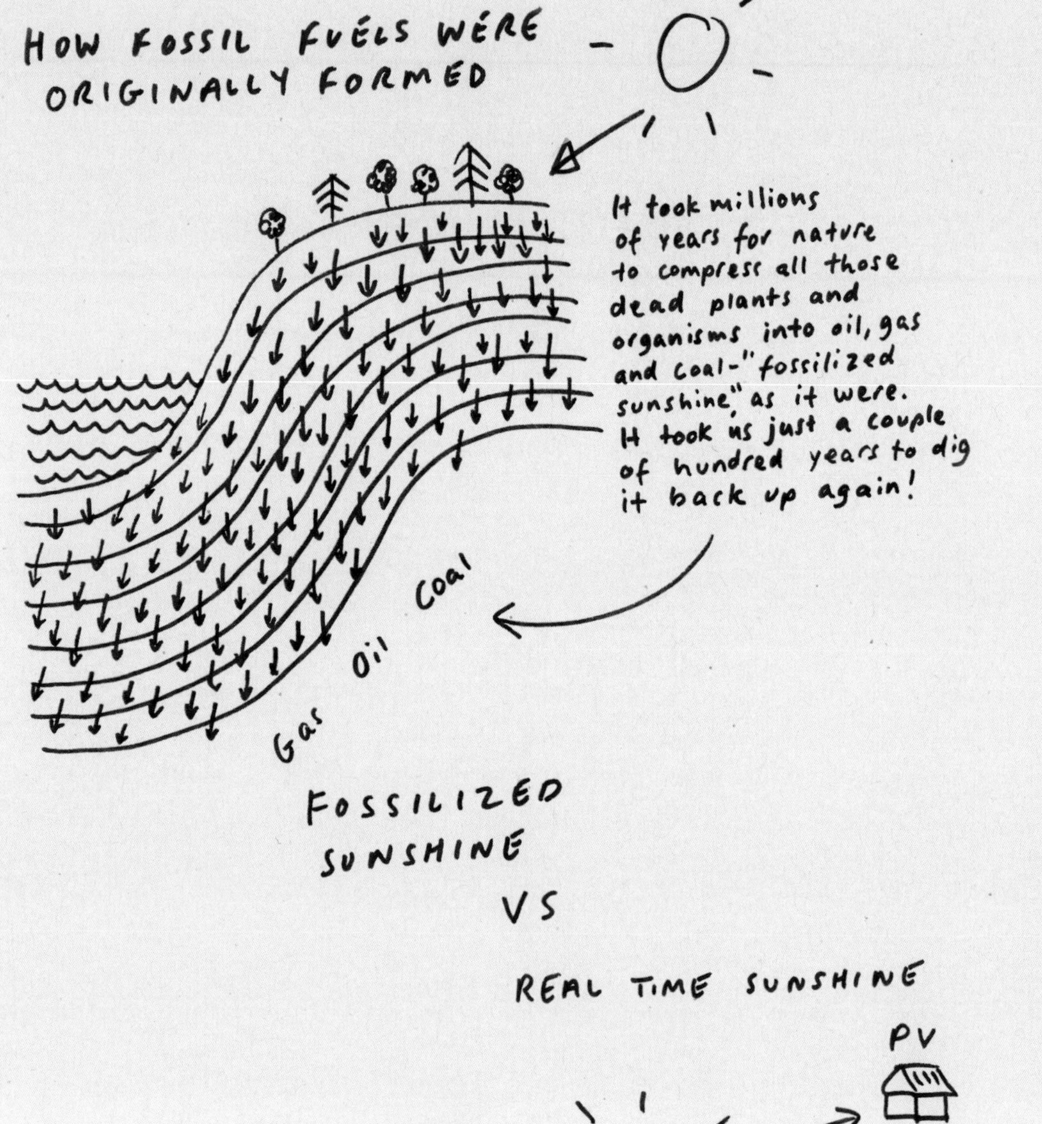

The sun provides enough potential energy in one hour to keep us going for an entire year: it's just taken us a long time to learn how to harness that incoming bounty without relying on the fossilized stuff.

PV

CSP

Solar Thermal

Water Tank

BIODIESEL IN THE PHILIPPINES

Raw material (coconut husks etc)

Trucks powered by biodiesel

Biofuel refinery

Coco-biodiesel

Coconut-fragranced air from car fumes

Coco-biodiesel was the fuel of choice by 2020 – which some people believe explains the sweet-smelling air in Manila!

The Philippines: a case study

Here's a case study that my researchers have unearthed. Back in 2015, the Philippines was a very poor country, made all the poorer by unconstrained population growth. So punitive was the cost of importing oil that the Philippines' government took the bold decision in that year to become the world's first all-renewables country. It already had a lot of hydro and geothermal power, to which it then added wind and solar on a vast scale.

But the real breakthrough came with the revolution in the use of biomass. As a predominantly agricultural country, the Philippines can call on huge amounts of forestry and agricultural waste from the production of rice, sugar, maize and coconuts. With major support from the Asian Development Bank, investment in biorefineries and biomass power stations (using rice hulls and straw, maize cobs and stalks, coconut husks and the like as fuels) took off in the early 2020s.

A mega-biorefinery in the Philippines, 2025.

17.02.2050

It's All in Our Genes

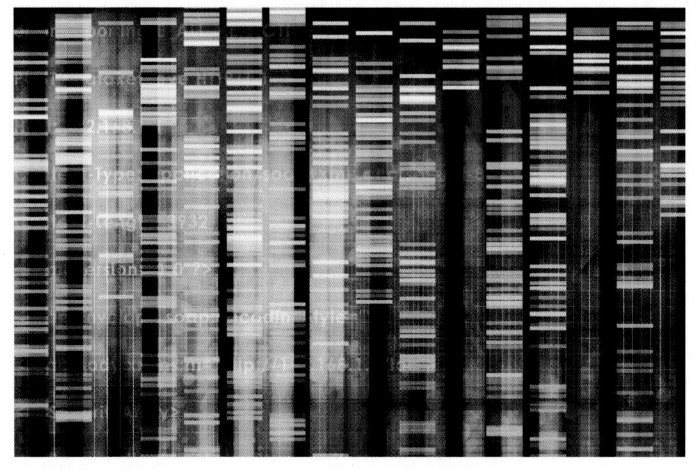

The field of genetics has proved the biggest disruptive force in modern healthcare.

It seems odd now, but I do remember feeling a bit nervous about having my genome sequenced in 2021. After all, I was only 21 years old, and not exactly worried about my health.

But I'd just come back from a year studying at Tsinghua University in China, where it was rapidly becoming something that Chinese students signed up to almost as a matter of course. It was cheap, and there was already a real buzz of excitement about digital health and personal genomics. If I hadn't done it then, I would have certainly done it later. By now, more than 90 per cent of people in my age group have had their genomes sequenced, and it will be 100 per cent for our children's generation. The benefits have been enormous in terms of early diagnosis, the development of new drugs and targeted treatments tailored to the individual. And it's had an equally big impact on lifestyles and diet.

It made me think a lot more about what I was eating, simply by identifying the conditions that I'm genetically susceptible to – in my case, obesity and Alzheimers. This made it all very personal when the debate about sugar exploded as a public health issue.

Alex McKay: Genetic Risk Factors (September 2021)

0-1%	>1-10%	>10-25%	>25-50%	>50-100%
Brain aneurysm You: 0.80% Avg. 0.64%	Lung cancer You: 8% Avg. 8%	Diabetes, type 2 You: 24% Avg. 25%	Atrial fibrilation You: 27% Avg. 26%	
Crohns disease You: 0.44% Avg. 0.58%	Colon cancer You: 5% Avg. 6%	Alzheimers disease You: 25% Avg. 9%	Obesity You: 38% Avg. 34%	
Glaucoma You: 0.7% Avg. 1.1%	Psoriasis You: 3.8% Avg. 4.0%		Osteoarthritis You: 41% Avg. 40%	
Multiple sclerosis You: 0.17% Avg. 0.30%	Abdominal aneurysm You: 3.9% Avg. 3.1%		Heart attack You: 46% Avg. 42%	
Celiac disease You: 0.01% Avg. 0.06%	Melanoma You: 2.3% Avg. 3.7%			
	Stomach cancer You: 2.3% Avg. 2.4%			
	Deep vein thrombosis You: 2.4% Avg. 3.4%			
	Rheumatoid arthritis You: 1.5% Avg. 1.6%			
	Macular degeneration You: 1.2% Avg. 3.1%			

My genome sequencing report

ARTIFICIAL MEAT

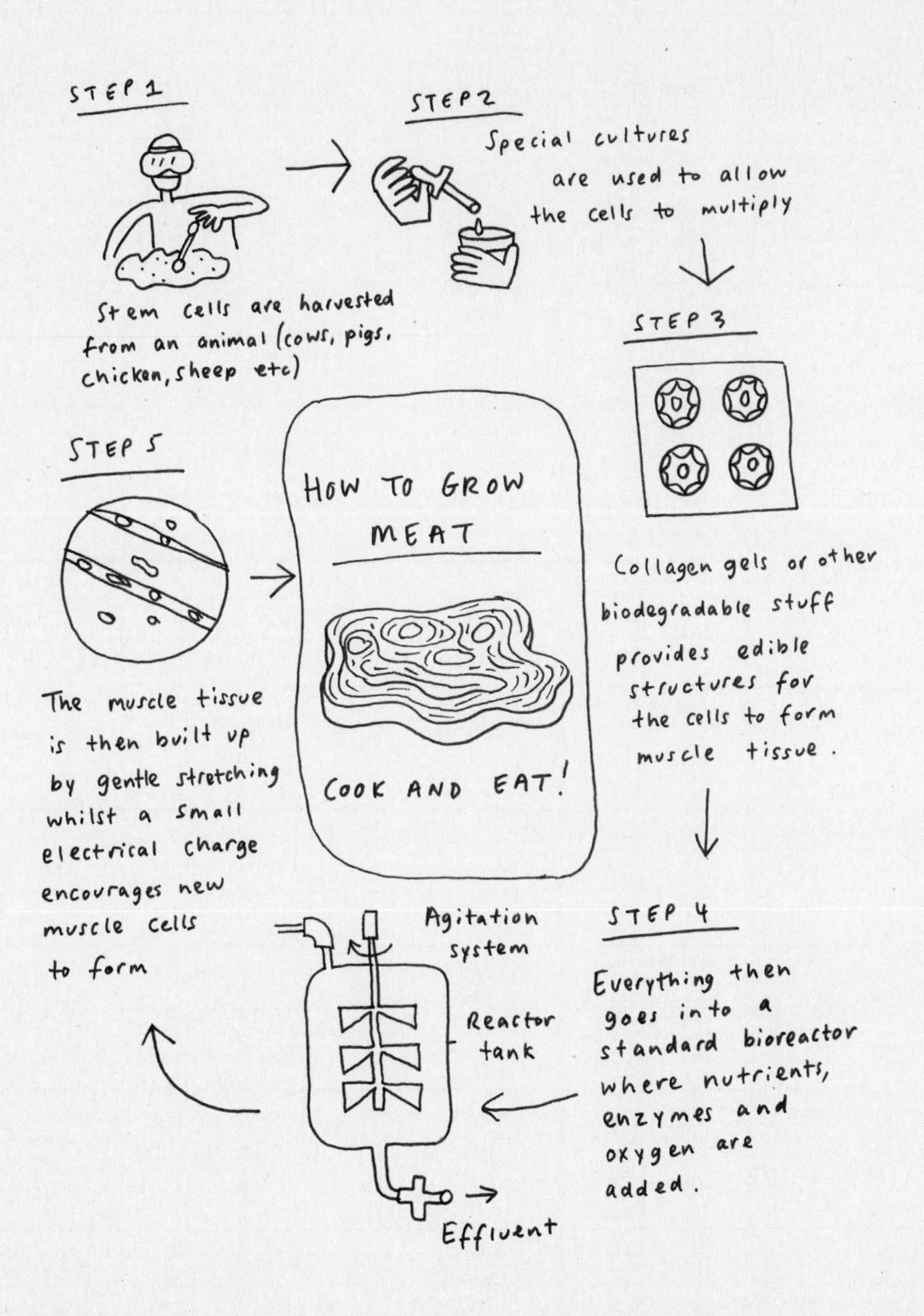

As early as 2010, there was growing concern about the massive increase in levels of obesity and, connected with this, the incidence of type 2 diabetes. This had already been labelled by some experts as the twenty-first century's major public health crisis, not just in rich northern countries but also in India, China, the Middle East and elsewhere. In 2010, 275 million people suffered from diabetes; by 2030, this had risen to nearly 500 million.

Today, this figure is back down to around 150 million, which is quite an achievement. The world's leading companies have worked hard, not just on developing better medication, but on encouraging preventative steps too, including dietary factors and a general reduction in the use of certain chemicals linked to the increase in obesity. Lifestyle changes have been equally important, especially amongst pre-diabetics – those identified as being at risk of diabetes. But it's all the conditions that people have developed as a consequence of diabetes (particularly cardiovascular disease) that are still causing the real problems.

Hence the focus on sugar. By 2015, many academics were already arguing that sugar was an addictive substance, and that the food industry – which was using this fact to its advantage – should therefore be regulated in exactly the same way that the tobacco industry was. But it wasn't just sugar – fat and salt made up the other two elements in this unholy trinity. What we called 'junk food' then – chips, hamburgers and the like – was very high in all three. The evidence that food high in sugar, fat and salt was altering people's brain chemistry (as other highly addictive substances do) got stronger and stronger through the decade.

Ironically, it was Denmark – a country with one of the lowest obesity rates in the developed world – where the government was the first to introduce a tax on fatty foods as far back as 2011. It didn't last long – the food industry saw to that – but other countries soon followed suit. In 2014, the US president, Barack Obama, imposed a 'soda tax' on all sugar-sweetened beverages – despite the food and soft drinks industries spending vast sums to try and scare him off.

In 2016, China simply banned the sale of all drinks and food stuffs that exceeded very strict sugar levels, so horrified was it at the rising toll of obesity. A decade later, governments all around the world were taxing, regulating and proscribing sugar, salt and fat – despite what they'd been saying a few years before about leaving it to the industry to regulate itself. The chronic disease burden caused by these dietary poisons has been slowly reducing ever since.

In policy terms, however, that was a mere stroll in the park in comparison to taking on the problem of excessive meat consumption. Just about everybody was refusing to face up to the sheer scale of the issue at the turn of the century, in terms of both the health and environmental impacts of eating meat. At that time, livestock farming contributed somewhere between 15 and 20 per cent of total greenhouse gas emissions, with massive impacts on water, soil and biodiversity. In response to these concerns, meat consumption had more or less stabilized in the rich world by around 2015 – but it was surging everywhere else, as economies grew. In 1962, the average meat consumption per person in China was just 4 kg a year; it was 60 kg by 2010 and 102 kg by 2030, roughly the same as in the USA.

MEAT CONSUMPTION
→ World

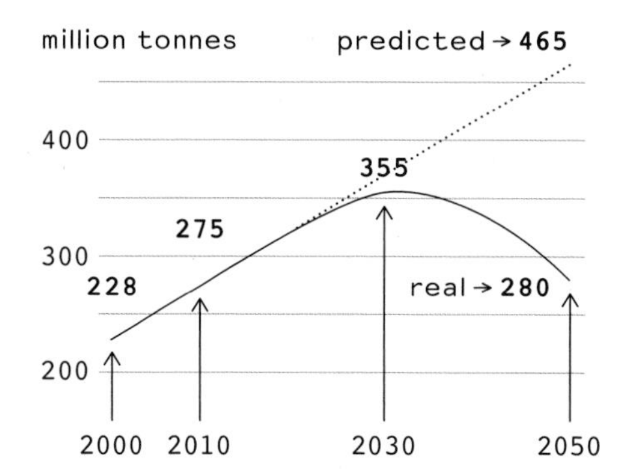

AVERAGE MEAT CONSUMPTION
PER CAPITA IN KG
→ USA

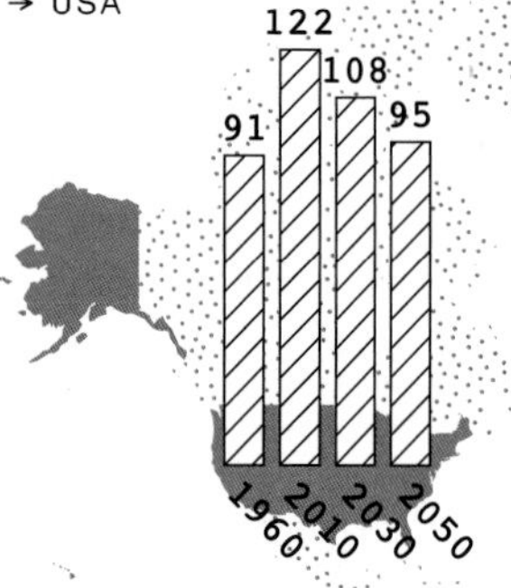

AVERAGE MEAT CONSUMPTION
PER CAPITA IN KG
→ China

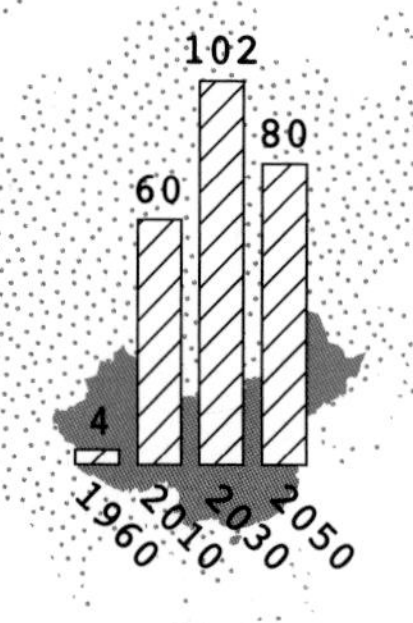

That kind of growth required the slaughter of tens of billions of animals every year. Despite the horrifying animal welfare impacts involved in factory farming, the experts were confidently predicting that meat consumption would grow from around 290 million tonnes in 2010 to around 465 million tonnes in 2050. Well, that didn't happen: instead, public opinion began to change, for both health and environmental reasons. Per capita meat consumption plateaued in 2030 at around 355 million tonnes in total – the 'peak meat' moment, if you like!

It's been gradually going down since then (especially red meat consumption) – a good outcome, if not an entirely fair one: rich countries (and rich individuals) still get to consume more meat than poor countries and poor individuals. A lot of this is down to the farmers themselves, who found all sorts of ways to reduce the amount of CO_2 and other greenhouse gases emitted from raising livestock – particularly through reformulated animal feeds. The chronic shortage of land was also a big issue: in 2020, livestock farmers had been using an astonishing 37 per cent of all productive land to rear animals and grow their feed, so change had to come. This figure is now down to little more than 20 per cent.

A rather different kind of breakthrough came in the early 2020s with the widespread take-up of artificial meat, made by culturing stem cells from cows, pigs, sheep and chickens (see p.44). This was promoted at the time as a major health innovation. However, being able to make the stuff was one thing: getting consumers to buy it was another thing altogether! Even now, some people can't get beyond the 'yuck factor', despite the fact that most cultured meats are actually healthier, often nutritionally enhanced with omega-3 fatty acids and other good things. Many environmentalists remain pretty sceptical too – on the grounds that people should go the whole hog (excuse the pun) and become proper vegetarians.

But artificial meat is here to stay: nearly a third of all meat consumed is already cultured, and with pressure on good farming land getting more intense, my bet is that this will soon be up to 50 per cent.

Personally, I've never been a big meat eater anyway. Maybe it was that DNA scan all those years ago revealing my particular disease susceptibilities that put me on the 'eat less meat' path – although I can't say it had quite the same effect in keeping me off sweet things! As the medical profession has got better at interpreting each individual's genome, it's become easier to fine-tune diets accordingly. So I know exactly what my optimum diet is – what I should eat lots of, what I should try to avoid and what I shouldn't touch at any cost.

25.02.2050

The Houston Concord on Climate Change

Newsweek, 21 May 2020.

The signing of the Houston Concord in 2020 was a huge step forward in reducing emissions of CO2 and other greenhouse gases. It was the first-ever comprehensive and binding agreement on greenhouse gas emissions supported by every nation on the planet! I'd love to be able to tell you that this was all about the science, but I'm afraid that just wasn't the case. The Houston Concord was all about politics and money – after all, the deal was done in Houston, Texas, the centre of the US oil and gas industry. And just a few months before the 2020 US presidential election.

But to understand how this happened, you have to understand why this was all about the USA. Since the late 1980s, the USA had blocked any progress on international negotations for nearly 25 years. As the world's only superpower then, the lack of leadership from the USA ensured total stalemate; China and India simply pointed the finger of blame, and the Europeans failed to break the deadlock.

From around 2012, the 'green arms race' between China and the USA started to become a big political issue. By 2016, a decade's worth of Chinese investment in renewable energy and every kind of green technology (or 'clean-tech') had achieved exactly what the Chinese had hoped for: increasing domination of what was then the world's fastest growing economic sector. During the presidential election of 2016, 'winning the green arms race' was a powerful rallying call, reinforced by higher energy prices that were really hurting US citizens. Securing the nation's energy supplies was a very hot topic indeed. Reducing dependence on imported oil and gas meant cutting back on all fossil fuels – including the USA's own supplies of shale oil, which had proved to be rather more expensive and difficult to extract than expected.

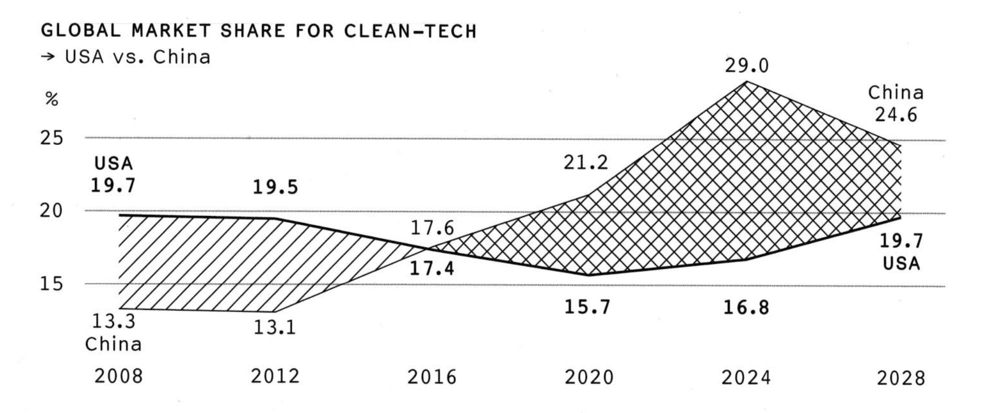

By looking at the data for each of the years where there was a presidential election in the USA from 2008 onwards, you can begin to imagine how that data was used in the electoral debates. The 'green agenda' was draped in the 'red, white and blue' of the US flag.

First and foremost, energy security meant energy efficiency – with the result that the need for energy efficiency came to be seen as the 'moral equivalent of war', an idea first advanced by a twentieth-century Democratic president, Jimmy Carter, some 40 years earlier. In 2016, this idea was taken up by everyone on the US political right, from the Evangelical Alliance to right-wing think tanks and the Republican Party at large, with the slogan: 'Energy is destiny: our energy in our hands'. This was music to the ears of US environmentalists at the time: places like the Rocky Mountain Institute had been campaigning for decades to persuade Americans to put energy security first, pointing out that it made no sense for the world's most powerful nation to be spending around 15 per cent of its GDP on oil – not counting the additional costs of maintaining a massive military presence in the Middle East (and fighting several wars) to ensure continued access to supplies.

There's one other factor we dug up in our research. Nearly everyone who had been denying the reality of climate change had shut up by 2016 – not so much because of the 2016 Emergency Report from the Intergovernmental Panel on Climate Change, but because of the weather in people's own backyards. From 2010 onwards, the only normality for US citizens was extreme abnormality; every year, things got a little bit weirder. Droughts got a little bit drier, floods got a little bit deeper, forest fires got a little bit fiercer. And storms that were supposed to be 'once in a hundred years' events were coming thicker and faster: Katrina in 2005; Sandy in 2012; Athena in 2015. So, when the third biggest insurance company in the USA went belly-up in 2017, unable to finance the stupendous level of claims, climate scepticism went belly-up with it.

As soon as voters really started to believe that extreme weather events were linked to a changing climate caused by greenhouse gases, 20 years of fruitless policy wrangling on Capitol Hill suddenly turned around. Emboldened by their triumph in the 2016 presidential election, a powerful grouping of Republicans in the House of Representatives (with strong backing from the Democrats) introduced the historic two-page Cap and Prosper Bill in 2017.

Even now, I just love the elegant simplicity of what they came up with. There were no bankers involved – people still despised bankers in those days – and no complex trading schemes for dealers to try and fiddle. Indeed, there was very limited scope for politicians to meddle at all. There were many more winners than losers, with dividends for the vast majority of US citizens worth far more than the increased cost of the fossil fuels that they used. As carbon permit prices increased (due to the cap coming down every year), so did the dividends that everyone received. In fact, Cap and Prosper has proved to be one of the most successful market-based policies in US history.

A lot of that success was down to the Rebuild America programme. This was dedicated not only to infrastructure renewal, but also to the retro-fitting of all existing housing and non-domestic buildings to minimize energy consumption. Funded by the Cap and Prosper scheme, the pay-back for the US economy in terms of jobs, skills and tax revenues, as well as reduced energy bills and increased efficiency, was astonishing. And the weirdest thing was that it was the Republicans that made it all happen, playing on every patriotic bone in America's body politic and doing everything in their power to 'protect America' from the chaos of global energy markets, see off China and get the economy going again.

So when it came to signing up to the Houston Concord (just a couple of years after Cap and Prosper had passed through both the House of Representatives and the Senate), it all went through pretty smoothly.

CAP & PROSPER: HOW IT WORKS

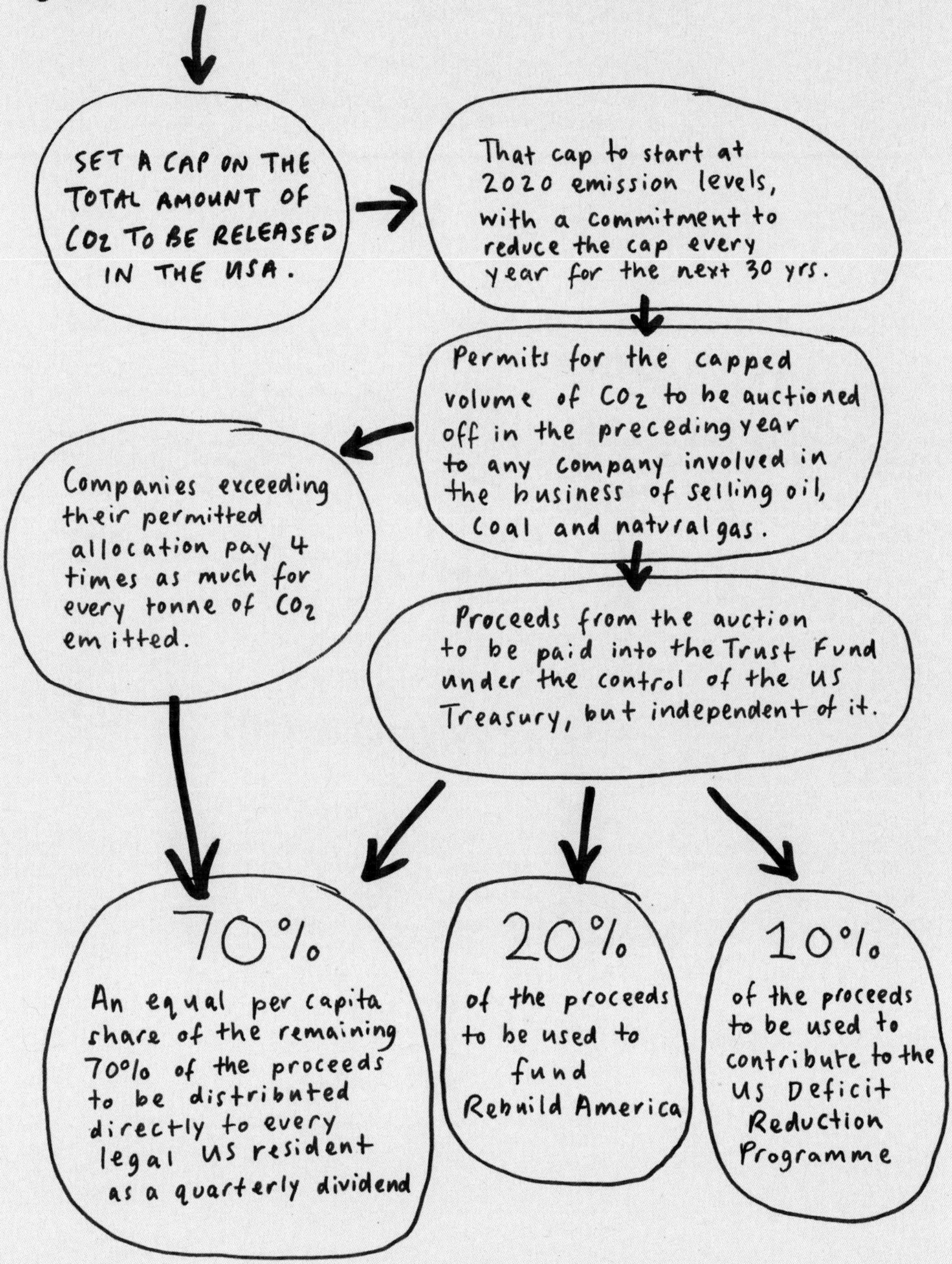

SET A CAP ON THE TOTAL AMOUNT OF CO_2 TO BE RELEASED IN THE USA.

That cap to start at 2020 emission levels, with a commitment to reduce the cap every year for the next 30 yrs.

Permits for the capped volume of CO_2 to be auctioned off in the preceding year to any company involved in the business of selling oil, coal and natural gas.

Companies exceeding their permitted allocation pay 4 times as much for every tonne of CO_2 emitted.

Proceeds from the auction to be paid into the Trust Fund under the control of the US Treasury, but independent of it.

70%

An equal per capita share of the remaining 70% of the proceeds to be distributed directly to every legal US resident as a quarterly dividend

20%

of the proceeds to be used to fund Rebuild America

10%

of the proceeds to be used to contribute to the US Deficit Reduction Programme

First came
CAP AND PROSPER
and then
THE HOUSTON CONCORD

But whether all that turns out to be
JUST IN TIME (!)
or TOO LITTLE, TOO LATE
is still a hugely controversial debate.

2050: GLOBAL GREENHOUSE GAS EMISSIONS
DOWN

84 %

ON 2020 LEVELS

After a period of 25 years during which the USA had systematically derailed every single international process aimed at getting a global agreement on climate change, the world looked on in amazement as the US president personally led the negotiations. With China, India, Brazil and Indonesia having all signed up to a similar agreement in the preceding years, a legally-binding global treaty to reduce emissions of all greenhouse gases by 90 per cent (on 2020 levels) before 2050 finally came into force on 1 January 2021.

By the end of last year, global emissions of CO_2 and other greenhouse gases were down to around 84 per cent of the 2020 level, with the Americans and the Chinese still competing for a bigger share of today's multi-trillion dollar clean-tech markets.

Introduced as part of the Cap and Prosper Act in 2017, Rebuild America had the support of both the Republicans and the Democrats.

04.03.2050

Companies, Cooperatives and Capitalism

My poor students! Here's the question that I asked them to look into: 'How was it that so many very clever people screwed up so spectacularly in the first decade of this century – and very nearly sank capitalism in the process?' Short answer: all warnings as to what was actually happening were systematically ignored.

The warning voices that most intrigued my students were those of concerned entrepreneurs who felt deeply uncomfortable about what was being done in the name of capitalism. Some of the billionaire gurus of the age (people like the legendary Warren Buffett and George Soros) made it very clear that the greed and irrational exuberance of the early twenty-first century would turn out to be a disaster. The title of a best-selling book at that time, 'Screw Business as Usual', summed up the appetite for change. Indeed, many of the most thoughtful chief executives could quite clearly see the idiocy of what was happening – but very few were prepared to talk about it in public.

The Enough! movement in 2018 changed all that. Concerned capitalists woke up to the realization that capitalism had to be actively defended against the greed and corruption of those who had messed it up for everyone else. Progressive business people took up the running from the Enough! campaigners and helped push through some major reforms (see p.56). Responsible capitalism became something worth fighting for.

Governments the world over introduced new legislation to incentivize the growth of socially beneficial forms of enterprise – employee share-ownership companies, customer stock-ownership schemes, cooperatives, community interest companies and social enterprises – all of which had previously just rubbed along as the economy's poor relations when the world was still dominated by unaccountable multinationals.

The emergence of what were then called B corporations (with the B standing for benefit) and their explosive growth through the 2010s did as much as anything to challenge that lack of accountability. Certified B corporations had to commit to much more ambitious environmental targets, meet higher legal accountability standards and be able to demonstrate that what they did was as good for society as it was for shareholders. By 2020, there were more than 5,000 B corporations (the majority of them in the US) with an increasingly influential role in the debate about the future of capitalism. We don't call them B companies today simply because they are now the norm.

The other real winner was the global cooperative movement. In the 2010s this movement was often described as a sleeping giant, in that it was already huge in terms of the number of people and organizations involved, but still largely invisible. In 2012, for instance, there were 1.5 million cooperative enterprises around the world, employing more than 100 million people, with more than a billion members and a turnover of several trillion US dollars. Three times as many people were 'member owners' of a co-op than were individual shareholders of listed companies.

Ghana's cooperative cocoa movement has successfully weathered all the ups and downs in the global cocoa market. It still has hundreds of thousands of farmers on its books.

FC Barcelona has been one of Europe's most successful football clubs for more than 60 years – as a fully-fledged cooperative! It has 150,000 members and 2,500 fan clubs around the world.

There are now around 450 million people working in cooperatives of one kind or another, and the success of the cooperative movement is one of the game-changing shifts that has altered the entire profile of the global economy.

There are still plenty of very successful multinationals – although fewer and fewer every year, it has to be said, as people around the world show their preference for more local and national businesses. There's still a huge amount of world trade going on, but what was once a very bitter debate about the role and obligations of multinationals has largely disappeared: if they're not operating as a force for good in the world today, they quite simply aren't operating.

So capitalism is still thriving, but in a very different way from 30 or 40 years ago. Nobody planned it that way, but with a billion wealthy people in the world today, plus more than four billion middle class people and another three billion or so aspiring to be able to live the way that the other five billion do, it should have been blindingly obvious to everyone that old-style capitalism was never going to deliver on that scale without the planet imploding. Given where we are now, something about today's more sustainable version of capitalism must be working.

Cleaning Up Capitalism

1. An end to tax havens

A Universal Taxation Convention was introduced in 2021, requiring any company operating in more than one country 'to declare all revenues and profits accruing in all countries where they operate, and to pay all taxes due on those revenues and profits solely in the country where they were earned'. This may not sound like much, but this one change made a bigger difference to poorer countries than any other measure introduced during this century. Who needs aid when you can get a fair price for the work your citizens do and the resources the world economy needs? It made a hell of a difference in the rich world, too. Many multinationals tried to get round the Convention, but they simply got hammered by one whistleblower after another.

2. An end to perverse subsidies

Another key event was the end of what were described as 'perverse subsidies' – the use of taxpayers' money to feather the nest of those businesses that were most actively involved in trashing the planet: the fossil fuel companies, for instance, or intensive agriculture.

A benchmark survey by McKinsey's in 2016 showed that $1.4 trillion US of public money was being handed over to such companies every year – an unbelievable sum at that time, in the middle of the Age of Austerity. At long last, the World Trade Organization started doing something useful, formally declaring many of these perverse subsidies to be illegal barriers to trade. By 2025, that figure was down to around $350 million US.

CLEANING UP CAPITALISM

Looking back over 80 years of nuclear generating capacity, it seems remarkable that we stuck with nuclear for SO LONG!

But the nuclear industry had always been incredibly successful at getting politicians to hand over countless billions of taxpayers' dollars - despite increasingly clear evidence that nuclear NEVER delivered in the way that it promised.

Of course, the world still has one fusion reactor at its disposal - the one 150 million kilometres away from the Earth! That one is still doing a pretty good job, as it will be for at least the next three billion years, all being well.

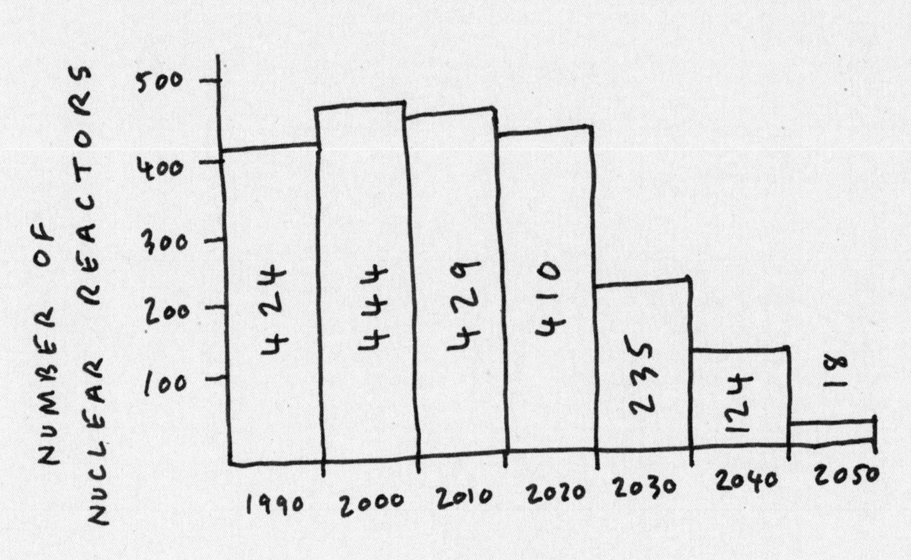

11.03.2050

Nuclear Power's Last Gasp

Natanz nuclear power plant, Iran, 2010.

In June 2019, five nuclear reactors in the US and two in the UK became targets of a devastating cyber-attack that took over the operating software of the reactors. Millions of people had to be evacuated from around the reactors, causing chaos and disruption. Astonishingly, as was revealed much later, the terrorist group involved chose not to exercise the 'nuclear option' available to them of causing reactor meltdown. Knowing that the economic damage had already been done, they instructed the 'worms' that they had inserted into the operating systems to self-destruct.

All the material that the Research Team has dug up around this theme just confirms the old adage: hindsight is a wonderful thing! General Keith Alexander, a former head of the Pentagon's Cyber Command, put it in context after the attacks in 2019:

> 'We and the Israelis got ahead of the game back in 2010 when we successfully infiltrated our Stuxnet worm into the operating systems of Iran's Natanz nuclear plant – at the time when we were still trying to stop the Iranians developing their own nuclear capability. But our lead didn't last very long, and since then, there have been countless attempts to infiltrate our energy and water infrastructure here in the US, using ever-more sophisticated worms. We thought our defences were sound – until now, that is.'

Although it would have been so much worse if the reactors had indeed melted down, the disruption that ensued was damaging enough: every reactor around the world (apart from those in China) was temporarily closed down to build in additional cyber-defences. By the end of 2021, the French economy was on the brink of collapse given its level of dependency on nuclear power at that time.

In the political firestorm that followed, the CIA also let it be known that an equally horrific nuclear attack on Saudi Arabia in 2016 had only just been averted. An al-Qaeda cell had fashioned two 'dirty bombs' using uranium from old nuclear weapons smuggled out of Ukraine and Belarus. One bomb was intercepted on the border with Iraq; the other was landed by sea close to the Ras Tanura refinery in Saudi Arabia and transported from there to the heart of the Qatif oil field. Miraculously, the three terrorists involved were unable to detonate the bomb – although they blew themselves up in the final attempt.

And that was it for nuclear power. 'Enough of this nuclear folly' was the collective cry around the world. The time was right for change: by the early 2020s, renewable energy was booming. There had been amazing advances in the storage technologies needed to smooth out the intermittency of renewables, such as solar and wind power, and energy efficiency savings were already at an impressive level. All in all, the deal that politicians had done on nuclear power after the Second World War – to turn 'atoms for war' into 'atoms for peace' – no longer looked like such a smart deal.

Signing of the Nuclear Decommissioning Treaty, Kiev, Ukraine, 2022. That was one grumpy group of people! And that's because none of those world leaders in 2022 felt particularly happy about signing up to an agreement that obliged them to phase out all their nuclear reactors. Yet there they all were – even Iran, even Israel, even China, even France.

So the Nuclear Decommissioning Treaty was signed by all the principal nuclear nations in 2022, in the Ukrainian capital of Kiev – a city that knew more than a bit about nuclear disasters, having suffered the fallout from the nuclear explosion at the Chernobyl reactor in 1986. The Treaty ruled out building any new reactors, with China the only exception: although it had just about come to the end of its own nuclear power construction programme, China negotiated a special deal to complete the three reactors that were then still being built.

All nuclear nations were allowed to run their reactors through to the end of their operating life, as determined against the 'strictest safety standards' by the International Atomic Energy Agency. That's why, even today, there are still nine reactors operating in China, five in India, three in France and one in Olkiluoto in Finland.

Nuclear Alternatives

The 'nuclear dream' didn't just quietly wither away. With this industry, there was always another 'potential breakthrough' just over the horizon, and plenty of dreamers who thought they might be the ones to make it happen. 'Generation IV' nuclear technologies excited huge interest before 2019 – technologies that would apparently solve all the problems associated with nuclear power, including the problems of nuclear waste.

Some pro-nuclear environmentalists got particularly excited about the idea of reactors powered by thorium rather than uranium – which did indeed seem to have some merit, as there's a lot more thorium in the Earth's crust than there is uranium. But as ever with nuclear technologies, the research and development took forever and cost far too much – and by the time it seemed ready for some kind of commercial development, the combination of renewable generation, storage and energy efficiency made it redundant before a single thorium reactor could be commissioned.

And as for that other big nuclear dream – fusion power – it too never recovered from the events of 2019. Especially as it was still said to be '40 years away' at that time, just as it had been '40 years away' in 1960!

Looking back on it now, it's clear that the cyber-assaults of 2019 did us all a favour by killing off such expensive fantasies, as well as closing down the working reactors.

17.03.2050

Spiritual Militancy

As my students keep reminding me, there will be some atheists who won't like this particular entry as they don't like to admit the contribution made by the world's religions and major faiths to achieving a more sustainable world. But the truth of it is (and I speak as an agnostic here) that it's been absolutely critical.

You can track this particular story right back to the 1980s, when the leaders of five major world religions (Buddhism, Christianity, Hinduism, Islam and Judaism) met in the Italian hill town of Assisi in 1986 and all signed up to a radical Environmental Statement. 25 years later, all the major faiths launched their rolling Generational Plans on climate action and sustainable development.

With momentum gradually building up, in May 2022 the leaders of all the world's religions and major faith groups (and many minor ones too) gathered in Lhasa, Tibet, to sign the Lhasa Declaration.

Faith and the Green Agenda

To be honest, the green agenda was far from central to the way in which faith leaders engaged with their followers at the turn of the century. As with that generation of politicians, it always looked and felt like an add-on. That was deeply disappointing to those environmental champions already actively engaged within their own faith communities.

Many 'green' Christians couldn't understand how their church leaders seemed more preoccupied with sexual mores and gender politics than with the fate of God's Earth. Many Muslims were horrified that the Qur'an's eloquent teaching on stewardship and common property was constantly obscured by battles between Sunnis and Shias. And while it's true that the majority of Orthodox Christians, Buddhists, Daoists, Hindus, Sikhs and Jains were more consistently committed to environmental faith practice, their influence was limited.

The failure of the world's religions to mobilize people through their faith meant that progress on the green agenda was much slower than it could have been – given that we are talking about at least four fifths of humankind involved in these faiths, with their correspondingly huge influence and their financial muscle (providing over 10 per cent of the world's total market for institutional investment). Perhaps it was the Enough! movement that finally got them all going – with the idea of 'enoughness' being perhaps at the heart of all religious teaching. As Mahatma Gandhi famously said: 'The world has enough for its needs, but not for its greed'.

MAY THE LORD MAKE US TRULY GRATEFUL

***

EVANGELICALS UNITE

....

FOOD WASTE IS A SIN!

....

Every tonne of food waste averted = 4 tonnes of CO_2 averted.

The average American family of four spends more than $600 a year on food that never gets eaten – it just gets chucked away. That's millions and millions of tonnes of good food that our God-fearing farmers have worked so hard to put on our plates. And vast amounts of energy, water and fertilizers are wasted in the process. We all know it's wrong, but we do nothing about it…

UNTIL NOW!

....

In 2015, the combined power of all the major faith groups in the USA was turned on the 'wicked' problem of food waste. Having got the faithful on board in terms of avoiding food waste in their own homes, they then moved on to supermarkets, restaurants, fast food outlets, hotels, hospitals and schools. Within just five years, food waste in the USA had been reduced by 70%.

After the Lhasa Declaration, politicians the world over found themselves on the receiving end of a different kind of faith-based advocacy, captured in the Declaration's three great exhortations:

SHOW REVERENCE FOR THE EARTH

GIVE SERVICE TO OTHERS

PRACTICE SIMPLICITY IN LIVING

Religious leaders at the signing of the Lhasa Declaration, 2022.

The Declaration committed all world faiths to a series of targets around environmental issues, poverty reduction and active engagement in the community. The choice of Lhasa was itself pretty startling given the historical stand-off between China and Tibet. But China had started rebuilding its relationship with the Dalai Lama five years before that, providing the first tentative steps in a hugely problematic journey that led eventually to a complete reconciliation between China and Tibet in 2041.

People forget just how deep China's own spiritual roots were even at that time. Its understanding of sustainability was always underpinned by the concept of 'harmony', inherited from the philosophical legacies of Confucianism, Buddhism and Daoism. There were some 40,000 Daoist monks in China in 2022 (with more than 50 million people following Daoist practices), and both Christianity and Islam were gaining new adherents all the time – with the unspoken blessing of the Chinese authorities.

The Pope authored a long, personal article in 'Time' on his return from Lhasa in 2022.

The Lhasa Declaration in 2022 could have been just another rhetorical flourish – but it wasn't. For instance, it had a profound effect on the Pope – and that was certainly the first time a Pope had been to Tibet. It was also central to the redefining of the role of Islam that had started with the Arab Spring in 2011, while the burgeoning Pentecostalist churches in the USA put it absolutely at the heart of their mission from that point onwards.

Many of the campaigns that followed on from the Lhasa Declaration had a major impact. The Indian government, for instance, found itself at the sharp end of renewed activism on behalf of the environment, with Hindus, Muslims and Sikhs working together to put an end to what was often referred to as 'the juggernaut of Indian industrialism'. As a direct result of this, the Ganges is now one of the cleanest rivers in the world. And in the USA, as we've seen, moderate evangelicals had already played a big part in making it possible for the Republicans to get their climate act together a few years earlier.

In a much more modest way, we can see that influence here in our own local community through the value that people of faith attach to recognizing that the whole of creation is sacred. We're all much more orientated towards living simply and avoiding waste or opulence, distinguishing between wants and needs, standing up against injustice and helping the least well off in society – because, in the end, it's better for all of us.

25.03.2050

The Material World

One thing that's really come back to me while doing the research for this project is the degree to which we were once obsessed with our IT kit. Embarrassingly, I can still remember the absolute thrill of getting my first R3 device at the age of 21 – R3 standing for 100 per cent repairable, recyclable or reusable. I can even remember the strapline that went with it: 'Because the future's worth it'!

I can honestly say I haven't been so excited about a particular gadget since then. All the devices I use today are at least 10 years old, quite simply because they still do everything I need them to do as well as I need it done. They're all but indestructible, the software on which they run is updated automatically or on command, and works just as well at home, at work or play, on display screens, handheld or retinal, activated by voice, movement or thought. 'One device for life' was one of those early slogans that seems to have worked out pretty well in practice.

Interestingly, even though people were obsessed with their IT devices at the turn of the century, they didn't seem to care much about all the waste these devices created. As sales of every possible comms device increased, most of them eventually ended up in what were then called 'landfill sites' as so much useless junk. Even materials like rare earth metals (naturally occurring metallic elements on which so much of the IT and renewable energy technology depends) met the same fate, despite periodic panics about their availability.

In 2010, less than 10 per cent of all the handheld devices sold were being channelled for recycling or reuse in other countries. More ambitious recycling initiatives were brought in from around 2010 onwards, but these were still hopelessly inadequate given the scale of the problem. It was only when the EU threatened all the device manufacturers with their very first MADD (Manufacturing Dissassembly Directive) that the hard work on designing out waste really started – with the initial focus on the raw materials mined in conflict zones in Africa and elsewhere.

This waste-to-energy plant opened in 2017, situated just about in the centre of Denmark's capital city, Copenhagen. It was then the city's tallest building! People loved the fact that its architect, Bjarke Ingels, made it double up as a popular ski slope. And it is still one of the world's cleanest and greenest plants.

Whole new supply chains had to be established. The manufacture of many components (batteries, screens, cameras and so on) had to be standardized. Adhesives had to be either completely reformulated or avoided altogether. The earliest disassembly plants for electronic and electrical goods were obviously fairly low-tech in comparison to today's state-of-the-art facilities – which now provide hundreds of thousands of very skilled jobs all around the world. (The much talked-about Disabots – or disassembly robots – just kept on making too many mistakes.)

I guess this is one of the best examples of how we've created all sorts of reuse loops – treating all industrial materials as precious, rather than just as junk to be chucked away. In 2010, for instance, the standard power tools so sought after by do-it-yourself enthusiasts (which, for some reason, were mostly men in those days) were each used on average for no more than 12 minutes. That would be seen as criminal these days! What's more, the vast majority of people owned their own power drills: these days, only tradespeople do; the rest of us just hire them.

The Circular Economy

As I discovered when I was studying at Tsinghua University in 2020, the Chinese were the first to coin the term the 'circular economy' 30 years earlier: putting back as much as possible of the raw materials into productive use, rather than being used once and then discarded. This way of thinking has revolutionized almost every sector of the economy – not least clothing.

At the start of the century, for reasons that it's hard to fathom now, clothing was just another throw-away industry. Items of clothing were worn just a few times (or sometimes not worn at all after purchase), then chucked out – with vast quantities of cotton, wool and synthetic materials completely wasted. No thought at all was given to all the energy, water and chemicals needed to produce these materials.

In the late 2010s, with the price of raw materials and energy rising all the time, a few pioneering retailers decided to call time on this insanity. 'Fashion forever' became the slogan for a decade's worth of innovation. New techniques were developed to design clothes for disassembly – in exactly the same way as was already happening with cars and electronic gadgets – so that garments could be reworked into new items of clothing just as attractive and functional as those made from 100 per cent virgin fibre. Today, some virgin fibre is still used, but only a fraction of what was once required.

By 2025 clothing recycling had freed up more than 20 million hectares of land to grow food instead of cotton. So we're now well on the way to our end goal: ZERO FIBRE TO LANDFILL!

Look at the story of aluminium. Before 2015, the best rate of recycling for aluminium was no more than 35 per cent globally, although some countries (and industries) had achieved far higher figures. The energy required to make a tonne of recycled aluminium is just one twentieth of the energy needed for a tonne of primary aluminium.

THE MAKING OF A COTTON T-SHIRT

THE MAKING OF A COTTON T-SHIRT USES AN AVERAGE OF 2,700 LITRES OF WATER

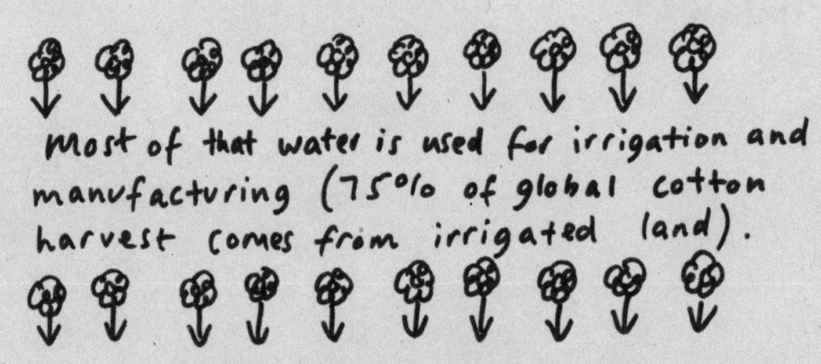

Most of that water is used for irrigation and manufacturing (75% of global cotton harvest comes from irrigated land).

And then there's all the pesticides needed. And the fertilizers. And all the energy required to make all those pesticides and fertilizers, and all the energy to manufacture the t-shirts themselves, and move all that raw material and finished t-shirts around, and all the greenhouse gas emissions from all that energy...

Ours is a world where nearly everything is repaired, recycled or reused – whether we're talking about clothes, electronics, cars, packaging or anything else that can be cycled through our circular economy.

It makes things cheaper, keeps things simpler, and massively reduces our impact on the planet.

This is because primary aluminium requires the mining of aluminium ore (a horribly messy business at the best of times), as well as all the smelting and processing. Today, global aluminium recycling is up to 85 per cent. And some of the best performing countries managed to get to nearly 100 per cent recycled by the mid-2020s.

That recycling story is one of the reasons why aluminium has turned out to be such a success story. The vast majority of today's vehicles, for instance, are made from aluminium (rather than the steel used earlier in the century). Funnily enough, however, there's actually a far lower volume of aluminium being recycled now than in the 2020s: reuse is what it's all about today. Even recycling is a very energy-intensive process, and the real 'closed-loop' processes only became possible when smart design and manufacturing enabled all sorts of standard parts and components to be reused – car doors, boots and bonnets, for instance.

A few decades ago, environmentalists had a favourite little saying when they were campaigning against the throw-away world: 'There's no such thing as waste in nature'. We haven't quite got to the point where we can say 'There's no such thing as waste in the human economy', but we're not far off.

31.03.2050

Restoring the Web of Life

4

National

The Guardian | Tuesday 17 August 2010

Telephone: 020 3353 4090
Fax: 020 3353 3190
Email: national@guardian.co.uk

The real butterfly effect: destroying nature will ruin economies and cultures, pleads UN

Biodiversity chief to push for more ambitious targets

Damage to natural world 'reaching tipping point'

John Vidal
Environment editor

Britain and other countries face a collapse of their economies and loss of culture if they do not protect the environment better, the world's leading champion of nature has warned.

"What we are seeing today is a total disaster," said Ahmed Djoghlaf, the secretary-general of the UN Convention on Biological Diversity. "No country has met its targets to protect nature. We are losing biodiversity at an unprecedented rate. If current levels [of destruction] go on we will reach a tipping point very soon. The future of the planet now depends on governments taking action in the next few years."

Industrialisation, population growth, the spread of cities and farms, and climate change are all now threatening the fundamentals of life itself, said Djoghlaf, in London before a UN meeting in which governments are expected to sign up to a more ambitious deal to protect nature.

"Many plans were developed in the 1990s to protect biodiversity but they are still sitting on the shelves of ministries. Countries were legally obliged to act, but only 140 have even submitted plans and only 16 have revised their plans since 1993. Governments must now put their houses in order," he said.

According to the UN Environment Programme, the Earth is in the middle of a mass extinction of life. Scientists estimate that 150-200 species of plant, insect, bird and mammal become extinct every 24 hours. This is nearly 1,000 times the "natural" or "background" rate and, claim many biologists, is greater than anything the world has experienced since the dinosaurs vanished nearly 65m years ago. Around 15% of mammal species and 11% of bird species are classified as threatened with extinction.

Djoghlaf warned Britain and other countries not to cut nature protection amid the recession. In a reference to expected 40% cuts in Britain's Department of the Environment spending, he said: "You may well save a few pounds now but you will lose billions later. Biodiversity is your natural asset. The more you lose it, the more you lose your cultural assets too."

Djoghlaf said 300 million people who depended on forests and the more than 1 billion who lived off sea fishing were in immediate danger. "Cut your forests down, or over-fish, and these people will not survive. Destroying biodiversity only increases economic insecurity. The more you lose it, the more you lose the chance to grow." He added: "The loss of biodiversity compounds poverty. Biodiversity is fundamental to social life, education and aesthetics. It's a human right to live in a healthy environment."

Djoghlaf criticised countries for separating action on climate change from protecting biodiversity. "The loss of biodiversity exacerbates climate change.

15% **Proportion of mammal species now facing extinction. The present rate of disappearance is 1,000 times the natural rate**

But it is handled by the poorest ministries in government, it has not been mainstreamed or prioritised by governments. Climate change cannot be solved without action on biodiversity, and vice versa."

The UN chief said that children were losing contact with nature. "In Algeria, children are growing up who have never seen olive trees. How can you protect nature if you do not know it?"

A UN report on the impact of biodiversity loss, out in October, is expected to say that the economic case for global action to stop species destruction is even more powerful than the argument for tackling climate change. It will say that saving biodiversity is cost-effective and the benefits from saving "natural goods and services", such as pollination, medicines, fertile soils, clean air and water, are between 10 and 100 times the cost of saving the habitats and species that provide them.

guardian.co.uk/biodiversity100

A Painted Lady butterfly. A new UN report due out in October will argue that protecting the increasingly fragile natural world is as important to the global economy and human culture as the prevention of climate change Photograph: Press Association

An article we found from The Guardian, Tuesday 17 August 2010, highlighting the importance of protecting our natural world.

Apart from climate change, no environmental issue has caused as much concern as the damage done to the natural world and its wondrous diversity of species. Over the decades, there have been endless conferences, 'landmark reports', research papers, international agreements and brilliant wildlife documentaries – all highlighting just how bad things have got. The details of our sorry situation are logged each year in the Red List, the official annual account of threatened species and their risk of extinction.

The relentless loss of species has been all the more extraordinary as so many people (particularly in the rich countries of the Northern Hemisphere) appeared to care passionately about biodiversity. For instance, there were said to be more than 60 million bird watchers in the USA in 2015, shelling out billions of dollars every year to catch the occasional glimpse of precisely those birds that their very way of life was putting at risk! Whale watching was even more of a guaranteed money spinner. Ecotourism just kept on growing and growing, even as the Red List got longer and longer.

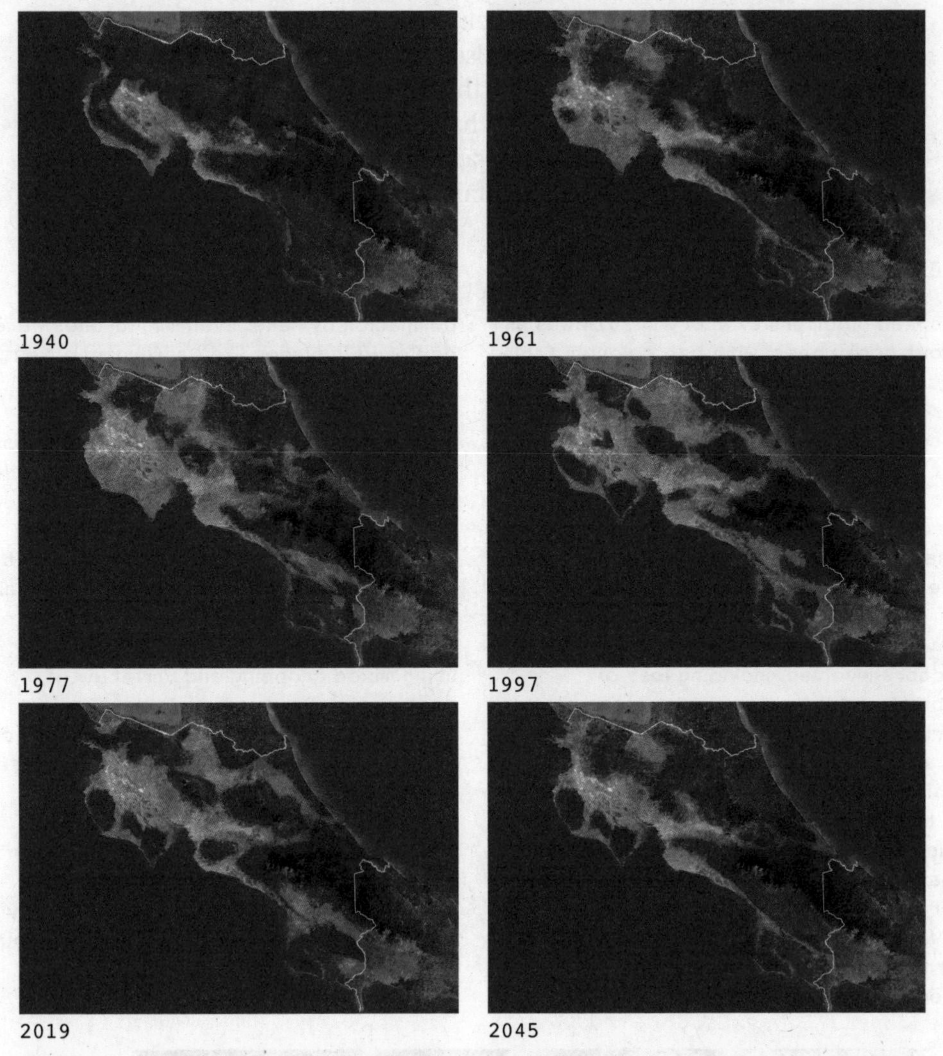

Satellite images of forest cover in Costa Rica, 1940–2045 (with reconstructions for 1940 and 1961).

There were, of course, some wonderful exceptions – as these satellite images show. Through its ground-breaking Environmental Services Payment Programme, by 2015 Costa Rica had regenerated more than 1000 square kilometres of tropical forest, including the Guanacaste Conservation Area, which became the world's most renowned facility for tropical forestry research. With Costa Rica becoming a major destination for ecotourism of every kind, the Costa Rica Conservation Trust Fund was also established, with an endowment of more than a billion dollars to 'protect in perpetuity' one third of its total land area.

Out of the 188 countries that had ratified the Convention on Biological Diversity in 1994, Costa Rica provided the only really convincing nationwide success story on offer when they celebrated the Convention's 20th anniversary in 2014. There was also special recognition for WWF International, whose 'Gifts to the Earth' campaign had by that time persuaded the governments of more than 100 countries to 'set aside' for special protection the equivalent of 250 million hectares. But for the most part, it was a grim picture of loss and failure.

Honey Bees

The lead biodiversity story in 2014 was all about honey bees, with bee colonies facing total wipe-out worldwide. What was known as 'colony collapse disorder' was first observed in European bees in the 1970s, but it became much more serious from the mid-1990s onwards and spread rapidly across the world. Adult bees would just disappear from the hive, leaving the young bees and queen without nutrition.

It was a complex story with many different factors involved, including loss of habitat and flowering plants, increasingly serious air pollution, the excessive use of agricultural chemicals and reduced resistance to parasites and pests such as the Varroa mite. With bees being the principal pollinator for 70 of the world's most important crop species, the loss of more than 60 per cent of bee colonies had devastating economic consequences. Some farmers gave up, while others resorted to desperate alternative measures, such as pollination by hand. Even mini-drones were deployed in places like California to carry out mechanical pollination.

But by 2014, a clear scientific consensus had emerged that new types of insecticide (the infamous neonicotinoids, applied for the most part as seed dressings) were to blame. More than 20 of the most suspect insecticides were banned virtually overnight. In addition, bee-friendly farming practises were re-introduced using mixed cropping and varieties of nectar-rich flowers in field margins. Thankfully, that all had the desired effect, and within a decade bee populations were almost back to normal.

The shock of the honey bee episode went deep and wide. People suddenly realized that conservationists had not been 'crying wolf'. When natural systems crash, our own prospects really are put at risk.

Pollinating trees by hand in Sichuan province, China, 2023.

It's strange that it was the humble honey bee that triggered a revolution in our approach to the natural world, rather than the wonderfully charismatic creatures such as the snow leopard, orang-utan and rhino that had been the focus of so much conservation attention. But it focused our minds, and from the early 2020s onwards, everything that had been learnt back in the twentieth century about creating buffer zones around special conservation areas, about Community Development Trusts, volunteer schemes and so on got to be rolled out on an unprecedented scale. Many of these schemes made good use of EarthCorps volunteers. But were it not for the International Financial Transaction Tax, introduced in 2022 (see p.225), it's difficult to imagine where the funds would have come from for this essential but demanding conservation work.

A cloned condor circling high in the Andes, 2043. The Frozen Zoo at San Diego now holds the genomes of more than 3,300 species. Boldly proclaiming that 'extinction needn't be forever', it's busy advocating various survival programmes – even though the reintroduction of genetically identical clones of a handful of iconic species has met with very mixed results over the years. There's a simple reason for that. If the habitat is still at risk, then the creatures in it are still at risk – cloned or not.

While this has been one of the great recovery stories of the twenty-first century, success seems to have bred complacency. Even though our global population has started to decline, there is still enormous pressure on scarce land. Biodiversity refuges, national parks, wetlands, bogs, grasslands, wilderness reserves, even rainforests, are all still seen by some politicians and economists as fair game for short-term economic development at the expense of long-term prosperity. Disappointingly but not surprisingly, the annual Red List of endangered species still shows a huge number of species still at risk. But the number is slowly coming down.

I know I'm biased, but in my view this all comes back to education. In 2005, a writer called Richard Louv wrote a highly influential book called 'Last Child in the Woods'. It attributed many of the problems that children and young people faced at that time to what he called 'nature-deficit disorder' (or NDD) – the inability to connect with the natural world in any meaningful sense. As the evidence base grew that contact with the natural world was indeed a crucial part of growing up, an ever-higher priority was put on enabling young people to get out more, with lots of places to play and interact with the natural world.

BIODIVERSITY HOTSPOTS
→ World

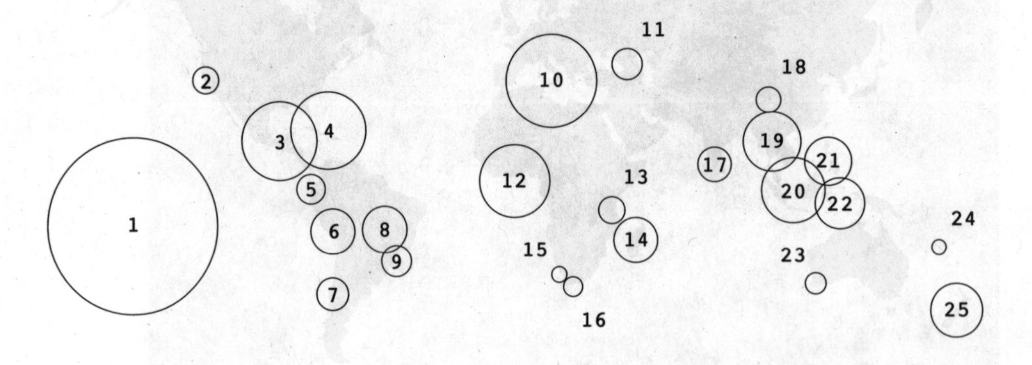

1 Polynesia / Micronesia
2 California Floristic Province
3 Mesoamerica
4 Caribbean
5 Chocó / Darién / Western Ecuador
6 Tropical Andes
7 Central Chile
8 Brazil's Cerrado
9 Brazil's Atlantic Forest
10 Mediterranean Basin
11 Caucasus
12 West African Forests
13 East Africa Coastal Forests
14 Madagascar
15 Succulent Karoo
16 Cape Floristic Province
17 Western Ghats and Sri Lanka
18 South-Central China
19 Indo-Burma
20 Sundaland
21 Philippines
22 Wallacea
23 Southwest Australia
24 New Caledonia
25 New Zealand

Scientists had long pointed out to politicians that if they provided proper protection for just 25 biodiversity 'hotspots' around the world, they would be halfway there in terms of protecting the Earth's most precious biodiversity. Those 25 hotspots represent no more than two per cent of the Earth's total land area – but they're also the places where more than 1.5 billion people now live. So no easy answers!

07.04.2050

Education Unlimited

Ashton Vale Community College, 2031. I took this photo on the first day I started teaching there.

I started teaching in 2022 and moved to Ashton Vale Community College in 2031 – a big, boisterous inner-city college, taking kids from the age of 10 upwards. The surrounding catchment area was among the most deprived earlier in the century, but in 2014 Ashton Vale was selected to become the UK's first Sustainable Community College, to mark the close of the UN's Decade of Education for Sustainable Development. It had a specific remit to shake up an educational system that had changed little in the preceding 60 years, preparing most young people for jobs that no longer existed, to lead unrewarding, self-absorbed lives in a world that was on the brink of collapse, economically as well as environmentally.

A very different kind of education has been at the heart of our journey to a more sustainable world – eloquently captured in the original Ashton Vale Mission (see p.83), which seems just as fresh and relevant as it was when it was written, 36 years ago.

Ashton Vale was built nearly 40 years ago, one of a new generation of schools and colleges that were expensive at the time, but built to last. A combination of durable materials and flexible design (so that all interiors can be easily reconfigured) makes it as good a building to learn in as it was 40 years ago. The College's mission statement from 2014 talks about providing young people

with the skills they need to thrive in the real world (see p.84). We have our own workshops, IT labs, kitchens and allotments; we generate our own energy, recycle all our waste, harvest all our rainwater, keep bees and grow 30 per cent of the food that we use in the school.

Most of the academic stuff takes place in the morning, while most of the technical, creative and vocational stuff is in the afternoon. We have plenty of teaching assistants, drawing on the widest range of skills across the whole of the local community.

That focus on the local community is absolutely critical. Every young person takes part in various community projects, working with old people or volunteering on urban nature reserves and in 'pocket parks'. And although security is still an issue, instant face-recognition systems mean that the barriers between us and the community that we serve can be kept to a minimum.

I don't quite know how, but I quickly got drawn into Ashton Vale's multiple food initiatives – despite the fact that I was actually employed to teach history! I have particularly strong memories of one ambitious project to take over some neighbouring wasteland (covering more than two hectares) and use it to grow our own food. We did it as 'guerrilla gardeners' to start with, without any permission, until it reached the point where the local planning authority decided it was a good thing anyway and gave it their blessing. Our 'incredible edible Ashton Vale' project is still going strong, 15 years on!

Most of the time, the young people design their learning programmes for themselves, with pretty much unlimited access to e-learning initiatives of every kind, involving hundreds of volunteers prepared to donate their time to tutor the students via Skype. (I think this was originally called SOLES, standing for 'self-organized learning environments', when the College was set up.) The College now has some of the highest attainment rates in the city and the lowest truancy rates.

Self-Organized Learning

I can vaguely remember my Dad telling me about various 'twinning' schemes that his school in Glasgow was involved in back in the 1970s – but they never actually got to see any of the kids in the school that they were twinned with. Via SkypePlus and various educational platforms including iLearn and the Young Makers' Programme, we're linked in with kids in Tibet and Bhutan when learning about wellbeing and Gross Domestic Happiness (GDH), and with communities in Bangladesh and California doing our climate logs; we swap growing tips and recipes (and even illicit packets of seeds!) with schools in India and the Philippines, and so on. And there's still a lot of competition to take part in some of UNESCO's OneWorld flagship programmes – the Global Chemistry Experiments remain extremely popular, as does the WomEn (Women in Engineering) Initiative. What were once called MOOCs (Massive Open Online Courses) blossomed into today's Learning Universe – where the 'ubiquity story' I outlined on p.30 really has transformed our world.

Lillian's Learning Lab

Lillian is one of the Research Team, and this is her mind map of her self-organized learning programme.

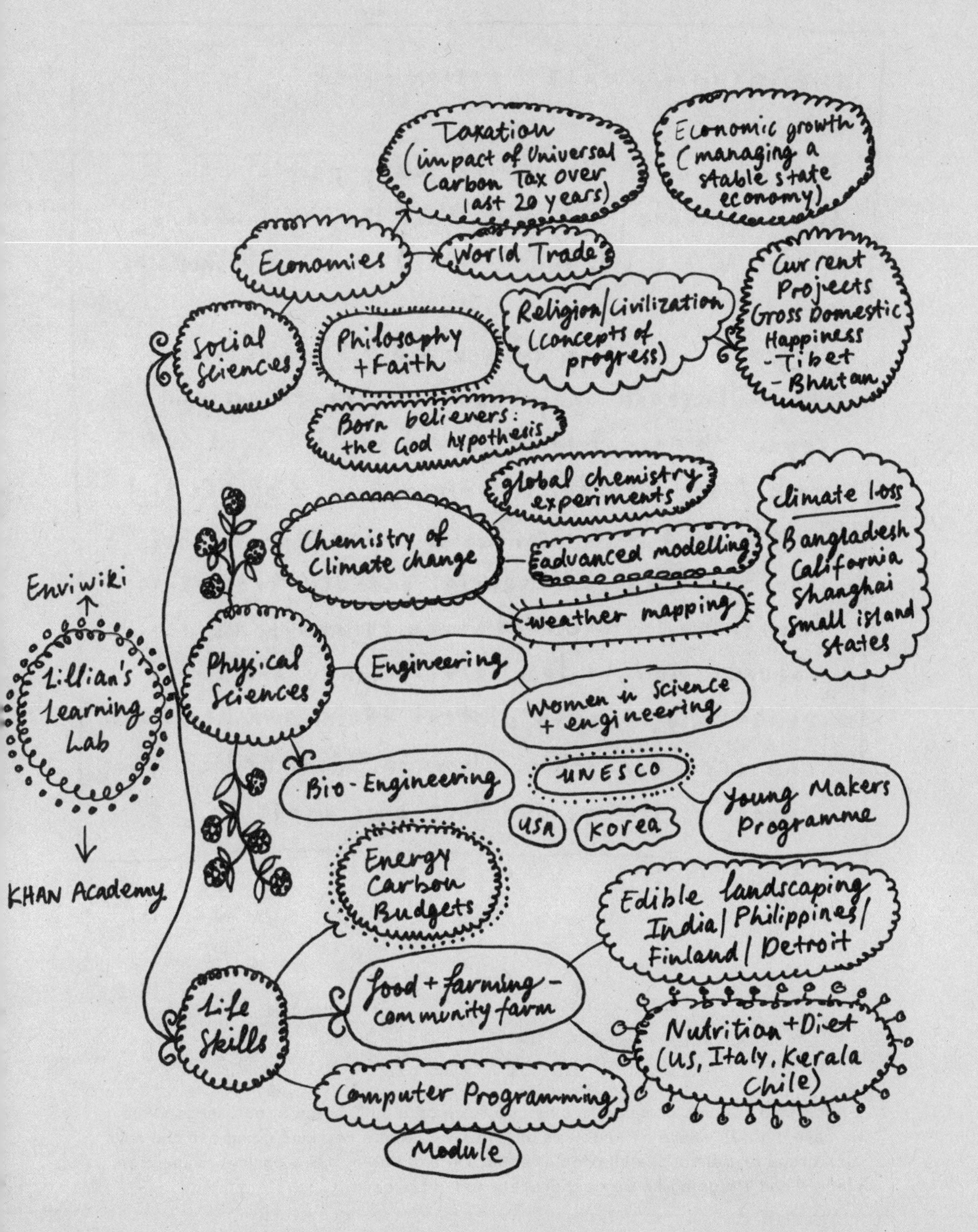

THE ASHTON VALE MISSION

Our mission is to provide young people with the knowledge and skills that they will need to thrive in the world as it really is, not as it once was.

We will help them to ask the right questions. We will teach them how to make things and repair things; how to grow food, love food and cook food; how to celebrate the gift of life and understand the meaning of interdependence; how to be entreprenеurial and self-organizing; how to build their community and to value nature; how to look after money and live generously; how to protect their own health and care for others; how to think critically, engage actively, and live passionately.

I hope this doesn't come across as too much of a puff piece about Ashton Vale. We have our fair share of problems all the time, with a few kids going off the rails with drugs or mental health problems. But on the whole, it's a caring, connected place – and I'm going to be desperately sorry to leave it.

For the kids at Ashton Vale, the exposure they get to lives a lot tougher than their own is what makes so many of them sign up with the EarthCorps (see p.189). As a former participant (I spent six months in Kenya with the EarthCorps in 2018–2019), I soon got to be the EarthCorps coordinator for Ashton Vale and the surrounding community. Once someone volunteers for the EarthCorps, they spend a whole year getting themselves ready, acquiring basic skills in agronomy and engineering, teaching and healthcare, or whatever.

Education For All

Kids at Ashton Vale get a real sense of the rest of the world from all their digital connectivity – and also a real sense of their own relative privilege here in the UK, compared to many other places where access to education still has to be fought for. Progress on the UN's Education For All initiatives had been much slower than hoped for earlier in the century, but it's now much better, even on challenging issues like equal access to education for girls and boys. Indeed, the amazing 'one tablet per child' worldwide computer initiative led by Nicholas Negroponte formally shut up shop in 2028 with the job more or less done. From a starting point of around 10 million computers delivered by 2010, the whole thing took off over the next few years, with the average price of a tablet coming down to around $20 by 2020. Given the shortage of teachers then, a lot of the benefit came from the same kind of self-learning approach we use at Ashton Vale.

Massive Open Online Courses were available across the entire world; by 2020, for example, UNESCO's Global Academy initiative was providing academic content at every level for more than 100 million kids. Game-based education was already well established, enabling really effective peer-to-peer learning – 'making learning addictive and wildly entertaining', in Negroponte's words.

The 'One Laptop Per Child' initiative was highly successful, with 10 million computers delivered in 2010 – including this group of kids in Ethiopia when it started back in 2008. 'One Tablet Per Child' built on that early momentum.

15.04.2050

The Great Famine

The effects of black stem rust on wheat.

A lot of contemporary historians seem to have opted for 2025 as the definitive turning point on our journey to a sustainable way of life. The seismic shock of what happened that year – only partly captured in a grisly death count of more than 10 million people dead – finished off the business-as-usual brigade once and for all.

It was not exactly unexpected. Scientists (including my Dad) had been warning for years of a potential 'perfect storm' of converging crises. Politicians had talked endlessly about the importance of food security and the efforts they were making to make sure everybody should have enough to eat – 'Zero Hunger' as they called it. Organizations like Oxfam and the World Resources Institute in the US issued warning after warning, but no one in power had really reckoned on all the crunch factors occurring at the same time.

Any one of the six crises (listed on p.89) would have been manageable on its own – after all, there had been periodic food shortages and occasional regional famines going right back to 2008. Food riots had become commonplace all around the world because of high food prices. But it was the combination of all those factors that caused the entire food system to collapse in 2025. What turned it into an apocalypse, rather than just another disaster, was the onset of a new variety of black stem rust (called Ug99), which wiped out the wheat harvest across the whole of Africa, the Middle East and parts of Asia.

THE SPREADING OF BLACK STEM RUST 2023 – 2025

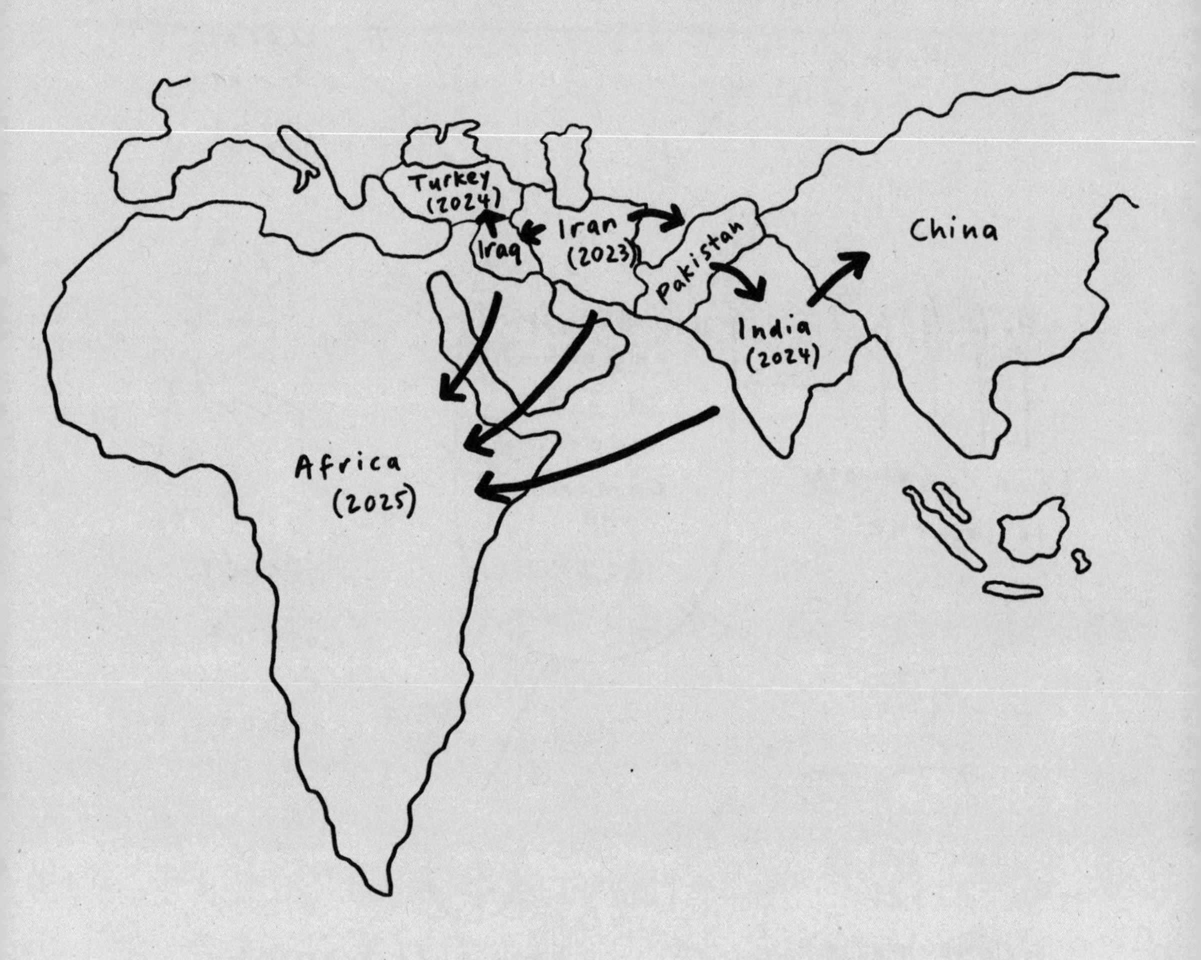

How the disaster unfolded:

New variants of Ug99 emerged in Iran in 2023 and spread rapidly to the north (into Iraq and Turkey), to the east (to Pakistan and India) and – most disastrously of all – on into the extensive wheat fields of China. Then it started to spread south into Africa. In total, more than 1.5 billion people depended on wheat in those countries.

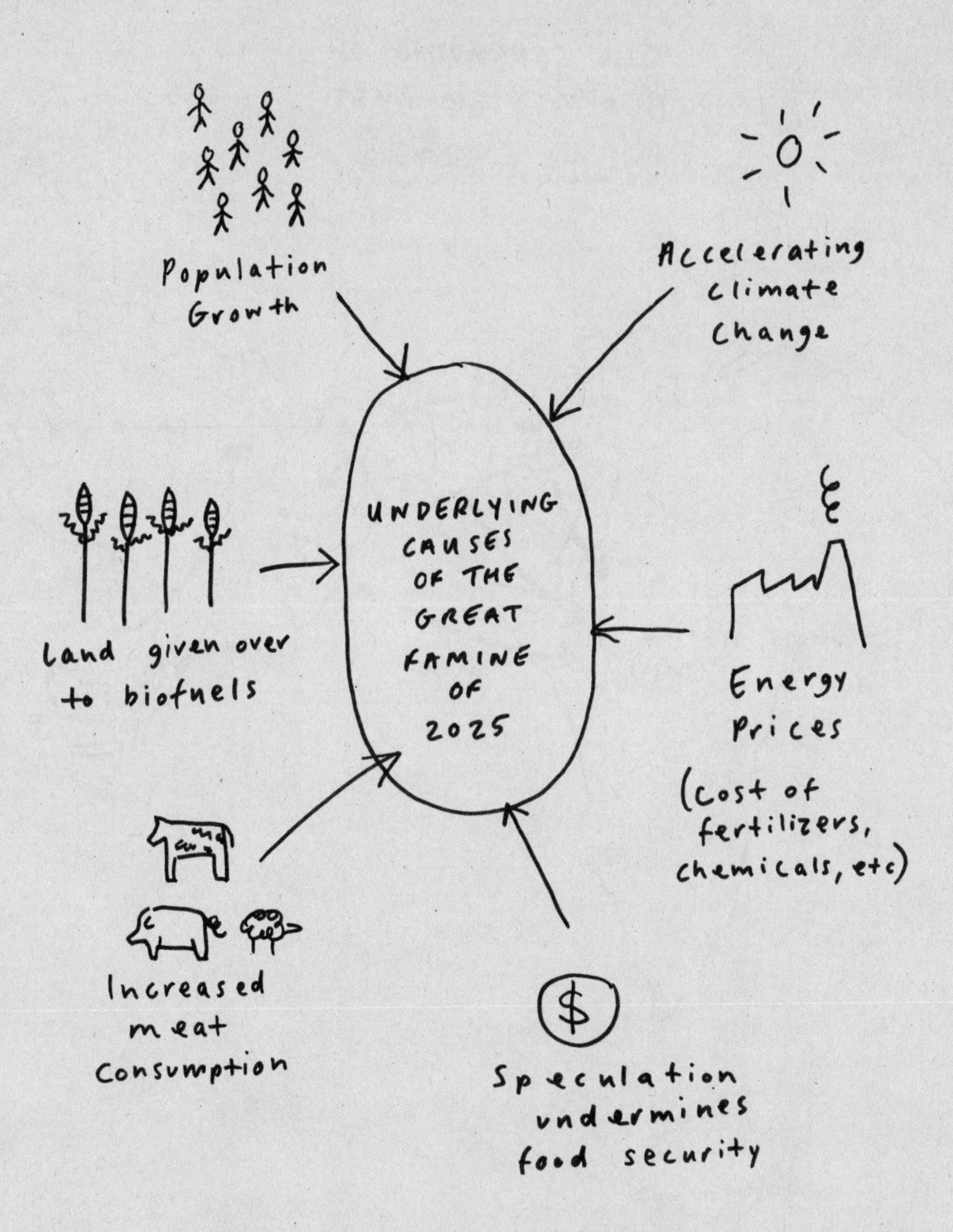

UNDERLYING CAUSES OF THE GREAT FAMINE OF 2025
Population Growth
Accelerating climate Change
Land given over to biofuels
Energy Prices
(cost of fertilizers, chemicals, etc)
Increased meat Consumption
Speculation undermines food security

Causes of the Great Famine, 2025

1. Climate Change
2024 was a particularly grim year, with severe drought affecting more than 25 countries. The devastating fires in Russia and the Ukraine (far worse than in 2010 and 2018) destroyed more than 75 per cent of their wheat harvest.

2. Energy Prices
Oil and gas prices hit their highest ever in 2023, and stayed high through to 2025. Production of nitrogen fertilizer was still almost entirely dependent on the use of gas for energy, so fertilizer prices went sky high, putting them beyond the reach of many farmers in poorer countries.

3. Speculation
Speculation had become a feature of many commodity markets since the turn of the century. Despite constant efforts by governments to regulate the role of hedge funds in basic commodity crop trading, the hedge funds were always too clever for them. (It was later revealed that 50 per cent of maize production and 40 per cent of rice production was under the direct control of speculators at that time.)

4. Meat Consumption
Growing crops for animals to eat was still just as profitable as growing crops for humans to eat. In 2025, 50 per cent of the world's grain was being fed to animals and meat consumption was still rising in China, India and many other countries.

5. Biofuels
Despite some astonishing breakthroughs with advanced biofuels, there was still a huge amount of prime land growing crops for fuel rather than crops for food. As food prices rose, farmers started to move back into food production – but too late to make enough of a difference by 2025.

6. Population
Grain yields had continued to grow by about 1 per cent a year throughout the second decade of the century. But the world's population kept growing by slightly more (at 1.2 per cent per annum), and demand for food was growing still faster, by an average of 1.7 per cent a year. It just didn't add up.

Drought in Kenya, 2025.

Throughout the 25 years since this particularly virulent fungus was first identified in Uganda in 1999, Ug99 had been causing problems. The great Norman Borlaug himself (the father of the Green Revolution back in the twentieth century) had warned that Ug99 constituted 'a greater risk to humankind than any other threat it faces'. Most strains of wheat had little resistance to it.

The problem was kept at bay for more than 20 years, but then the disaster struck. New variants of Ug99 emerged in 2023 to which not one single strain of wheat had any resistance. The first effects were felt in 2024, but the full fury came in 2025. Yields were slashed by more than 80 per cent, and there was simply no making up the shortfall. Food stocks had been at an all-time low anyway, and the US harvest had been very poor both in 2023 and 2024. As the scale of the disaster became apparent, wealthy countries committed billions of dollars to famine relief, although there simply wasn't enough food to buy on the open market: all sorts of export bans had instantly been put in place by governments worried about their own food supplies.

At the same time, thousands of volunteers were mobilized to support countries that were simply unable to cope, helping distribute what food was available and planting new crops. The lives of millions were saved. I was one of those volunteers. As soon as I could get away, I returned to the same town in Kenya where I'd served with the EarthCorps just a few years earlier. Already weakened by several years of below average rainfall and reduced fertilizer use because of very high prices, East Africa lost the whole of its wheat crop for three years in a row. Many of the children I had taught didn't make it.

There have always been those who argue that we humans only ever learn through failure and pain. Right up until the world famine in 2025, most 'experts' continued to argue that we could still expand our way out of any potential food shortages – even though their model of oil-dependent, chemical-dependent intensive agriculture was shrivelling up in front of their eyes. They continued to argue that we had enough land for rising meat consumption <u>and</u> increased biofuel production <u>and</u> more food.

Those cornucopian fantasies were forever dispelled in 2025. Not only did more than 10 million people die as a direct consequence of the famine, but thousands more were killed in food riots in more than 70 countries. Supply chains were thrown into total chaos as prices soared, and governments had to introduce various kinds of rationing even in some of the world's wealthier nations. Riots on that scale weren't seen again until 2032 – but by then, the world was much closer to achieving genuine food security. The lessons of the Great Famine had been well and truly learned.

20.04.2050
Putting Nature to Work

People today forget just how controversial the debate about biofuels was at the start of the century. The original decision by the US government to subsidize its corn farmers, if they produced ethanol rather than food from their corn, ignited a 'food versus fuel' debate that went on for more than two decades.

When food prices spiked for the first time in 2008, the fact that more than 30 per cent of US corn at that time was being used to make ethanol instead of food caused outrage. Over the next 10 years, the Americans came to accept that it made no sense subsidizing their corn farmers to produce a form of ethanol that did almost nothing to reduce emissions of greenhouse gases, while sticking a punitive tariff on the much lower carbon ethanol from Brazil! All subsidies were phased out after that, though production still continued right through to the Great Famine in 2025.

But the basic idea of biofuels was right, even then. In fact, we didn't really have much choice, as everyone accepted that we had to dramatically reduce our dependence on oil for transportation. There were only three ways of doing that: improve the internal combustion engine so that it became super-efficient; go all-electric; or substitute biofuels for fossil fuels. In the end, it turned out we did all three!

A state-of-the-art biorefinery in Brazil, 2035.

One country stands out as the driving force behind the transition to biofuels: Brazil. Brazil first started making ethanol from sugar cane back in the 1970s, when the priority was to reduce its dependence on very expensive imported oil. From 2000 onwards, it was by far the most efficient producer of bio-ethanol (with the lowest carbon footprint), using both the sugar and the waste products from making that sugar to produce ethanol.

Despite having huge oil reserves of its own, the Brazilians established leading positions on a variety of different biofuel molecules (including bio-butanol, which has significant advantages over ethanol), working with a range of commercial companies to achieve this. They also pioneered the production of a whole host of 'second generation' biofuels using cellulose-based feedstocks from perennial grasses (such as switchgrass and elephant grass) to fast-growing trees.

Brazil wasn't alone in this biofuels revolution. All around the world, biotechnology companies worked out how best to break down the cellulose in plant materials, using highly specific enzymes and other chemical 'battering rams'. Start-ups in the UK, USA and Italy (which pioneered the use of Arundo cane) soon established themselves as market leaders, but the competition got a lot fiercer when both China and India entered the market. And as paper production continued to decline, even Russia, the Nordic countries and Canada got in on the act, directing more of the available pulp into advanced biodiesel.

Year on year, these second generation biofuels got cheaper, more efficient (in terms of fuel density), more reliable and with better carbon balances in terms of CO_2 emissions per unit of energy produced. By 2020, most car engines were designed to run on 85 per cent biofuel blends (15 per cent oil-derived fuel), or even on 100 per cent biofuel. This was still controversial, simply because these second generation fuels needed land for growing the feedstocks, and that meant there was still some competition with food. There was also a limit to the amount of agricultural waste that could be turned into biofuels without damaging soil fertility.

However, in general, it all worked reasonably well as a substitution strategy. And not just for the rich world: many poorer countries (with relatively low per capita consumption of petrol and diesel) put biofuels at the heart of their own liquid fuels strategy from the start – using locally grown feedstocks for local markets. The result was a completely decentralized production model based on plants like jatropha, agave, camelina and sweet sorghum.

However, by the end of the 2020s, demand for food was so great that even the most efficient second generation biofuels couldn't really justify the amount of land they were using. That's when the pioneering work of people like Craig Venter (see p.94) in developing 'advanced biofuels' came into its own and began to take over.

At about the same time, various air-capture technologies (to make use of all the CO_2 in the atmosphere) began to kick in, using algae that need just sunlight and CO_2 to synthesize fuels such as bio-butanol. We can now make this work at any scale, right down to local community use. Neat stuff – although not without continuing controversies on the air-capture front, as I'll explain on p.142.

AIR-CAPTURE TECHNOLOGY FOR BIOFUELS

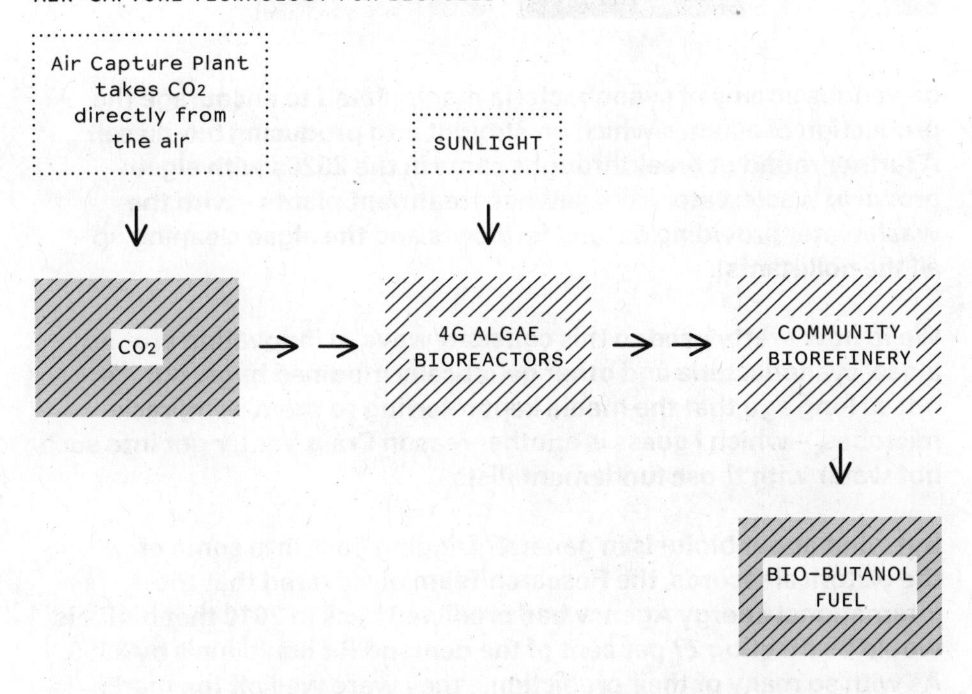

There had been countless false starts, of course, with untold amounts of venture capital eaten up in the process. Even Craig Venter's Synthetic Genomics Inc. had worked its way through around $500 million of ExxonMobil's cash before its first commercial success with SynAlgo in 2017. Venter's team had eventually succeeded in synthesizing novel algae – single-celled organisms that turned CO_2, hydrogen and nitrogen into carbohydrates and natural oils (or lipids) – as a direct substitute for petrol and diesel.

As has happened so often over the last 40 years, that one breakthrough seemed to open the floodgates for everyone else. Some technologies focused on algae of every conceivable type; others

Craig Venter was one of the great entrepreneurs of the first half of the twenty-first century – and one of the first to use the techniques of synthetic biology to create completely new organisms. To say this was controversial is an understatement! Venter himself very nearly gave up his work in 2016, when his lab was destroyed by arson and his life was threatened on several occasions by a Christian fundamentalist sect for having dared to 'take God's law into his own hands'.

on various strains of cyanobacteria manipulated to encourage the production of alkanes which go straight into producing bio-diesel. A further round of breakthroughs came in the 2020s with algae grown in wastewater from sewage treatment plants – with the wastewater providing natural fertilizers and the algae cleaning up all the pollutants!

We're now pretty used to this constant wave of innovation around algae, cyanobacteria and other genetically modified bugs. But it's not so long ago that the media kept referring to them as 'miracle microbes' – which I guess is another reason Craig Venter got into such hot water with those fundamentalists.

But what about biofuels in general? Digging back into some of the historical records, the Research Team discovered that the International Energy Agency had predicted back in 2010 that biofuels would be meeting 27 per cent of the demand for liquid fuels by 2050. As with so many of their predictions, they were well off the mark: that figure was surpassed back in 2035, and total market share is now hovering at around 85 per cent – of a much smaller total market, of course, given the dominance of electric vehicles (see p.144).

27.04.2050

Security in a Cyber World

This is a century that started conventionally enough in terms of warfare. The US was still in the business of imposing its 'Pax Americana' on the rest of the world, and on the Middle East in particular. The war in Afghanistan (2002–2015) cost around $4 trillion; the war in Iraq (2003–2008), a mere $2.5 trillion. For a country that had been technically bankrupt for years, this was folly on a grand scale – and only possible because China continued throughout that time to buy up US Treasury bonds and bills, without which the US couldn't possibly have financed its military ambitions.

The end of the war in Afghanistan marked the end of this inglorious period in US history. Barack Obama began the cutbacks in defence spending in his second term as president, and those reductions continued for the next 20 years. It got easier to make those cuts as the US became progressively less dependent on oil from the Middle East – which meant it no longer had to maintain massive firepower in that part of the world. Unfortunately, a significant share of those savings had to be redirected into spending on cyber-warfare – going right back to the attack on Iran's Natanz nuclear facility in 2010.

Natanz nuclear plant, Iran – the target of the first US cyber attack back in 2010.

The 2010 Stuxnet cyber-attack carried out by the US on Iran's uranium enrichment plant at Natanz is recognized today as the first clear escalation in the era of cyber-warfare – the first time any nation carried out an explicit 'act of war' on another nation using computer software.

It turned out soon afterwards that many nations had been hard at work developing their own cyber-capability. China, for instance, was already very actively involved in probing weaknesses in Western defence systems. It's now known that it was China, not the US, that disabled North Korea's entire nuclear capability in 2017, when it looked as if the latest outbreak of hostilities with South Korea was on the point of escalating into a nuclear exchange. By that time, even China had had enough of its erstwhile client state, and although it took another 20 years, the re-unification of Korea was born of that moment.

Both India and Pakistan had been quick to ramp up their cyber-warfare capabilities, leading to what seemed like an endless sequence of tit-for-tat spoilers on each other's military forces. It could have been worse (in that it could at any time have turned into a nuclear confrontation), but it seriously weakened peace efforts throughout that time. Worse, it helped train up dozens of frighteningly talented specialists in cyber-warfare – a number of whom ended up putting that talent at the disposal of terrorist organizations, as was the case with the attack on US and UK nuclear reactors in 2019 (see p.59).

The costs of maintaining defences against cyber-terrorism over the last 40 years have been staggering. And I still don't think we know the half of what's actually been going on. What really worries communities like ours is the risk all this poses to day-to-day things like telecoms, power stations and water supply. What happened to France in 2022 really brought that home to people. A previously unknown terrorist group based in Algeria carried out a devastating cyber-attack on the SCADAs (supervisory control and data acquisition systems) used at that time to operate all the biggest water treatment plants in France. Because the software was standard across the industry, the vast majority of water companies all around the world had to completely replace their security systems.

That one incident caused water bills across Europe to increase by an average of five per cent. A year later, China was hit by an equally devastating attack on both chemical plants and air traffic control systems, organized by one of the many dissident groups operating in China at that time. There has been one indirect upside here: cyber-threats of this kind reinforced the willingness of politicians (and their electorates) to move towards a much more decentralized world. Taking out a nuclear power station is one thing, but who's going to bother with a community wind farm?

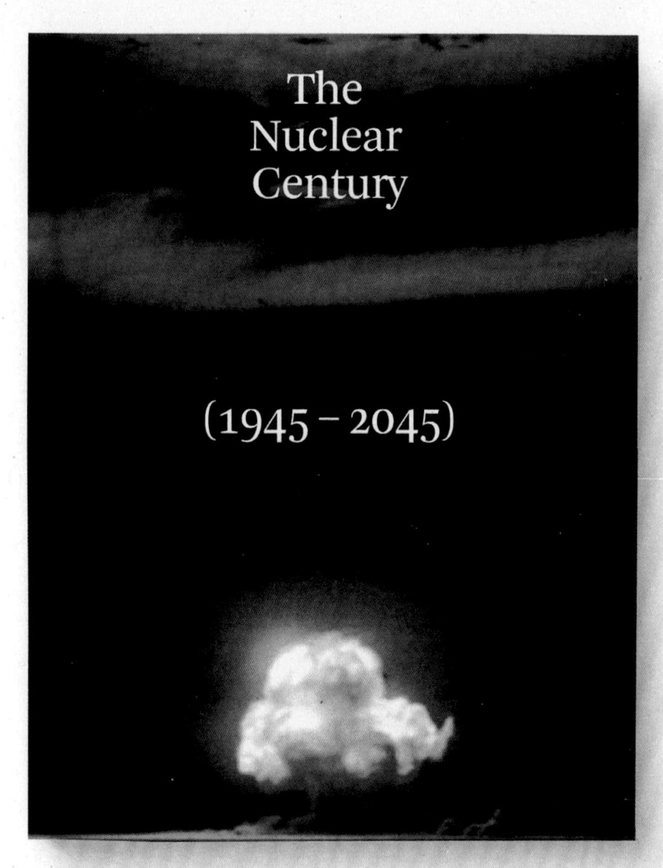

It's more than 100 years now since the scientists involved in the Manhattan Project witnessed the detonation of the first atomic bomb, in July 1945. One of them, Robert Oppenheimer, was forever haunted by a verse from the Bhagavad Gita: 'I am become death, the destroyer of worlds'.

In other words, nobody was immune, however powerful. Politicians soon came to the conclusion, particularly in the US and China, that any cyber-aggression on the part of any one nation was inevitably going to be a game without winners, in that it made it so much easier for other nations to follow suit.

Negotiations on CONCYBA (the Convention on Cyber and Bio-Aggression) started in earnest in 2023, and the Convention was eventually signed (by all nations) a few years later, in 2027. In itself, this did little to deter terrorist organizations, but it helped to put a cap on escalating expenditure and made it possible for countries to collaborate on keeping a closer check on the terrorists.

So much for the cyber-story, which still looms over us all in a pretty gloomy way. However, on other security issues it's a much better picture. Some spending still goes on nuclear weapons, but – as my students keep reminding me – at least there are far fewer nuclear weapons than there were at the turn of the century, and those that exist are in the hands of fewer countries: just the US, Russia, China, India, Pakistan, Israel and Iran. But not France and not the UK!

The 'top brass' of the armed services in the UK, on their way to a meeting with the Prime Minister in 2021 to confirm plans for phasing out nuclear weapons.

When the vast majority of top-ranking officers across the UK armed services, whether serving or retired, came to the conclusion that the maintenance of our nuclear deterrent was the biggest single threat to our future defence capability, the phase-out process at long last got underway in 2022.

Despite the UK's disastrous involvement in the Iraq and Afghanistan wars at the start of the century, we also had a formidable reputation as one of the few nations that could take on often dangerous peacekeeping missions around the world. With Trident gone, that became an even more crucial part of our foreign policy. In recent surveys of what it is that makes us feel proud about our country, more than 50 per cent of people in the UK put our role in international peacekeeping close to the top of their list. And that's why a lot of young people today are still so keen to enlist in the armed forces.

A 21ST CENTURY PEACE DIVIDEND (sort of!)

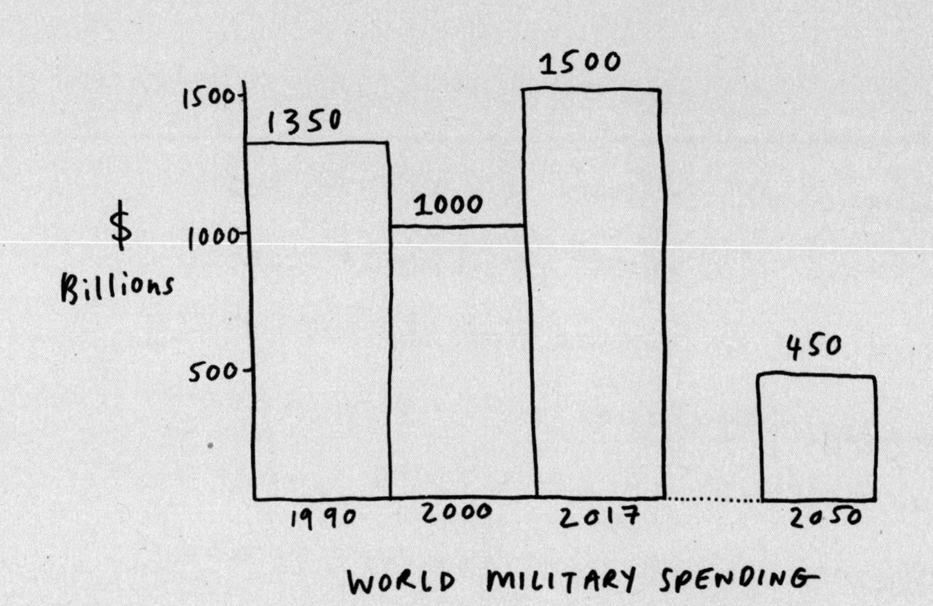

Total global spending on defence has been gradually coming down from a high of $1,500 billion in 2017.

No country at that time could really afford to divert such huge percentages of net wealth into military expenditure.

Slowly but surely, spending on conventional warfare has been reduced to the much more manageable level we have today – around $500 billion.

That's good news for all of us, though many people are still deeply concerned about the continuing 'improvements' in both drone and cyborg capability.

As with the splitting of the atom in the twentieth century, giving rise both to the 'benefits' of nuclear power and the horror of nuclear weapons, the splitting and splicing of genomes has given us an even more significant treasure chest – or Pandora's box – of potential benefits and horrors.

05.05.2050

Containing the Biotech Genie

Cyber-terrorism wasn't the only security threat that world leaders were facing in the 2020s. There was already widespread agreement on the urgent need to tackle the equally grave threat of bioterrorism.

This story goes back to the start of the century. The 'biotech revolution' turned out to be exactly that, in more ways than people realized at the time. No sooner was it possible to map the genome of organisms than it became possible to make synthetic copies of the genomes of simple organisms – bacteria, viruses and so on – and then to create entirely new organisms.

I've got to admit this stuff still scares the hell out of me – and my Research Team! I hope I've been even-handed in covering all the extraordinary advances these techniques have led to (in terms of human health, zero-carbon biofuels and other food and energy breakthroughs), but I'm still not sure we've really weighed up the risks and benefits in the right way.

Shortly after Craig Venter engineered the first synthetic copy of the genome of a bacterium in 2010, scientists in the USA and the Netherlands created a number of different variants of the deadly H5N1 bird flu virus in their labs. Their motives for doing this were wholly benign: to help scientists the world over to improve vaccines and other defences against H5N1, so that when the next outbreak emerged (as everyone knew that it would), we would be better prepared to manufacture new and more effective vaccines. Only then did the world wake up to what had been going on for at least a decade in laboratories all around the world. 'Mutant flu' horror headlines proliferated, and there was a furious storm about whether the results of the work should even be published (in case they got into the wrong hands, providing handy tips for aspiring bioterrorists). Predictably, this was followed by earnest commitments to tighten up biosecurity arrangements to 'eliminate' (the word they used at the time) any such risk of a terrorist outrage.

Many people at that time believed that there should be at least a moratorium (or even a ban) on all such research and development. But they were ignored – not least because it was already too late: hordes of bright young graduates were already taking part in competitions and research programmes of every kind in genetic engineering and synthetic biology. There was even a 'garage biology' movement for amateurs to get involved in tinkering with DNA.

To their credit, many of the pioneers of this revolution in biotechnology had been calling for a comprehensive regulatory regime for a long time. But the limited controls that were in place were easily avoided as they relied far too much on the goodwill and self-discipline of the researchers involved. The 'mutant flu' furore prompted a complete overhaul of biosecurity systems – with the admirable intention of controlling every bit of the supply chain of research requirements, from the DNA synthesis machines and the chemicals they used to the labs and the scientists working in them, all the way through to the synthetic organisms themselves and the knowledge that was generated.

But where there are human beings, there is always error. It was accidental viral releases that caused the biggest problems – in southern Russia in 2018, for example, followed by a much more serious incident in China just a few years later. (China had agreed to follow the new biosecurity rules, but had remained implacably hostile to any external surveillance.)

A decade later, in a random border check between Mexico and the USA, officials from the US Biosecurity Agency discovered and confiscated material that turned out to be a genetically modified variant of the Spanish flu virus – which had caused the death of some 50 million people in 1918.

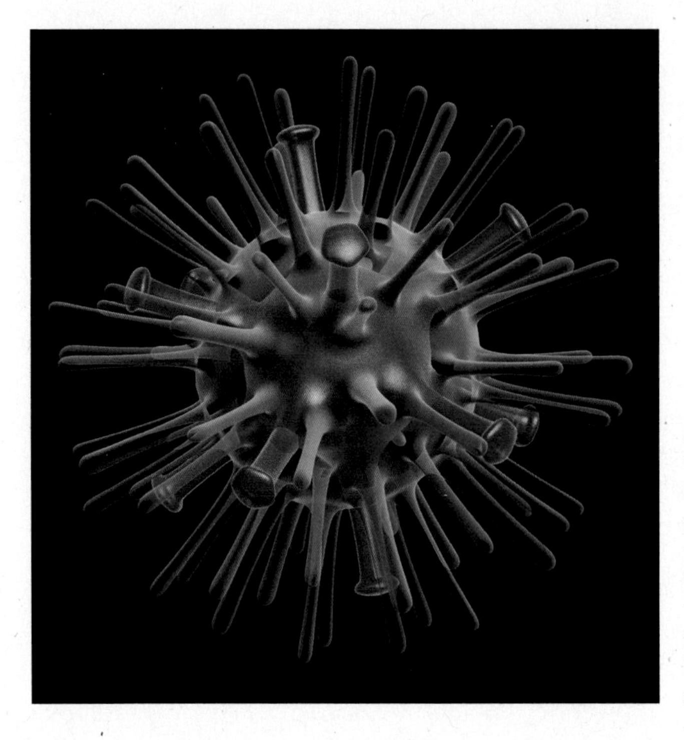

A mutated strain of the Spanish Flu virus, 2028. In the 1990s, scientists recovered the genome of the Spanish flu virus so they could use it for research purposes in both the USA and Canada.

The now-infamous terrorist Luiz Hernandez was arrested, although to this day it remains unclear what he was planning to do with the virus. There was little doubt that the impact of any release would have been horrendous.

The Biosecurity Agency's investigations revealed a complex trail, starting from a disaffected scientist working at the Institute for Infectious Diseases in Ottawa, Canada, then to a shadowy group in Afghanistan (dubbed the 'real al-Qaeda' by Western intelligence agencies), through Pakistan (where the synthesis was done in a laboratory that had never appeared on any official register), and on to Venezuela and ultimately to Hernandez, who was based in Mexico.

GM SPANISH FLU (2024): A TERRORIST TRAIL

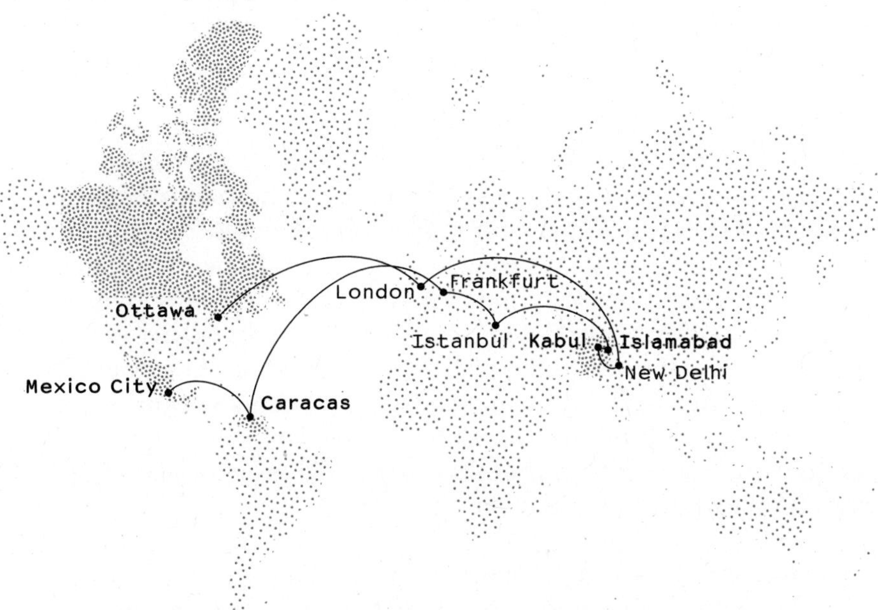

At that point, in the mid-2020s, world leaders finally decided to take effective action. The monitoring and surveillance regime they agreed to was the toughest ever seen – far more rigorous, for example, than that used by the International Atomic Energy Agency to try to contain nuclear proliferation. At the same time, the Biological Weapons Convention (which came into force in 1975 as the first ever multilateral disarmament treaty) was completely revised and made equally restrictive.

So far, to everyone's continuing relief, it seems to have worked pretty well. There certainly haven't been any major life-threatening incidents since then, but many people are still hugely uncomfortable about the risks involved in this kind of research – including me.

12.05.2050

Water For All

Water issues have always been a big deal for me – ever since my father's death in the water riots of 2017. So I'm going to break this down into a kind of progress report on some of the key aspects of water use that ensure it's used as efficiently as possible – irrigation, conservation, purification and desalination.

Irrigation

Domestic water use represents around 15 per cent of total water use today. Another 15 per cent is used by industry and manufacturing, which leaves roughly 70 per cent of the world's available fresh water for use in agriculture. That's much the same as it's been for decades, but these days the most efficient drip irrigation schemes achieve an amazing 80 per cent efficiency – in other words, 80 per cent of water used actually gets to the crops (we'll never achieve 100 per cent because there's always some run-off and evaporation). Even countries like China and India, where it's much harder to use drip irrigation, have pushed up their average efficiency levels to 65 per cent and 55 per cent respectively.

But the real story here isn't about about technology itself, but about ownership and responsibility. In the early part of the century, environmentalists used to go on about something called 'the Tragedy of the Commons', based on an article by some eco-doomster written in the 1960s. Its message was depressingly simple: left to their own devices, people who depend on shared resources – land, water, forests and so on – will always put individual self-interest (in terms of what they can gain from those resources) ahead of their shared interests in keeping those shared resources in good heart. With water use, this has turned out to be wrong: in country after country, local water users' associations have taken over responsibility for managing irrigation systems from ineffectual government agencies. The trail-blazers here were countries like Mexico, Indonesia, Spain and Tunisia, and although there are many fierce disputes, subtle and complex governance arrangements have often delivered what no government could possibly have done. So, far more of a triumph than a tragedy.

For sentimental reasons, I've kept this little doodle that we found in my father's papers when they were returned to us after his death.

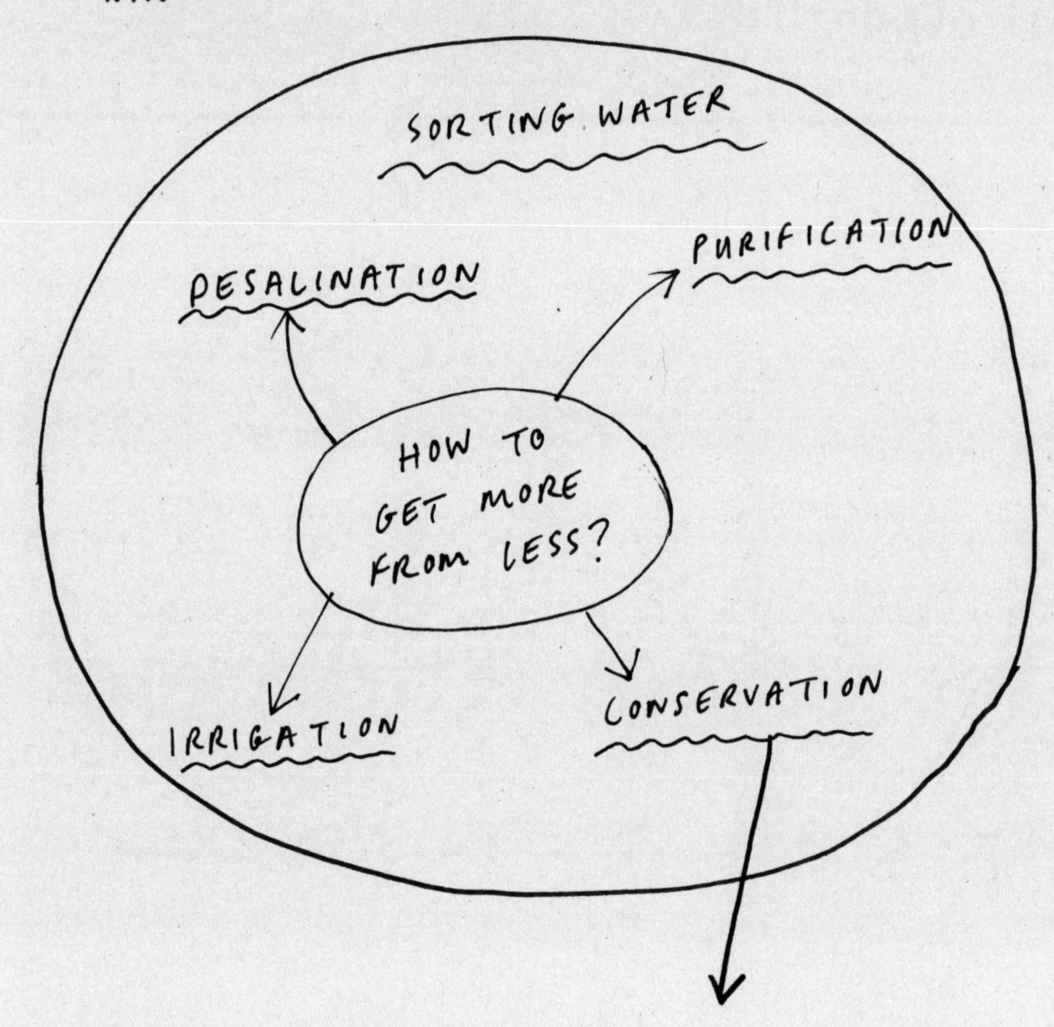

Conservation

Over the last 30 years, every aspect of domestic and industrial water use has been transformed, driven by the need for efficiency. For one thing, the more we use, the more we pay these days – although most countries still have special tariffs to protect the less well-off.

This is not just a rich world story. As my Dad always argued, providing drinking water and basic sanitation is not ROCKET SCIENCE: it just needs INVESTMENT. As soon as funds for this work really started to flow (partly because of the introduction of the International Financial Transaction Tax in 2022), rapid progress was made in meeting the targets set in 2000 (see p.225).

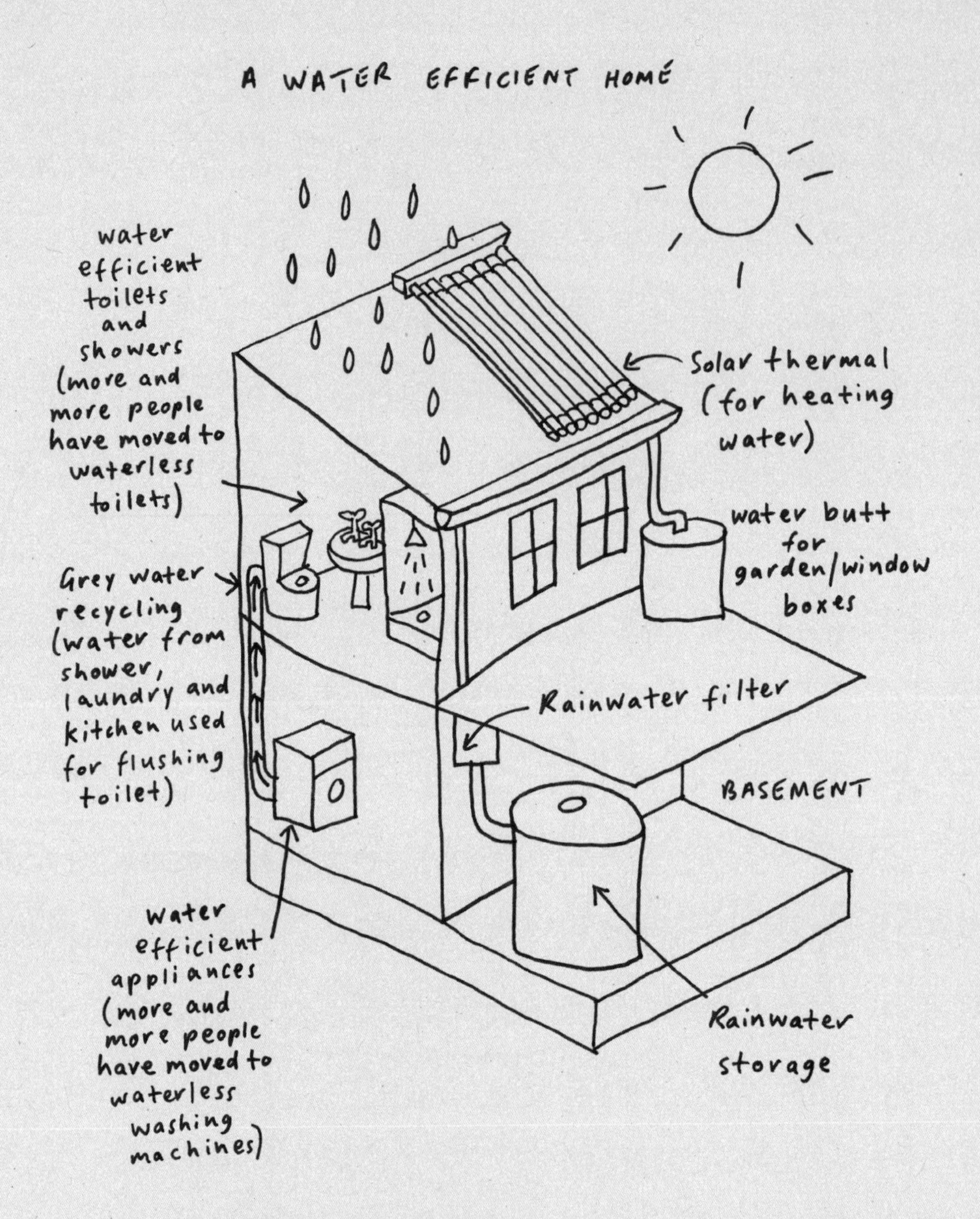

In the old days, 100% of the water delivered to homes in the rich world was clean enough to drink, despite the fact that less than 10% was actually used for drinking or cooking. The amount of energy wasted (and greenhouse gases emitted) in the process beggars belief! Since the mid 2020s, all new housing has been designed very differently, with drinking water separated from the water used for laundry, bathing and dishwashing. All that water, topped up by rainwater harvesting where that's feasible, is then recycled for watering the garden and flushing the lavatory – for those who haven't yet moved over to waterless toilets.

Watercone technology uses simple solar stills to turn saline brackish water into drinking water. It's still as popular today as it has been over the last 50 years.

Purification

However efficiently we use it, people still need their water to be clean. This is just a brilliant story, because from 2010 onwards there was a tidal wave of innovation, creating one device after another – Pure-it, LifeSaver, Slingshot, Swach, Aquapure, Aquaver, Vivreau, Waterlogic, Solvatten, Watersafe and so on – to clean up water in even the most challenging environments, rural or urban. When nanofilters became easily available a few years later, even heavy metals and toxic elements like arsenic (a massive problem in countries like Bangladesh) could be dealt with at point of use.

The best thing about many of these innovations is that they're dead cheap – and quick. Intelligent sensing devices provide instant information for people about the state of their water, which means that the kind of water-related health problems which were standard in the early half of the century have largely disappeared.

One of the smartest ways of reducing losses through evaporation was first introduced at scale in the 2020s: installing PV panels over the top of big irrigation canals. The PV energy provides the electricity to pump the water, while shade from the panels greatly reduces evaporation from the canals – this was the first installation of its kind in Punjab, India.

Desalination

Finally, there's desalination (or 'desal' as we call it). Astonishingly, there are now more than 1.5 billion people all around the world who depend on desalinated water.

Singapore's story is the one that jumped out at us during our research. Keen to reduce its dependence on water imported from neighbouring Malaysia, it set a target in 2010 to meet 30 per cent of its water demands from desal by 2060. When we checked, they had already reached 50 per cent – partly because increased efficiencies in all water uses means that their demand is a lot lower than projected. They will soon be up to one million cubic metres of desal a day – and, since 2035, nearly all of it has come from plants powered by renewable energy, including offshore wind and solar. Singapore also leads the world in reclaiming clean water from sewage wastewater, both for industry and (blended with rainwater in reservoirs) for drinking water.

The use of renewable energy for desal is now standard, both for large plants and the ubiquitous mini-desals. Improvements in the conventional 'reverse osmosis' desal technology (using components such as nano-membranes, ion-exchange resins and chlorine-resistant polymers) have helped to bring both prices and energy consumption right down, making it a much more attractive investment – even for countries that are rather less prosperous than Singapore.

Elsewhere, a rival technology based on membrane distillation (linked to some of the big solar plants in North Africa, southern Europe and California) has also made impressive breakthroughs. But it's not all high-tech: simple solar stills remain vital to many smaller coastal communities and to people inland who have to cope with saline or brackish water (see p.107).

So what happens to all the concentrated salt that's left over? It's still a problem, especially in areas where increased salinity can affect the quality of reefs and other sensitive eco-systems. But some smart chemists in the 2020s found a way of using at least some of the salt as part of new electricity storage technologies, based on the kind of molten salt batteries first invented by the Germans during the Second World War back in the twentieth century!

So, there's still some way to go here – but I think my Dad would be fairly astonished by the progress that's been made.

19.05.2050

Defusing the Population Time Bomb

WORLD POPULATION
→ based on 2025 projections from the UN Population Division

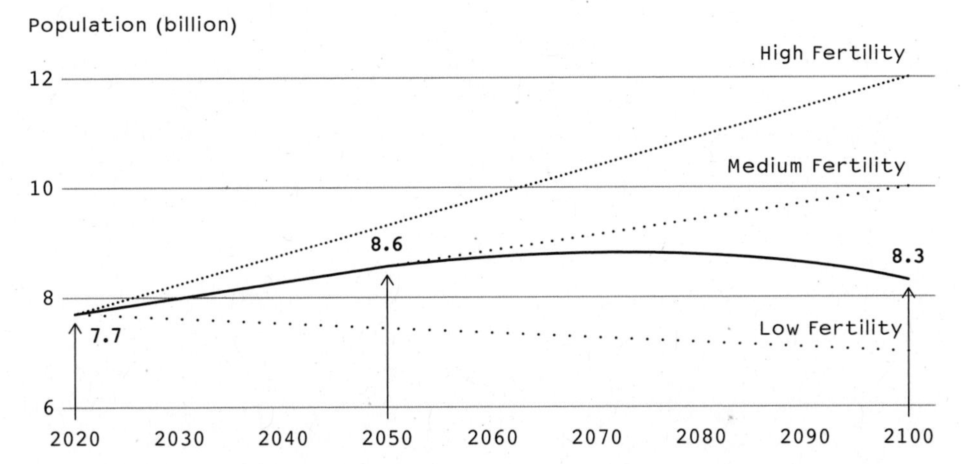

Here's an interesting set of figures that we came across recently: the population projections published by the UN Population Division back in 2025. They're not bad, as projections go: world population today stands at 8.6 billion – in line with the medium population variant you can see on the graph.

This graph may not look like a big deal, but has to be one of the major success stories of the twenty-first century. If birth rates hadn't changed so dramatically over the last 35 years, our population today would be much closer to 9.4 billion rather than 8.6 billion – a difference of more than 800 million people. And all the experts now believe that world population will peak well below 9 billion (instead of the 10.5 billion peak that people thought was likely back in the 2020s), before declining gently to 8.3 billion at the end of the century.

To discover the origins of this turnaround, we delved back into the past. The Research Team found there had been a bit of a stir about population back in the 1970s, and a lot of very successful family planning programmes had been introduced at that time. In 1994, the UN Conference on Population and Development in Cairo seemed to confirm a readiness on the part of politicians to redouble those efforts – but instead, astonishingly, family planning pretty much dropped off the agenda. With Republican presidents in the White House decreeing that not a dollar should go to any family planning organization anywhere in the world that wasn't implacably opposed to abortion, funding pretty much collapsed.

Equally hostile to addressing population issues was a great army of environmentalists and left-wing politicians in Western countries. For the next 20 years after the Cairo conference, they argued that population was 'a distraction' – that the real issues were poverty, injustice and over-consumption in the West. They also claimed that the population explosion was over – despite the fact that there were roughly 80 million more people at the end of every year than at the start of it!

This kind of approach was not just stupid, but cruel. It was reckoned in those days that there were more than 200 million women who were unable to manage their own fertility because of lack of access to contraception. An estimated 50 per cent of pregnancies were unplanned or unwanted, resulting amongst other things in more than 20 million unsafe or illegal abortions every year.

And the economics told a clear story: no country ever got itself out of poverty without first addressing population growth. Those countries with high average fertility (as measured by the number of children per woman) stayed trapped in poverty, with a massive knock-on impact on health, education, life expectancy and security. Once women know that their children have a reasonable rate of surviving into adulthood, non-coercive family planning – allowing women to choose both the timing and the number of children they have – has always been the soundest foundation on which health and prosperity can be built.

To be honest, it was a shameful period. But from 2015 onwards reality began to kick in. The reappearance of famine in East Africa; food riots in literally dozens of countries; resource shortages resulting in high and very volatile prices; competition for land; even fiercer competition for water; and the inexorable build-up of greenhouse gases in the atmosphere – those physical limits made people focus on population all over again.

And then something else happened – a bit of a miracle, in fact. In 2016 the still relatively new Pope decided to revisit the Vatican's teaching on the use of contraception. He set up a new Pontifical Commission to review the landmark 'Humanae Vitae' from 1968. That was the nearest the Church had come in modern times to changing its teaching on 'artificial contraception', but it was defeated by conservative factions in the Vatican.

As in many African countries, a toxic combination of war, corruption and male dominance meant that family planning programmes in Uganda were hopelessly under-funded at the start of the century. In 2010, its population stood at 33 million people, growing at an extraordinary 3.2 per cent per annum, with an average of 6.2 children per woman. It wasn't until the early 2020s that sanity belatedly prevailed, and radical family planning programmes were imposed. Uganda's population peaked at 62 million in 2044, and is now steadily declining.

By 2010, Bangladesh had already done an amazing job in reducing the number of children per woman from 6.3 in 1975 to 2.3. But the population at that time (of around 145 million) was still growing, and would have reached 220 million by today without some truly heroic interventions from the Directorate General of Family Planning and a generation of inspiring women politicians. Bangladesh's current population is just 175 million. But with more and more land lost every year to rising sea levels, it's still a very hard life for many Bangladeshis.

And nothing happened for the next 50 years, despite the fact that the vast majority of Catholics in Europe, South America and elsewhere simply ignored that teaching. The fact that Italy had one of the lowest average fertility rates in Europe throughout that time must have been a constant affront to the Vatican! However, it's relatively easy for well-educated Italians to ignore the Pope – but not so easy for impoverished peasants in South America or the Philippines.

One person who really understood all this was Melinda Gates – herself a devout Catholic, as well as the wife of top businessman-turned-philanthropist Bill Gates. In 2012, she launched a campaign to ensure that all women could have access to contraception, wherever they lived and whatever their religion. Amazingly, the Bill and Melinda Gates Foundation is still providing funds for that cause even today.

I like to think Melinda Gates might have had a bit of an influence on the Pope! Whatever the reason, in 2018, symbolically marking the 50th anniversary of 'Humanae Vitae', he decreed that Catholic teaching on contraception should henceforth be that it is a matter of private conscience rather than papal direction (as it already was for most Catholics, anyway).

From the UN's point of view, the timing couldn't have been better: the 2019 Conference on Population and Development (25 years after the original conference) was attended by no fewer than 78 world leaders, and binding commitments were made to dramatically increase funding for family planning programmes in all those countries that had been desperate for financial assistance for so many years – particularly in sub-Saharan Africa, the Middle East, North Africa and Pakistan. The success of women-centred family planning programmes in countries as diverse as Cuba and Costa Rica, Thailand and Taiwan, Tunisia and Iran, provided all the inspiration those other countries needed.

The real success of all this lies not only in today's total population figure of 8.6 billion, but also in the fact that unmet demand for contraception has been all but eliminated all around the world, empowering hundreds of millions of women to lead lives that would otherwise have been unavailable to them. And all for a few billion dollars.

POPULATION + PER CAPITA INCOME (Thailand + the Philippines)

	2010		2045	
	Population	Per Capita Income	Population	Per Capita Income
Thailand	69 million	$4,600.00	66 million	$17,300.00
Philippines	93 million	$2,200.00	148 million	$10,800.00

As we know, the Philippines is still one of the most troubled countries in Southeast Asia, despite all the brilliant things it's done on renewable energy. After decades of completely unsustainable population growth, its forests have been largely destroyed, its coastal fisheries totally depleted and much of its farming land severely degraded. You only have to compare that tragic story with the continuing success of Thailand to understand the significance of getting population growth wrong.

Most Chinese politicians are scientifically trained, and a lot of them are engineers – so the laws of physics and chemistry still sort of matter to them!

Most American politicians (even now) are either lawyers or business people – or career politicians who've never done anything else other than politics.

While it was clear to Chinese politicians as early as 2010 that coal would have to be phased out as soon as it was practically possible (because of its high carbon content), most politicians in the USA at that time were still clamouring for more coal and denying that climate change was even happening!

27.05.2050

A World Without Coal

By around 2040, coal was dead in China – as it was in the US, which had also gone over to gas. Of the three big coal-burning countries, that just left India – which is still releasing around half a billion tonnes of CO_2 from coal-fired powered stations (like the one above) every year, to the growing fury of the international community.

30 years ago, in 2020, the International Reinsurance Industry Association (IRIA) published the graph you can see on the next page. It became one of the most controversial and widely discussed 'exhibits' in the climate debate over the following decade or more. The text that went with it was even more controversial: 'Some people say we can't afford a war against carbon. Yet climate-induced disasters in the twenty-first century have already cost us more money than every war fought in the twentieth century'. You'd expect stuff like that from Greenpeace, but not from the IRIA.

They updated that data five years later, in 2025. As you can see, there were two events that were particularly influential in getting the USA and China to move against coal as the most carbon-intensive of all the fossil fuels: first, Hurricane Wilma in 2021 (which caused as much damage to Miami as Hurricane Sandy had done in New York, and killed 10 times as many people as Katrina had killed in New Orleans), and then the Shanghai Inundation in 2024.

GLOBAL ECONOMIC LOSSES CAUSED BY CLIMATE-RELATED DISASTERS (1994–2025)
→ Data from the International Re-insurance Industry Association

$ (billion)

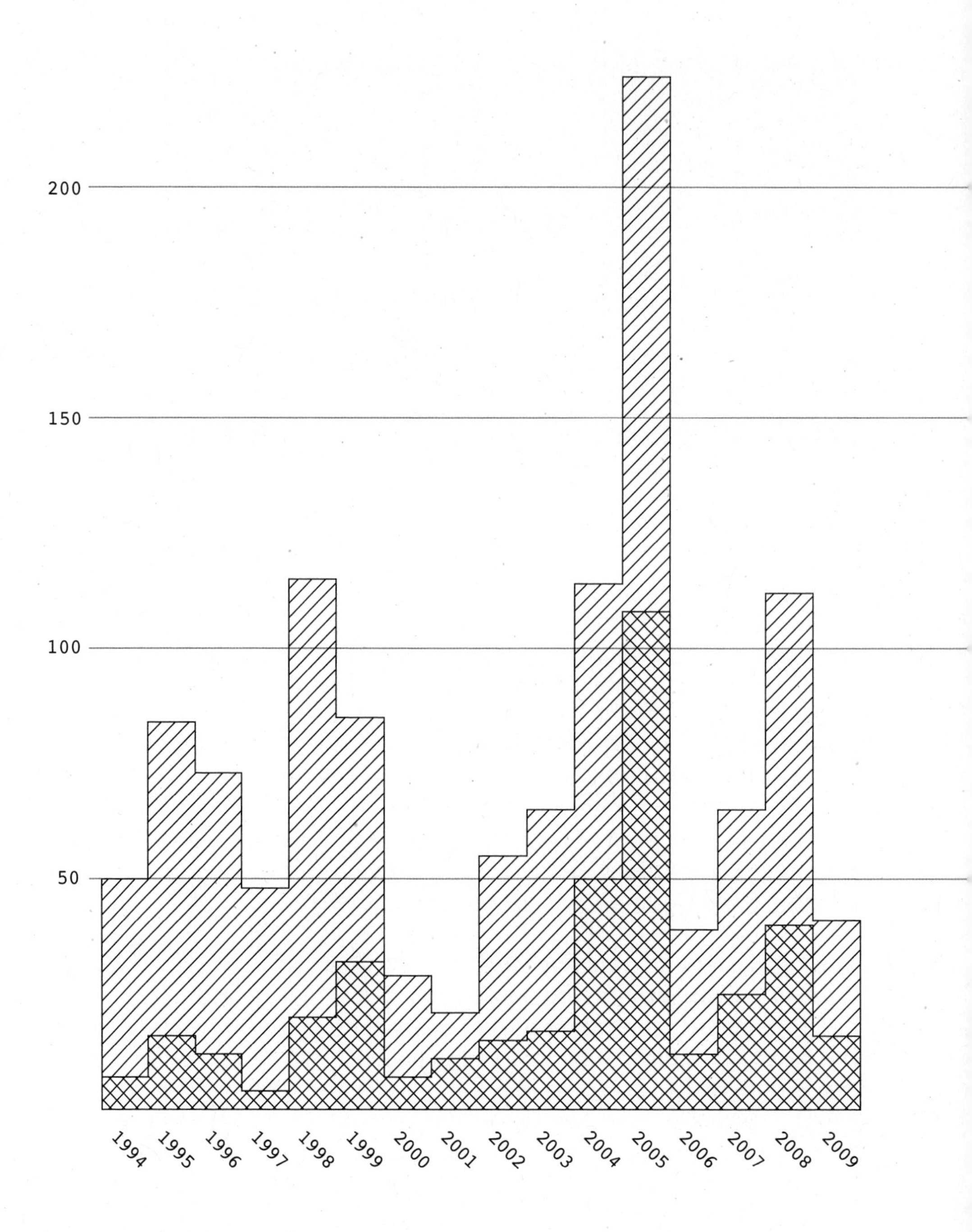

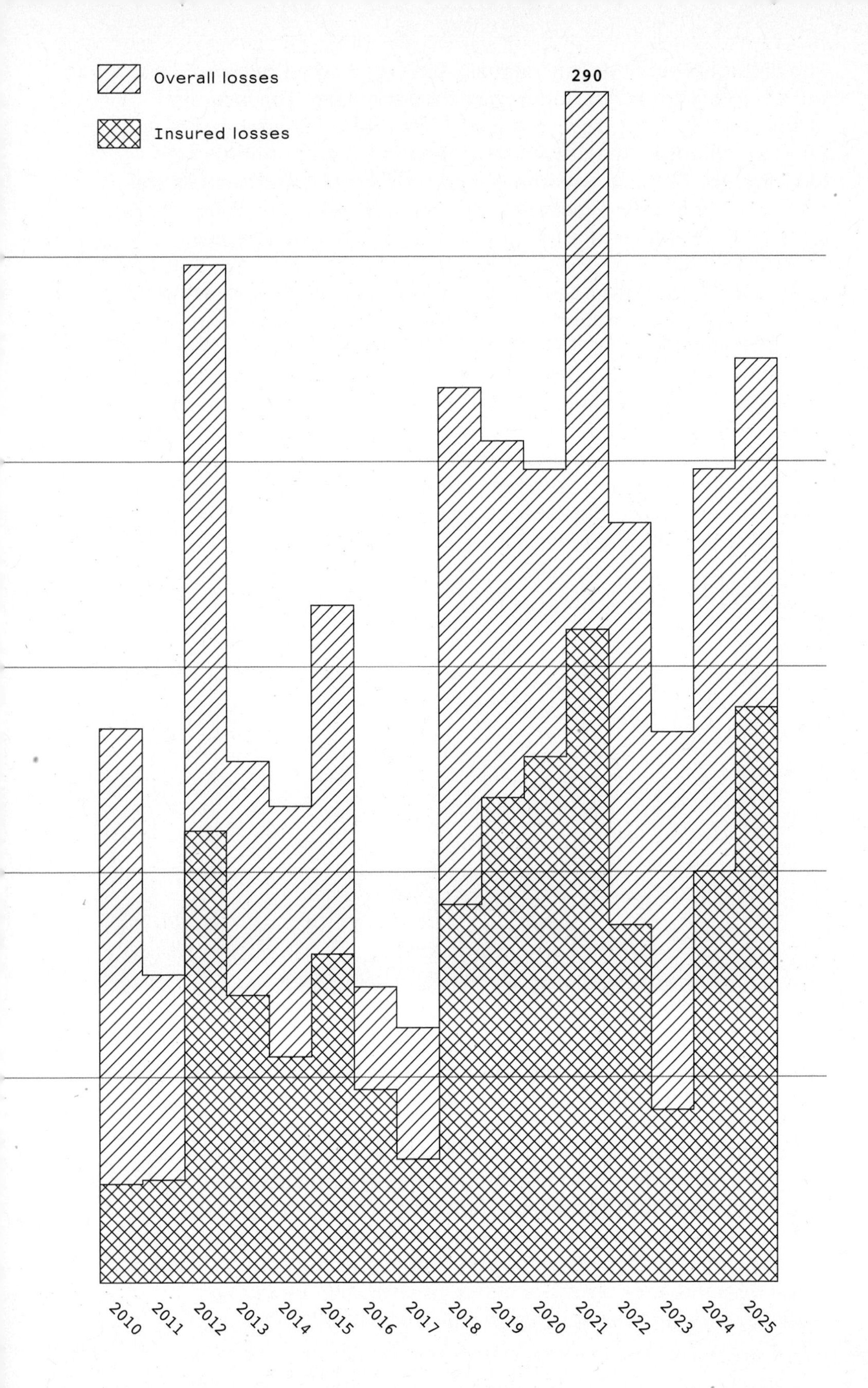

Overall losses
Insured losses
290
2010
2011
2012
2013
2014
2015
2016
2017
2018
2019
2020
2021
2022
2023
2024
2025

The Shanghai event doesn't actually look too bad on the graph, but the implications for China were truly shocking. The incursion of sea water into the fresh-water aquifers around Shanghai was far more extensive than revealed at the time. It was only 10 years later that the Chinese government admitted that it had been on the point of ordering the evacuation of at least 50 per cent of Shanghai's metropolitan area, amounting to more than 20 million people.

In retrospect, therefore, the decision by China in 2025 to close down all coal-fired power stations by 2040 wasn't all that surprising. There was a lot already going on in China that made the decision less daunting. For one thing, the roll-out of wind power was working astonishingly well: China had 125 GW of installed wind power (on and offshore) by 2025, far more than any other country in the world. Although it was Germany and the USA that first developed the new TurbineMax (using different superconducting wires instead of standard copper, tripling average efficiency), it was China that was the first to roll them out at scale.

Wind power drove China's renewables revolution between 2015 and 2040.

When details of the 15th Five Year Plan emerged in 2026, the Chinese government announced that it was going to massively increase the amount of wind power in China. It was a lot cheaper, a lot more reliable and a lot less complicated than either coal or nuclear. They also decided to build thousands more AAD plants (advanced anaerobic digestion), producing both biogas and heat for local networks, as well as animal feeds – a technology, by the way, which has transformed the lives of farmers globally. To sort out remaining urban demand, they opted for super-efficient gas-fired power stations, with carbon capture technology built in.

The Chinese already knew a lot more than any other country about using carbon capture and storage (CCS). Up until then, CCS was often talked about as the technology which would 'keep coal alive' by preventing its emissions of CO_2 from getting into the atmosphere (the 'capture' bit), and ensuring that the CO_2 could be safely buried underground (the 'storage' bit). The Chinese had more than 20 CCS installations up and running by 2020. It worked fine technically, but the costs were very steep: coal-fired power stations with CCS installed lost 25 per cent of their energy output to provide the energy for the carbon capture and storage processes. By contrast, CCS on gas-fired power stations worked much better – not least because gas produces far lower emissions than coal.

So much for coal. Gas, of course, proved to be a very different story. At one time, there were around 350 large gas-fired power plants working on the same basis as the Indonesian example on the next page. Using gas like this was often described as 'the least-worst transition' from the Age of Fossil Fuels to the Solar Age. There are far fewer like this now: countries keep them running for as long as they are cost-effective, but they're never actually replaced once they come to the end of their operating life.

That's how the transition was done. With the best will in the world, it just wasn't possible to go straight from a world that was almost completely dependent on fossil fuels (as it was back in 2010) to a world that's now 90 per cent dependent on renewables. We still needed a lot of gas to get us through – and there was still a lot around at that time. Vast quantities of what were known as 'unconventional' gas reserves (in particular, shale gas) had become available as a direct consequence of new horizontal drilling techniques at the turn of the century. 'Fracking' was controversial then and is still controversial today, despite the best efforts of regulators to force the industry to clean up its act – particularly by preventing the gas leaking from the wellhead into the atmosphere.

So although shale gas was far from ideal, it had its advantages: it was available in lots of countries, and cheap enough and clean enough to kill off all the remaining coal-fired power stations in the USA by the early 2020s. In the end, it was really gas that killed coal – just as it's renewables that have now more or less killed off gas.

LOW CARBON ELECTRICITY FROM INDONESIAN GAS

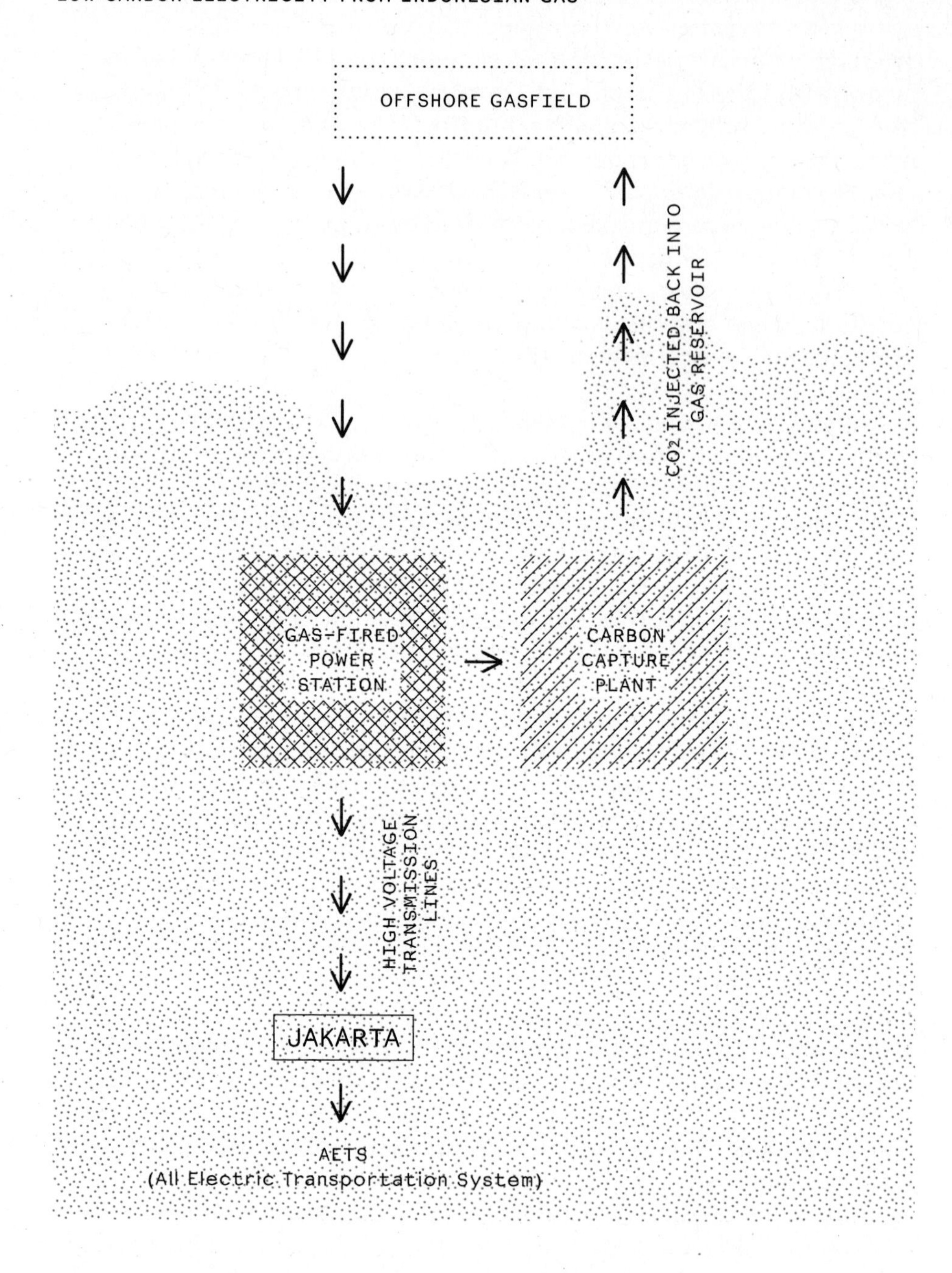

This is a diagram of a gas-fired power station just 160 kilometres away from Jakarta – 'state of the art' when it was commissioned 20 years ago, with a carbon capture and storage plant built in. The gas is extracted from a huge offshore gas field, burned in the power station to provide electricity for Jakarta's all-electric transportation infrastructure, with the CO_2 duly captured and injected back down into the reservoir from which the gas was extracted in the first place. The company involved calls this 'near zero-carbon electricity' – generated from a fossil fuel!

01.06.2050

Minds and Machines

Robots of all sorts were already fairly commonplace 25 years ago – and these days they are as much part of our lives as our pets are, both in the home and the workplace, where remote-controlled 'tellies' (or telepresence robots) became increasingly commonplace from the early 2020s onwards.

Our son's Litbot. Ben was into robotics from a very early age. For whatever reason, he just wouldn't learn to read. Eventually, when he was eight, we got him this, one of the latest Litbots, and I have to admit it worked like magic. Litbots aren't programmed with any fixed methods of teaching reading; they simply respond to whatever it is that works well with any particular child – or adult. They have something like a 90 per cent success rate – and sure enough, within nine months, our son was reading anything and everything that came his way.

Most people are pretty comfortable about all the advances still being made in robotics today. Although our own all-purpose home robot doesn't look so different from those in the 2020s, its computing power is a million times greater. Scarily, that's rather more than the computing power of the human brain, which makes us feel somewhat guilty that we are only using a minute fraction of its 'intelligence'! Robots have simply become as natural an extension of our lives as a car or a fridge – and there's no denying the fact that people do get very attached to their robots. As the 'companionability' of very cheap standard robots has increased, it's become more and more natural to think of them as 'friends' of a sort – but somehow not as people. I think that's the main reason why most people today like their robots to look like robots – not like people!

Our home robot – getting on with stuff!

I recently went with my mother to visit her oldest friend, living alone since her husband died 12 years ago. She was always a rather cantankerous soul, but she honestly sounded much happier with her robot than with her husband! Not just because of the way it copes with the fetching and carrying, cleaning and cooking and so on, but because it manages all her social networks and games. She seems to have legions of friends/rivals all over the world with whom she engages in every conceivable kind of competitive activity! It also deals with her regular healthcare: all her tele-med sensors are connected via her robot straight through to her doctor.

And that's what 'peace of mind' means to a lot of old people these days. Twenty years ago, there were endless debates about the pros and cons of such developments. While psychologists urged people to look at the very positive impact of robots on loneliness (particularly among the ever-larger numbers of older people), faith leaders and politicians kept worrying about what this meant for society and communities. There's not much debate on that these days. For most people, it's the continuing controversies around augmented human intelligence that seem to loom much larger, with an increasingly fierce debate in society about where to draw the line between what's human and what's not.

Ben (now 23) is immersed in this world – which has certainly provided us with some telling insights. He's employed by a company in Los Angeles that designs personalized virtual worlds. By all accounts, he's one of their best 'gatekeepers', fixing up clients' Intell augments and guiding them and their avatars in and out of their virtual lives. Whatever the latest mind augmentation fix is, he's on it.

Some of the early augmentation breakthroughs (in the 2020s) emerged in the field of mental health. After years of experimenting with deep brain stimulation (DBS), scientists came up with a range of implanted devices that very effectively treated clinical depression, ADHD and extreme anxiety. DBS has also done more to delay the onset of Alzheimer's and other forms of dementia than any other kind of treatment.

And it's pretty amazing to see what's now possible in terms of the direct conversion of signals from the brain into mobility and communication software. Controlling robots, computers and artificial limbs by brain signals alone was once the stuff of science fiction, developed initially to help those with severe spinal injuries or degenerative diseases. Today it's absolutely standard.

The most sophisticated EEG headsets on the market today make it possible for people to communicate directly with each other via wireless networks. Just last week, the BBC's sponsored telepathon raised more money than ever before, with more than 10 million people around the world sharing reactions to support the victims of the most recent Bangladeshi floods.

It's not all upside, however. After the horrifying revelations regarding the Last Frontier project in the early 2020s (see p.31), human rights campaigners have had to be even more vigilant in monitoring invasive techniques on the part of big IT companies. Over the years, there have been many scandals about ruthless employers 'inviting' employees either to have implants fitted or to start using the latest intelligence-enhancing drugs to improve their productivity or 'competitive instincts'.

Even more worryingly, it seems university students and even school children have been circumventing the ban on brain implants below the age of 23. There are now growing concerns about 'personality shifting', as more and more evidence emerges that such major changes to cognitive functions in the brain can have a profound effect on people's personality and sense of identity.

No surprise then that our politicians seem to be completely flummoxed as to how best to manage such a fast-moving area of technology. So we just carry on muddling through!

08.06.2050

Urban Makeovers

Doing the research for this entry, my students could hardly believe how much money was frittered away in the old days, even in the so-called Age of Austerity – or 'Age of Profligacy, more like', as one of them put it.

One example: in 2010, more than 40 per cent of total energy consumption was used by buildings – a lot of which was completely wasted because the buildings were so inefficient. It was, in effect, like taking piles of cash (the paper notes they used back then) out of the bank every day and setting fire to them! Why taxpayers and shareholders put up with it is something we could find no explanation for in any of our research.

Then energy got a lot more expensive, and by 2020 sanity had prevailed. Without really trying very hard, the top 40 cities around the world had reduced total energy consumption in their non-domestic buildings by around 35 per cent over the decade. By 2030, it was down by another 25 per cent. 'Retrofitting' was the key idea. Not as exciting as building completely new cities from scratch (see p.127 and p.130) or regenerating large swathes of cities that had seen better days, but it was the most important way of achieving better energy efficiency quickly. Nearly 80 per cent of the buildings in cities like ours had already been built by 2015, so retrofitting was really the best option available to city planners.

It's funny how it was New York's old Empire State Building that ushered in the age of urban retrofitting. The efficiency savings its retrofit achieved back in 2010 (more than 40 per cent on a before and after basis) provided a benchmark for the many schemes that followed. Its pioneering use of super-insulated glass (remanufacturing the building's 6,514 glass windows on site) encouraged further innovation in glass technology. It also took full advantage of the latest improvements in lighting: at that time, lighting alone accounted for 19 per cent of the world's electricity consumption, so the scope for relatively easy efficiency savings was massive.

This is one of my favourite eco-cities: the Korean city of Songdo International Business District, still a relatively new metropolis built from scratch on a man-made island in the Yellow Sea between China and South Korea. What made it unique was its 'digital plumbing': during construction, every single part of the city was wired up with routers, switches and fibre-optic filaments, so that from the beginning the city has literally run on information. For instance, it has just one utility centre, with all water, energy, transportation and ICT systems bundled together and internet-enabled. It was also the first city in the world to standardize wireless electricity.

SUSTAINABLE CITIES

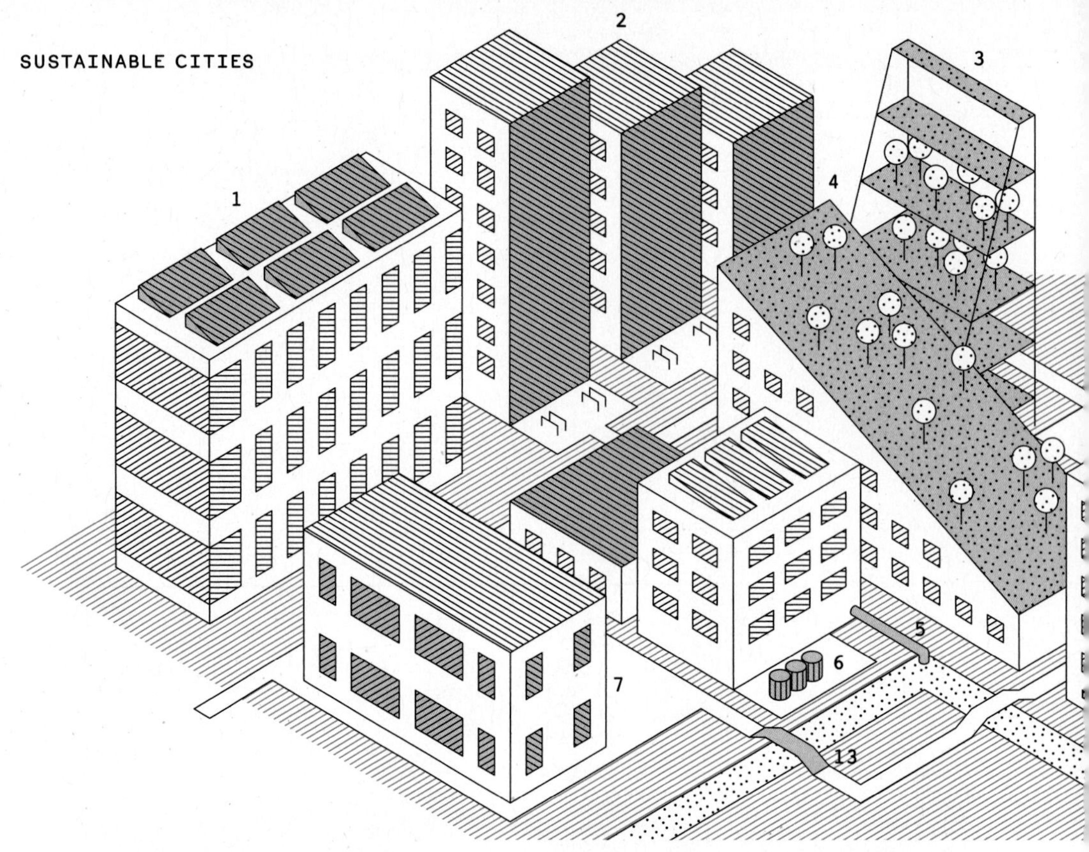

1 SOLAR POWER
Both rooftop photovoltaics and concentrated solar power have become more and more efficient over the years, enabling most buildings to generate most if not all of the electricity they use – including air-conditioning. However, rising average temperatures in most cities mean that demand for air-conditioning continues to rise.

2 SOLAR CLADDING
Sheets of thin-film photovoltaics have been standard on south-facing walls for the last 25 years. Photovoltaic glazing (using dye-sensitized solar cells) is also widely used.

3 VERTICAL FARMS
Vertical farms are now a more and more familiar element of the urban landscape (see p.172). Rainwater harvesting and recycling reduces water consumption to the absolute minimum required.

4 GREEN ROOFS/WHITE ROOFS
Some rooftops are planted up with shrubs, grasses and small trees to improve insulation, help manage storm water and promote biodiversity. And some are painted white to reflect sunshine, which marginally reduces the cost of keeping buildings cool.

5 WATER EFFICIENCY (SEE P.106)
Ultra-low-flow toilets, showers and kitchen appliances, as well as waterless urinals, have reduced water consumption to astonishingly low levels. But there is still real anger at very high water prices in many cities.

6 RECYCLING
Volumes of urban trash are a fraction of what they once used to be, with levels of recycling up above 90 per cent in most cities today. All food waste is composted for use in city farms or digested to provide reliable and cheap supplies of gas for urban gas grids.

7 SELF-CLEANING BUILDINGS
A wide range of titanium-dioxide coatings have become very popular. Sunshine releases highly reactive 'free radicals' from these coatings, which then oxidize a wide range of airborne pollutants. Self-cleaning windows have been standard for more than 30 years.

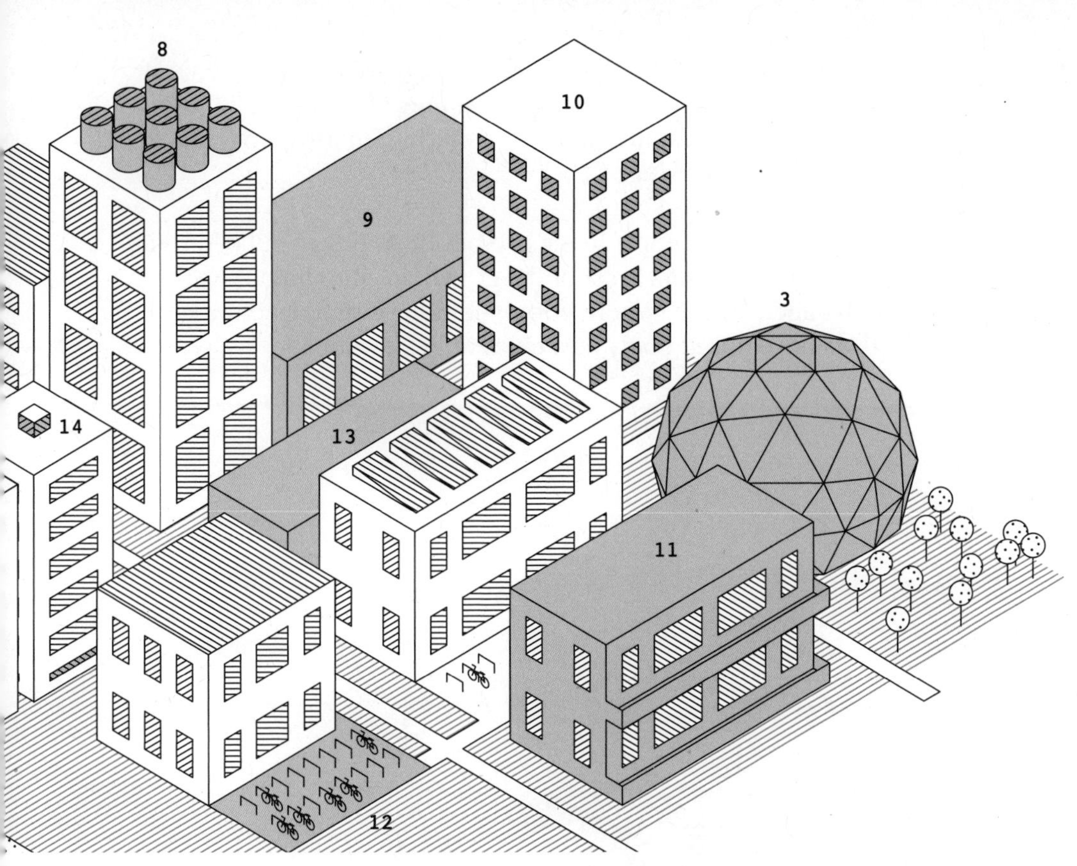

8 **SOLAR THERMAL**
Super-efficient solar thermal tanks (providing hot water for all non-domestic buildings) have been mandatory in most countries since the early 2020s.

9 **CONCRETE**
Zero-carbon concrete has to be one of the most important innovations of the century. The keys to this breakthrough are today's magnesium-based cements, which actually absorb CO_2 in their manufacture – the older limestone cements released a tonne of CO_2 for every one and half tonnes of cement!

10 **SUPER INSULATED WINDOWS**
The latest super-insulated windows (see p.126) are the key to today's zero-carbon office and retail buildings.

11 **GREEN LEASES**
Rental values in most cities are increasingly determined by the scale of contribution a building makes to energy efficiency, renewables, water consumption and waste reduction – as well as its rating on the latest Healthy Buildings Index. The healthier and more efficient a building is, the more attractive its rental value.

12 **BIKE CITIES**
Almost without exception, today's cities put bikes first – then buses and trams, then cars. Congestion charges are still widely used, but generate little income (as there are so few privately owned cars per head of population), and priority on use of parking spaces is given to car clubs.

13 **SELF-HEALING CONCRETE**
The old kind of concrete used to degrade over time. Today's concrete mixes contain microfibres which absorb moisture from the air, expand and then harden, filling any cracks that may have developed. This has been a godsend in terms of maintaining bridges and other concrete structures.

14 **NATURAL VENTILATION**
Many buildings now use natural ventilation systems (based on designs taken from different aspects of the natural world) to provide part or all of the cooling they need.

Some of the world's biggest contracting companies started offering energy performance guarantees on all the retrofits that they did, making full use of improvements in processes such as smart metering, energy performance management and remote sensing.

There are nearly 6.5 billion people living in cities these days – out of a total global population of 8.6 billion. Most of the growth in cities has taken place outside the USA and Europe (where populations have remained fairly stable), and this has required many new cities to be developed.

Masdar City, Abu Dhabi, 2037.

There was already quite a lot of excitement about sustainable cities early in the century. Masdar City in Abu Dhabi was perhaps the best known of these, although it's now just as famous for the research work on sustainable technologies done there over the decades as for the city itself.

But most new cities have had to rely much more on high-rise buildings to minimize the total amount of land required. If you can't keep spreading out, you have to build upwards! And many of today's 'super-tall' buildings (those over 600 metres – it used to be 300 metres until 2025) have become beacons of sustainable construction in their own right.

This is the New Petronas Tower, completed in 2042 in Kuala Lumpur. It is 750m tall, generates 92 per cent of its own energy and is completely water neutral, using the latest aquacycle technology.

Songdo International Business District (see p.127) has become the template for dozens of cities across China and Southeast Asia. Some people call them 'symbiocities', emphasizing the mutual dependencies between natural cycles and the built environment – first pioneered by Swedish cities, but then taken up by hundreds of Chinese cities. In India, the city of Lavasa (just under 100 kilometres from Mumbai) provided the role model for new urban developments, eloquently demonstrating how the principles of biomimicry (see p.212) help to regulate water, energy, waste and biodiversity in a genuinely 'circular' urban economy.

One of the biggest energy guzzlers early in the century was air conditioning (AC). As average temperatures rose, so too did the use of AC – and the associated emissions of CO_2 and other greenhouse gases. It took people a long time to innovate their way out of that vicious circle: the answer was ultra-efficient AC units powered directly by concentrated PV or CSP, on roofs wherever possible. But these days, more and more people are relying on alternatives to AC, and over the last 30 years we've seen the widespread roll-out of what are called phase change materials (PCMs) – gels and other natural materials that can absorb or release large amounts of energy to help regulate temperatures in passively heated and cooled buildings.

So the truth is that we got pretty good at managing the energy efficiency side of urban development – but just a little bit late in the day. Unfortunately, sea levels are still rising and many of the world's coastal cities remain very much at risk. The new Thames Barrier (completed in 2037 at an astronomical cost) and the Five Barriers system designed to protect New York are now typical of the kind of defences that cities are having to invest in.

For some, as we know, it's already too late – so let's just pause for a moment to remember that once-great city of New Orleans, which had to be permanently evacuated in 2035.

16.06.2050

Of Men and Money

UNICS, the universal currency.

The kids I teach today describe my generation as 'the pay-back generation': in their eyes, we seem to have spent most of our lives paying off our parents' debts. From the 1970s through to 2008, they did all the partying – and we got the hangover!

It's hard to summarize just how utterly different things are today. For one thing, money as such (as in notes and coins) doesn't exist. Practically everywhere in the world now relies on three electronic currencies: a local currency (a few of which already existed in the early part of the century, but were not taken very seriously); a national currency – still the principal means of oiling the wheels of our economies; and a global currency called UNICS (short for Universal Currency Services).

UNICS is essentially the currency of international trade and investment – and the source of almost all the revenues generated through the International Financial Transaction Tax. It's used primarily by international banks handling corporate accounts and large-scale project investments.

I suppose I should also mention a fourth currency used by all those 'virtuals' out there in i-space, living multiple alternative existences. By some estimates, there are now more than two billion virtuals involved in intensive gaming or simulated activities of one kind or another, so we are talking about a lot of virtual money here. This is the world in which Ben, as an expert Intell gatekeeper, seems to make a lot of his money.

Japan turned out to be the real game-changer on electronic currencies. There were already more than 65 million 'wallet phones' in circulation there in 2013, with most retailers already set up to accept payment via people's cell phones. It just spread from there, out of convenience as much as anything else – although the two big flu pandemics in the early 2020s added a powerful incentive for hygienic, 'no-contact-necessary' transactions, which became very attractive to people amid all the panic.

Another bottom-up change was the 'citizen finance' initiatives started up some 40 years ago, when organizations like Zopa in the UK, the Prosper and Lending Club in the US and Smava in Germany started to cut out all 'middle men' by directly linking up lenders and borrowers. Many of these initiatives have had a rather rocky ride over the years, but by some measures more than 30 per cent of today's credit is created on this type of peer-to-peer basis.

On the investment side, everybody still worries about their pensions – that seems to have been a constant factor over the last 50 years! Over and above the state pension (which really is pretty basic these days), almost everybody has their own investment-based personal pension, and I guess it's a sign of the times that LRLR (Low Risk Low Returns) portfolios are so dominant. Five-year municipal bonds are just about the most rock-solid investment you can make these days, but the huge growth in Shariah investments and various cooperative funds means that these are also popular choices.

If that all sounds very humdrum, it's probably because it is. Money matters a lot less than it once seemed to do, not least because we're much more realistic these days about what a good standard of living really means.

Following Japan's lead, China introduced the 'e-RMB' (electronic Renminbi) in 2018. All notes and coins were phased out by 2026 – the first country to go all-electronic.

Getting Over the Hangover

Unfortunately, the fallout after the 2008 economic crash lasted a lot longer than anyone had predicted in the 2010s. The 40-year binge leading up to the crash wasn't paid for out of income, but on credit. The scale of the accumulated debt (personal, corporate and national) was almost beyond comprehension.

But here's the extraordinary thing: this definitive and very painful turning point undoubtedly changed things for the better. For so many people of my parents' generation, living beyond their means was not just acceptable but respectable. A preoccupation with competitive consumption was the norm, along with instant retail gratification. And governments were on the same binge too: in 2015, total public debt in the USA amounted to $58,000 per US citizen – imagine trying to get all that back onto an even keel!

Every one of the big banks that dominated the financial scene at that time has disappeared since then, transformed into very different entities: mutuals, cooperatives, credit unions and wealthcare managers, operating at either the local or regional level. All of these are doing what was once described as 'boring banking' – savings, deposits, loans, mortgages, current accounts, payment systems, financial advice and so on.

Something else has changed too. People simply didn't understand how credit worked at that time. Instead of governments themselves (through their national banks) providing credit at zero interest, they allowed banks to create almost all of the money supply by making interest-bearing loans. For the banks, that interest was pure profit – as the rest of us got deeper and deeper into debt. There was no law that said the money supply of a country had to be managed in such a way that the rich benefitted at the expense of the poor. But it wasn't until 2026 that we finally got a law ensuring that the public money supply would from then on be created by national banks (like the Bank of England or the Fed in the US) or local banks serving the common interest.

The truth of it is that politicians of that era largely handed over the stewardship of the capitalist system to an army of greedy profit-maximizers. They had no real interest in investing in proper wealth creation, and were perversely incentivized to make money out of speculation, currency exchange and market manipulation.

26.06.2050

Fixing the Climate

When we did the research for this, I can honestly say that no other topic has made my students more angry than this one. They wanted to use a very different title for this entry – '25 Wasted Years' – but I persuaded them that that would be just too negative.

The 25 years in question were between 1997 – when world leaders first recognized the significance of climate change – and 2022, when they finally recognized the significance of having done so little about it over the preceding 25 years! And that's why we're now having to spend huge sums to get some of the CO_2 we put into the atmosphere during that time back out of it again – in effect, engineering the climate on a planetary scale. And that's why young people today are so angry.

Once the world woke up to the fact that we had no option but to get much of the CO_2 that we'd put into the atmosphere back out of it, the innovation cycle kicked in with a vengeance. In fact, it was like the worst kind of gold rush! Every conceivable kind of carbon cowboy, vested corporate interest and obsessive billionaire piled in with their own pet ideas. Countries like Russia, China and the US started taking the law into their own hands, trying out schemes that attempted to alter levels of incoming solar radiation (rather than reduce levels of CO_2 in the atmosphere). The result was that, for the best part of a decade, the UN Security Council was having to deal with one geoengineered mess after another.

This wasn't surprising, when you recall that these schemes included using giant hoses to pump sulphur dioxide particles into the atmosphere, to help reflect incoming solar radiation back into space. This was bad science at its worst. But once it was demonstrated that just two years' worth of large-scale experiments of this kind was having a seriously disruptive effect on the South Asian monsoon, all further unauthorized experimentation was prohibited at the fourth Global Geoengineering Summit in Dhaka in 2031.

GEOENGINEERING (THE GOOD STUFF)

TECHNOLOGIES THAT REDUCE GREENHOUSE GASES IN THE ATMOSPHERE

1. BIO-ENERGY WITH CARBON CAPTURE AND STORAGE

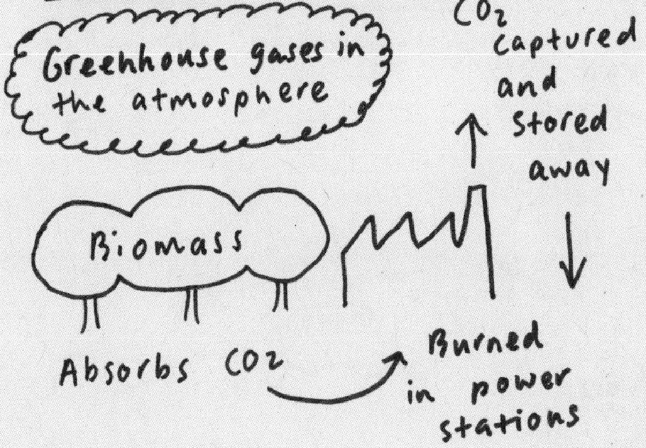

Greenhouse gases in the atmosphere

CO_2 captured and stored away

Biomass

Absorbs CO_2

Burned in power stations

2. OCEAN FERTILIZATION

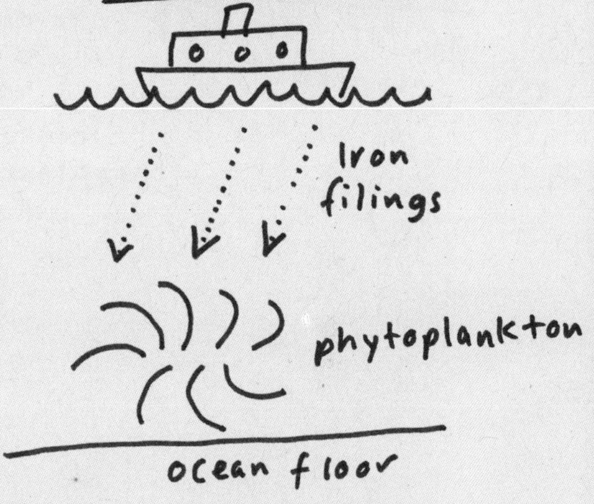

Iron filings

phytoplankton

ocean floor

Spreading nutrients (such as iron filings) to stimulate growth of phytoplankton which take CO_2 out of the atmosphere. When these short-lived blooms die, they take the CO_2 to the ocean floor.

3. BIOCHAR

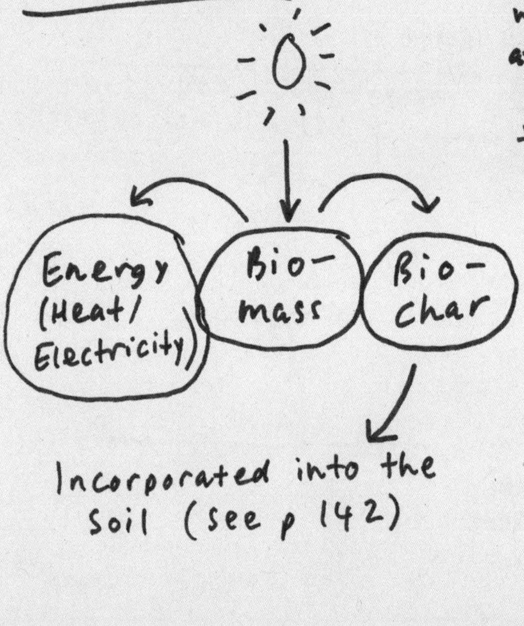

Energy (Heat/ Electricity)

Bio-mass

Bio-Char

Incorporated into the Soil (see p 142)

4. DIRECT AIR CAPTURE

(See p 140)

GEOENGINEERING (THE BAD STUFF)

SOLAR RADIATION MANAGEMENT

1. GIANT ORBITING MIRRORS

(to reflect back incoming solar radiation)

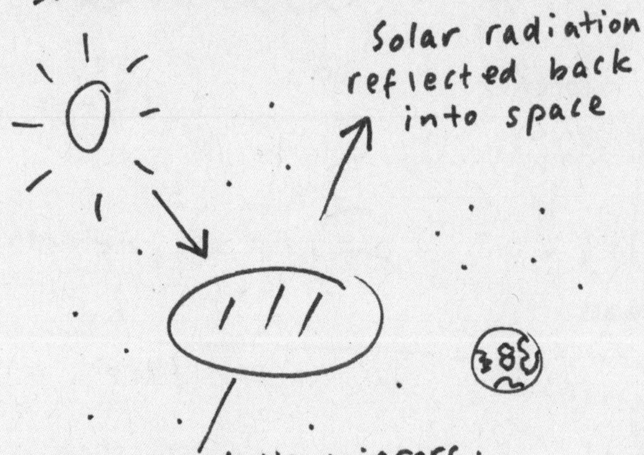

Huge parabolic mirrors.

2. SPRAYING SULPHATE AEROSOLS INTO ATMOSPHERE

(either by tethered boom system or from planes in the upper atmosphere)

3. CLOUD WHITENING

(water droplets used to change composition of clouds to reflect solar radiation – but just doesn't work!)

4. PAINTING ALL ROOFS WHITE

to reflect solar radiation (works ok but minimal effect)

The first Geoengineering Summit in Dhaka, Bangladesh, in 2022, formally ushered in the era of geoengineering. It was still hugely controversial at the time. Environmentalists had fought long and hard to stop gullible politicians getting all excited about the potential for geoengineering, knowing they might well use it as a further excuse to avoid doing the difficult stuff on reducing emissions in the first place. But by 2022, it was too late for that.

That was the harsh reality facing the Emergency Session of the UN General Assembly when it convened the first Global Geoengineering Summit. And this was the core of the communiqué that was published at the end of the Summit:

1. To have a reasonable chance of avoiding irreversible climate change, all nations will need to work together to stabilize concentrations of greenhouse gases at an even lower level than we believed would be sufficient at the time of 2016 Emergency Report from the Intergovernmental Panel on Climate Change.

2. We will need to do this as soon as is technologically possible and as cost-effectively as possible. But cost must no longer be a barrier to concerted action.

3. The above considerations mean that we must both redouble our efforts to reduce current emissions of greenhouse gases and commit energetically to reducing existing concentrations in the atmosphere via geoengineering schemes.

4. Our best estimate is that we will need to draw down a minimum of 5 billion tonnes of CO_2 a year for at least the next 50 years.

5. This will impose a substantial negative burden on the global economy during that time. Further delay, however, cannot be countenanced, as it is impossible to put a cost on the collapse of civilization.

Bit by bit, appropriate regulatory structures were put in place and reasonably cost-effective schemes to remove CO_2 from the atmosphere were soon being scaled up. Apart from all the work done on carbon capture and storage (see p.121), a number of technologies were pretty much ready to go immediately. From around 2010 onwards, many eminent scientists had been pioneering different kinds of direct air capture (DAC) – 'scrubbing' the CO_2 straight out of the air. In essence, they were using some fairly standard chemistry, but the engineering challenge was still huge.

A direct air capture (DAC) plant in South Africa. The air is drawn in through the large drum and passes over an ion exchange resin, where the CO_2 reacts with sodium hydroxide to form sodium bicarbonate, from which the CO_2 can be easily washed out. The CO_2 is then stored in underground salt domes found in this region of South Africa.

Farmers digging biochar into the soil, Honduras, 2023.

Apart from DAC, there have also been a number of successful ocean fertilization schemes where iron filings are scattered over the surface of the ocean, encouraging the growth of phytoplankton that then pulls CO_2 out of the atmosphere and takes it down onto the ocean floor when they die.

One equally controversial alternative in the 2020s and 2030s was capturing carbon from biomass-based power stations. Burning any organic matter is more or less 'carbon-neutral', with no more CO_2 released than is taken in by the plants and trees as they grow. Capturing and burying the CO_2 before it is released into the atmosphere makes the whole thing 'carbon-positive'.

A huge amount of timber ended up being 'co-fired' in power stations from 2015 onwards, especially in the US, Canada and Russia. One of the worst early consequences of accelerating climate change was the death of hundreds of millions of trees in northern latitudes through uncontrollable infestations of bark beetles of one kind or another. With far fewer really cold winters, the beetles could survive through the winter, and could also push farther and farther north as it got

warmer. This turned into an unprecedented ecological disaster, but at least some small good came of it from using the dead timber to generate power.

The other technology that was 'good to go' back in 2020 was biochar – partially combusted organic matter (trees, agricultural and forestry waste, food waste, sewage sludge and so on). Using a process called pyrolysis – 'burning' without oxygen (and thus without producing CO_2), in a similar way to traditional charcoal-making – it's possible to generate energy while producing a char that can be buried under the soil to lock the carbon away.

We did a lot of biochar between 2020 and 2040. But it's rather gone out of fashion over the last few years, given that we now have so many other technologies we can make good use of. It was also proving to be a bit of a problem getting access to enough organic matter – indeed, there was fierce resistance to setting aside large areas specifically to grow trees (even very fast-growing GM trees) specifically for biochar.

Twenty years on, we've sort of got used to all this experimenting with geoengineering. And it's reached right down to the community level. We've now got our own commi-DAC (community-scale direct air capture plant), using the captured CO_2 to help produce algae-generated biofuels for local use (see p.93). Thankfully, the deeply scary cost projections for DAC to capture the billions of tonnes needed proved to have been greatly exaggerated. And progress is good: last year, DAC systems of one kind or another captured an extraordinary 9 billion tonnes!

So, good ideas won out in the end – and the fact we're now feeling reasonably confident that we can avoid irreversible climate meltdown owes more to this 30-year war on carbon than to anything else.

01.07.2050

Electric Motion

We're so used to vehicles being carbon neutral, we forget how controversial the debate about 'the future of the car' was, even 20 years ago.

Throughout the 2020s and 2030s, there was a battle royal going on between the internal combustion engine (using petrol, diesel or biofuels) and electric vehicles (EVs). It's only in the last decade that EVs have finally won out. The key period was between 2010 (when IBM challenged the world with its 'Battery 500' project to find the first EV to achieve a range of 500 miles between recharges) and 2023, when the lithium-air battery first became available in a mass-market car. This sounded the death knell for its predecessor (the lithium-sulphur battery), which itself had evolved from primitive lithium-ion batteries. Twenty-five years on, today's EVs are still using super-refined versions of lithium-air technology.

This really isn't my bag, but I'm told all that may be about to change. For the last 30 years, the Formula-E Grand Prix has provided a showcase for the latest high-performance EVs – all of which have to be fitted with speed-limiters to keep them well below their top speed of 350 km per hour. Last year, the winning team was powered by a new range of supercapacitors, rather than batteries, which even the latest Lola-Drayson EV couldn't cope with.

Formula-E race car, Rome, 2023.

In contrast to worrying about the carbon footprint of cars 20 years ago, most people today are much more worried about the impact of personal jetpacks in terms of noise and intrusiveness - we still have loads of them buzzing around in our airspace, despite a 10-year campaign to get them banned!

V2G (VEHICLE TO GRID) TECHNOLOGIES

V2G systems – capable of feeding electricity back into the grid – were first pioneered more than 40 years ago. Some of the earliest mass-market EVs were able to provide that kind of two-way capability.

This was brilliant in terms of balancing supply and demand at the local level, smoothing out the problems associated with the fact that most renewable energy sources are only available for some of the time.

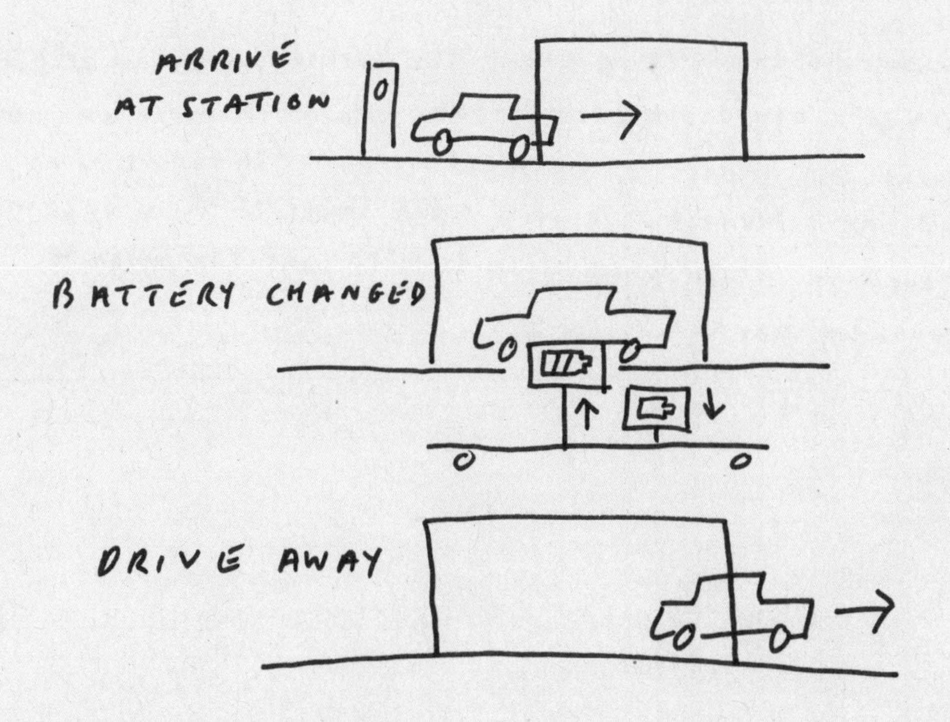

But we have to go back a bit first. There were big concerns before 2020 that lithium would run out as demand from EV manufacturers increased, but that never happened. Huge new reserves of lithium became available, not just in the 'Andean triangle' of Chile, Bolivia and Argentina, but also in China and the USA. And from 2019 onwards, all lithium batteries (whether for use in electronic goods or in cars) had to be designed to allow the lithium to be recycled – another example of the closed-loop economy in practice.

Prices for batteries kept on falling throughout the 2020s, which dramatically accelerated the move towards battery leasing systems rather than outright ownership – which in turn led to universal leasing systems for the vehicles themselves. These days, it's only a few crusty old nostalgics who still insist on owning their own cars.

Electric vehicles come in all shapes and sizes these days, some using standard battery technology, some based on more sophisticated hydrogen-powered fuel-cell systems. Hydrogen plays an important role in the liquid fuels market, but it never provided the economies of scale on which hopes for a much bigger 'hydrogen economy' were once based.

I've never owned a car myself, as it happens, having joined my first car share scheme in 2018. These days, I key in what kind of journey I'm planning, with an hour's notice, and the most appropriate vehicle (based on my personal preferences) is delivered to the door. When done, I either drop it back at our local community sub-station, or they come and pick it up. It's dead cheap, on a per-mile basis, and I get to choose between three different local schemes.

As far back as 2025, the Danish island of Bornholm went to 92 per cent renewable energy through a simple combination of wind power and grid-integrated EVs. PV is now incorporated invisibly into traditional Danish roof tiles.

As it happens, we hardly ever use a car, as we prefer our bikes for local use or our hydrogen fuel-cell scooters if we're feeling knackered. Driving isn't exactly fun, anyway, given that so much of today's road system is now auto-drive – you just get yourself on track, switch over to auto-drive and get on with other stuff until you arrive. That, of course, has had a dramatic impact on the rate of traffic accidents all over the world, reducing the number of people killed on the roads from more than a million in around 2010 to fewer than 50,000 per annum today.

There was a time when many people thought that breakthroughs in battery technology would completely kill off the internal combustion engine, with its continued dependence on carbon-based fuels – but the challenge of having to compete with EVs clearly worked wonders! By 2020, before the lithium-air revolution, the first zero-emission, 100 per cent biofuel, 100 miles per gallon, mass-market, super-lightweight vehicles became available. It was weight that proved to be the critical factor here, just as it had been since the turn of the century: in the old days, two-thirds of a car's fuel use was due to its weight!

Most of those early models still relied on conventional biofuels. But as I've already mentioned (see p.91), it wasn't long before a new generation of biofuels became available, some based on genetically-modified algae feeding on waste CO_2 in bio-reactors to produce oils that could then be converted into butanol-based biofuels, and some on pyrolysis systems converting waste biomass directly into fuels. As efficiencies increased, prices fell, giving new EVs a serious run for their money.

So the internal combustion engine lives on – but for how much longer? When large stretches of our central electricity grid were decommissioned in the late 2030s, almost all electricity was generated, distributed and used locally (except for some large-scale manufacturing plants still served by renewables such as offshore wind and wave power, the Severn barrage on the estuary between the Welsh and English coasts and mega-PV farms).

Balancing supply and demand at the local level remains a very tricky business, despite all the computing power we can now chuck at it. This is where EVs showed an extra advantage: the community electricity station that recharges our vehicles (using advanced solar and biomass schemes) can also draw on the electricity stored in their batteries at times of peak demand – as on the Danish island of Bornholm.

EVs had 30 per cent of the market in the EU and the USA in 2030; now it's 80 per cent. At its crudest (forgive the pun!), that's one reason why there's still so much oil still left in the ground.

08.07.2050

Nature's Balance Sheet

The RED Rocks Convention in Ecuador in 2035 – one of two international conferences that I've attended on behalf of Ashton Vale Community College – was hugely significant. Ecuador was one of the first countries to do a proper RED (Reducing Emissions from Deforestation) deal: money – lots of it – in return for the forest being completely protected. If I remember rightly, it was about $1 billion a year. A lot, even in those days.

Celebrating RED – two identical photos from 2013 and 2033, used by the conference organizers in 2035 as a device to demonstrate that the forest remained completely protected between those dates.

Before that, there had been much talk but not much action, despite all the fantastic work done by a coalition of organizations and individuals – including, as it happens, the former British sovereign, Charles III, or the Prince of Wales as he was in those days. But it was controversial. How would the interests of indigenous people be properly protected? What would happen if countries took the money but still cut the trees down later on, as the Democratic Republic of Congo kept on doing? The scope for corruption and fraud seemed limitless, and some of the early schemes ended up accelerating the loss of forests as the money was directed into new commercial plantations of eucalyptus, pine or acacia.

But Ecuador was different. Since 2008, it had had a constitution that recognized both human rights and the rights of nature. Despite doing some dreadful deals with Western oil companies, it had also created some of the most important biosphere reserves in the world. And the success of its RED scheme in keeping 20 million tonnes of CO_2 locked up in the forest provided just the role model everyone had been looking for.

Yasuni National Park, Ecuador, taken on my visit in 2035.

It was satellite surveillance that made it possible to police these deals. By 2015, forest protection agencies worldwide could home in on every single square metre of the land they were responsible for – and even detect what was going on beneath the tree canopy. Ecuador still has incredibly rigorous scrutiny systems in place because, without that kind of guarantee, why would people keep on providing the financial support?

We all find it a bit difficult these days to understand why economists back then were blind to the whole idea of 'nature's balance sheet'. It seems obvious: keep your natural capital intact, and nature will keep on providing all the raw materials and services that we need. Economists in the USA seemed to be especially blind: the big turnaround there didn't come until the mid-2020s, driven by a succession of natural disasters in places like the Mississippi Delta.

ANNUAL LOSSES OF BRAZILIAN RAINFOREST

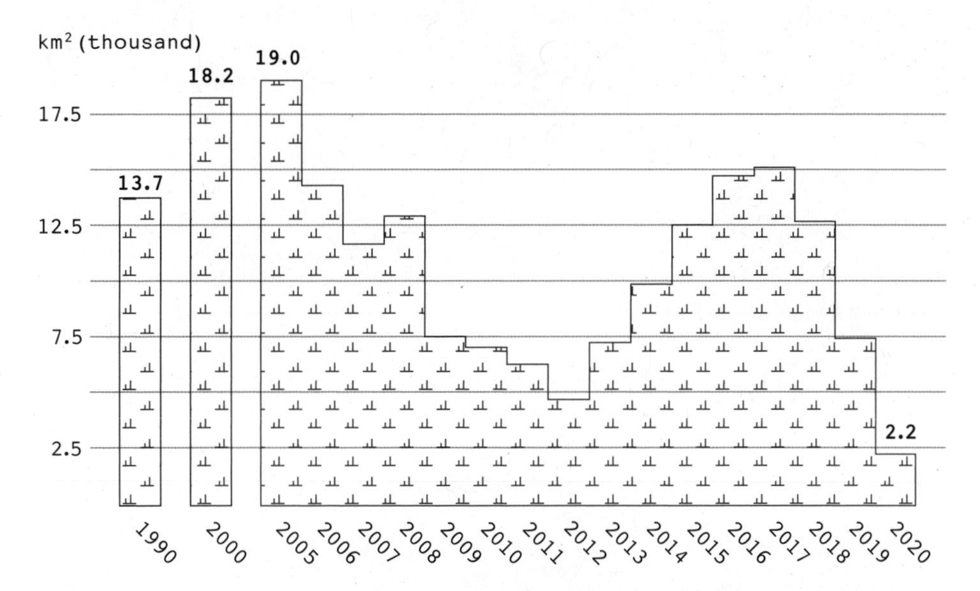

This graph shows how much progress Brazil made in reducing deforestation in the first decade of the twenty-first century. It then went back to its old ways as demand for farming land kept on growing. What swung it around again in 2020 wasn't the NGO campaigns or even the government, but Brazil's powerful soya farmers – precisely the people who had caused so much damage to Brazil's forests in the first place! When the soya harvest failed catastrophically in both 2014 and 2017 because of severe drought, farmers discovered the hard way that no rainforest meant no rain. That dramatically changed the equation, as a rather weak Brazilian government found itself on the receiving end of aggressive soya farmers demanding a total ban on any further deforestation.

The Mississippi used to be one of the most over-engineered river systems in the world. But by 2015, hundreds of kilometres of levees and other protective barriers were simply unable to cope with constant flooding – and the damage done to the Mississippi Delta, starved for decades of the rich soil that was once swept downriver, had become more and more severe. Over a 20-year period, the US Army Corps of Engineers gradually got rid of all the barriers and allowed the Mississippi to return to its old meandering ways, with huge amounts of farmland turned back into flood plains. And guess what? Restoring the Mississippi to its former glory also meant that the run-off of fertilizer and pesticides from intensive farming was reduced – simultaneously reducing the size of the 'dead zone' that had devastated fishing in the Gulf of Mexico for decades (see p.154).

What a price we've paid for decades of dumb economics of this kind. Capturing the full economic value of all the services that nature provides is now taken for granted. No developments are permitted that undermine the healthy functioning of these services – but we're still working hard to undo the horrendous legacy of earlier generations who ignored that basic rule.

These dead zones (the bright turquoise areas hugging the coastline) form when blooms of algae feeding on pollutants die and decay, dramatically reducing levels of oxygen in the water. At 22,000 square kilometres, the dead zone in the Gulf of Mexico was certainly a big one, but nothing like as big as all the dead zones in the Baltic Sea, which once covered a staggering 120,000 square kilometres. In fact, there were more than 500 dead zones all around the world by 2020, causing enormous economic damage in terms of lost fisheries, impact on tourism and so on. Dramatic reductions in the use of agricultural chemicals means that the oceans are now recovering – but only slowly.

NUMBER OF DEAD ZONES
→ World

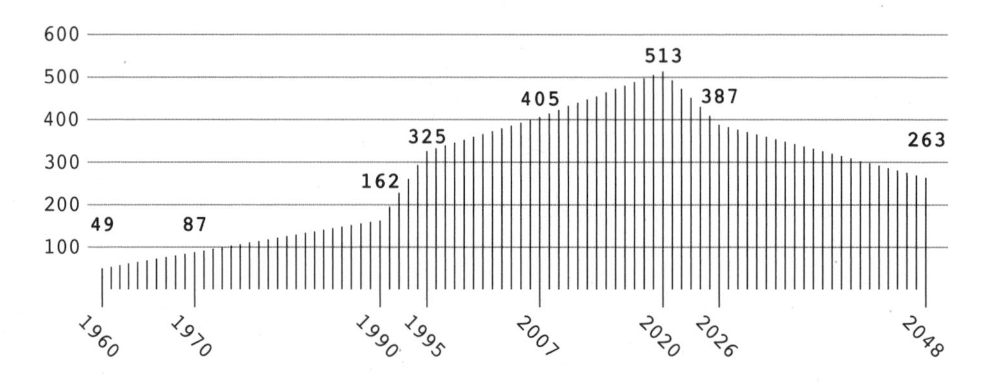

15.07.2050

Fisheries Bounce Back

I don't eat a lot of meat – very few people do these days. But I still eat a lot of fish, and I no longer feel guilty about it. All the fish we eat today (all around the world) comes from sustainable sources. Let's face it: if we hadn't got this one right, the whole idea of sustainable management – living off the interest of nature's wealth, not its capital – would be dead in the water, literally!

The origins of this particular revolution go back more than 50 years to the creation of the Marine Stewardship Council (MSC) in 1997 – one of the very first multi-stakeholder initiatives we've heard so much about since then. WWF and the global food giant, Unilever, got together at that time, targeting consumers with the simple message: if you like fish, buy it only from sustainable sources. The MSC logo gradually went global, and at the same time the number of fisheries certified as sustainable increased: by 2015, there were some 250.

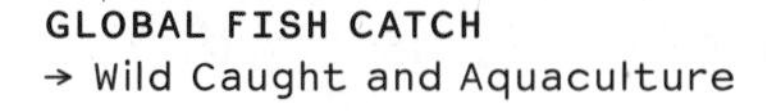

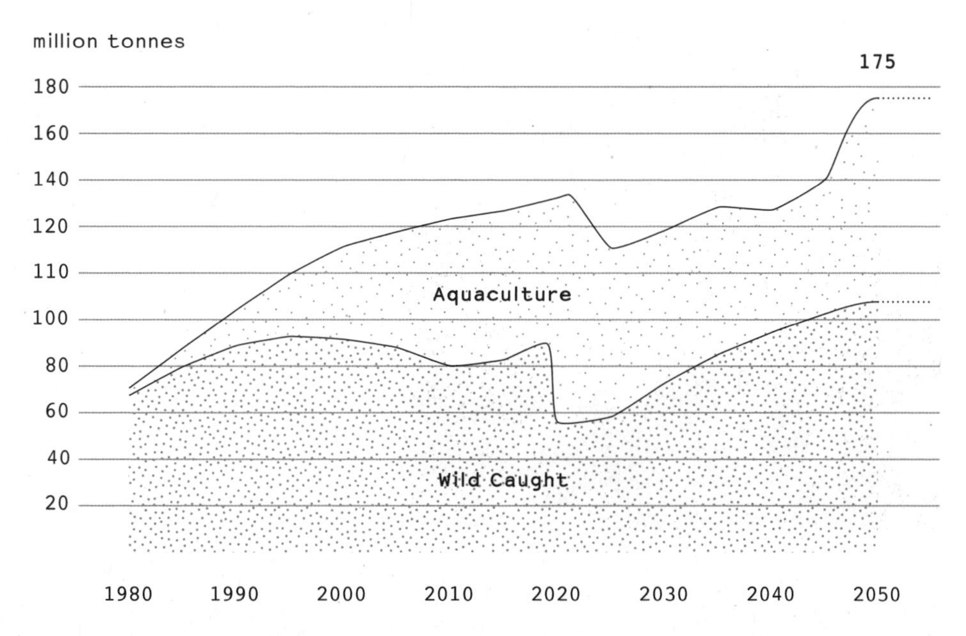

The Marine Stewardship Council logo.

But most of the fishing done then was still hopelessly unsustainable. The EU's old Common Fisheries Policy was the worst offender in those days, causing unbelievable wastage from 'discards' – the millions of tonnes of fish caught but then chucked back into the sea because of quota limits. That's when the chefs of Europe got involved.

In 2015, after another pathetic attempt to reform the Common Fisheries Policy, 2,182 chefs (led by Hugh Fearnley-Whittingstall, Raymond Blanc and Ferran Adrià) descended on Brussels. They numbered amongst them more than 1,500 Michelin stars and countless accolades in their own countries! Having already secured the support of an astonishing 4 million EU citizens who signed up to their e-petition, half of the chefs occupied the EU parliament while the other half occupied the Commission building itself – for four whole days.

At that point, even EU fisheries ministers got the message! A revised Common Fisheries Policy was finally adopted in 2018, marking the end of decades of unsustainable insanity by Europe's fisheries.

Hugh Fearnley-Whittingstall, indefatigable campaginer for fisheries the world over, berating EU Commissioners in Brussels in 2015.

MARINE RESERVES 2050

1 Greenland Sea
2 North Atlantic
3 Mediterranean network
4 Azores Mid-Altantic Ridge
5 Sargasso Sea/Western Atlantic
6 Northeastern Pacific
7 Moana Marine Reserve
8 Southeastern Pacific
9 Antarctic-Patagonia
10 South-Central Atlantic
11 Vema Seamount-Benguela
12 South Africa-Agulhas Current
13 Central Indian Ocean-Arabian Sea
14 Bay of Bengal
15 Northwestern Australia
16 South Austraila
17 Ross Sea
18 Lord Howe Rise and Norfolk Ridge
19 Coral Sea
20 Western Pacific & Greater Oceania Marine Reserves
21 West Oceania Marine Reserve
22 Kuroshio-Oyashio Confluence

In 2010, the UK somewhat astonished the world by announcing the creation of the world's largest marine reserve around the Chagos Islands in the Indian Ocean, banning all commercial fishing, coral collection and the hunting of turtles. Twelve years later, at the time of the Vigo Declaration, this was extended to include all of the ocean around the Maldives – the only exception being the sustainable 'pole and line' tuna fishery that had been operating there for as long as anyone could remember. It was far-sighted decisions like this that got us to where we are today, with 35 per cent of the world's oceans protected.

Unfortunately, none of this happened in time to avoid a calamitous crash in the worldwide fishing catch in 2019, as you can see on the graph on p.155. A combination of extreme climatic events, a near-total collapse in Pacific and West African fish populations (after years of over-fishing by EU trawlers, which had devastated local fishing businesses), plus the plagues of jellyfish that devastated the Mediterranean, South American and Japanese waters, brought the total fish catch that year to its lowest level since 1977. The price of fish (and fishmeal) rocketed, and the livelihoods of millions of people were seriously affected.

Somehow, this combination of environmental disaster and consumer engagement, plus brilliant campaigning by Greenpeace, WWF, the Blue Marine Foundation and other NGOs, emboldened governments to do what they should have been doing for decades: get it sorted!

Three years later, in 2022, the Vigo Declaration was signed, with its binding commitments to bring fisheries back into a healthy and productive state. All nations (including waverers such as China, Japan and the USA) eventually put their name to the Declaration. The majority (65 per cent) of the global fishing fleet was essentially paid off through a new international Fisheries Recovery Fund.

Unlicensed fishing was cracked down on in a quite draconian way: all fishing boats above a certain size were fitted with tracker devices, and if any fishing boat was detected at sea without an appropriate quota-based licence, it was tracked to its next destination, where the boat was impounded and sold for scrap to the highest bidder. The International Fisheries Inspection Agency was also established, with powers to board and inspect boats of any nation, anywhere in the world, at any time.

New protection regimes rapidly came into force in different regions, and the number of marine reserves went from around 2 per cent of the world's oceans in 2015 to around 35 per cent today. The case for 'no-take' marine reserves was pretty clear, even in those barbaric days: the average body size of fish inside such reserves is greatly increased, as is the number of species and the sheer biomass of all the plants and animals there.

At a more humble scale, the growth of local aquaponic schemes (growing fish and vegetables together as an integrated aquatic system) has been amazing, even in big cities – as pioneered in New York, San Francisco and Chicago. Community-supported fisheries (where members guarantee a certain amount of business up front and take a real interest in the fishery) have also become commonplace.

The latest figures from the Food and Agriculture Organization show that all these protective measures are costing us around $10 billion a year – but that's only about half of the $19 billion that politicians shelled out every year to subsidize the fishing industry earlier in the century!

With its deep historical knowledge of farming carp going back many centuries, China took the lead at the turn of the century in growing their fish-farming industries. The techniques they used became widespread across Southeast Asia, India and South America, and included many different plant-eating species such as tilapia and catfish. Doing the same for carnivorous fish species (salmon in particular) wasn't quite so easy. But the use of yeast-based feeds and magmeal products (a protein-rich meal produced from grinding up housefly maggots) reduced the amount of wild-caught fishmeal required by 75 per cent.

And here's one more brilliant statistic: the Scripps Institute of Oceanography announced earlier this year that the populations of almost all shark species are back to their 1990 levels. There's still long way to go, but it's unbelievable now to think that we once killed more than 40 million sharks a year – mostly to meet demand in China and East Asia just for soup made with sharks' fins!

22.07.2050

Feeding the World

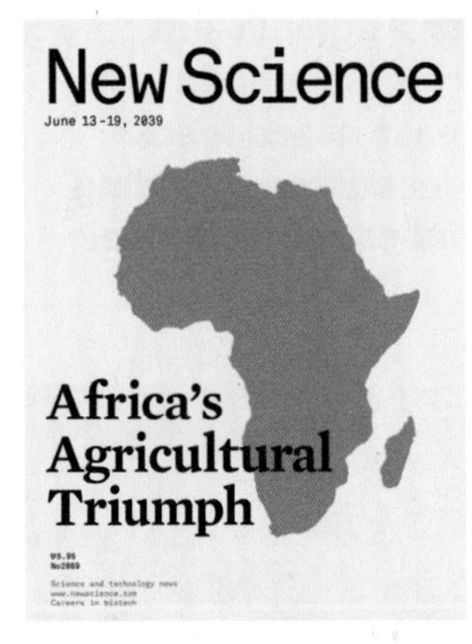

New Science, 13–19 June 2039.

Today, almost all of us have a hand in growing some of our own food, as I'll explain next. But commercial agriculture is still a huge global business.

The famines and food shortages of the 2020s and 2030s shocked us all into a radical rethink about food and land use. The overall result is that food waste has been all but eliminated, per capita meat consumption is at its lowest point ever, and the vast majority of today's 8.6 billion people are reasonably well fed, with reasonably balanced diets. Many of my friends see this as the greatest achievement of the first half of the twenty-first century. And as long as our population continues to decline (albeit on a rather gentle downwards curve), we should now be all right from a food security point of view.

But there's been no one 'big thing' that made this possible – as there was back in the twentieth century when the 'Green Revolution' massively increased yields of almost all the key crops we depend on. Many people at the start of this century were convinced it was going to be the science of genetic modification (GM) that would deliver that one big thing for the twenty-first century – but it's all turned out rather differently.

Many of the early GM strains promised much but delivered little: yields didn't increase very significantly, while many of the 'pest-resistant' breakthroughs did little to reduce the overall use of pesticides, as many of the targeted pests soon developed resistance to whatever was being thrown at them. There was next-to-zero benefit for the consumer in terms of lower food prices, and the GM-potato crisis in 2017 (which caused the death of more than 40 people across Europe) was a massive blow to consumer confidence.

Behind the scenes, however, the research focus had already shifted away from making profits for agri-business to creating solutions for the world. And the biggest solution of all came in the form of nitrogen-fixing (NF) wheat.

The fruits of 20 years of research at the John Innes Centre in the UK: a close-up of nodules on the root system of a wheat plant, demonstrating the technical feasibility of wheat being able to 'fix' its own nitrogen.

Nitrogen fixing was always the special preserve of legumes – peas, beans, clover and so on. Bacteria called 'rhizobia' lodge in their roots and draw in nitrogen from the atmosphere, turning it into useful nitrogen compounds. In return for the nutrients they need, the bacteria provide the plants with their own supply of nitrogen-based fertilizer. Symbiosis at its best! But other plants, including wheat, never acquired that trick – hence the need to keep on applying synthetic nitrogen fertilizers to get high yields, using vast amounts of natural gas in the process.

In that year, after more than 20 years' work, scientists at the John Innes Centre in the UK finally cracked it. They'd worked out how to transfer a key nitrogen-fixing gene from peas into wheat, and had trialled their new strains with both conventional and organic farmers – whose tireless campaigning against the use of synthetic fertilizers led many of them to see nitrogen-fixing wheat as the lesser of two evils.

At one level, this just looks like any old fully automated combine harvester – but this was actually the very first commercial harvest of nitrogen-fixing wheat back in 2022. A zero-till system with zero fertilizers applied – and above-average yields!

Nitrogen fixing split the organic movement down the middle – especially as another bunch of scientists at John Innes had also achieved extraordinary breakthroughs via completely conventional cross-breeding methods, producing varieties of wheat that flower that much earlier in the year and increase yields by up to 25 per cent. But NF wheat worked, with no impact on the environment, let alone on human health. By 2040, the use of nitrogen fertilizers on wheat crops had fallen by more than a quarter. It continues to decline, even now.

As it happens, there haven't been that many clear-cut GM breakthroughs over the years, despite the fact that all GM research was open-source from 2020 onwards as part of a much more rigorous global regulatory regime. Drought-resistant maize, sorghum and millet have proved beneficial, and cassava has been significantly improved. Bio-fortified rice has also made a difference in addressing vitamin A deficiency. But for all the billions of dollars chucked at one GM 'silver bullet' after another, that's not what made it possible to feed the world.

Instead, increasing productivity on small farms is what's made the biggest difference. And nowhere more so than in Africa – the only part of the world that had any serious capacity to expand its farming at that time. There are now around 450 million more hectares under cultivation across Africa than there were in 2015.

Not that this looked very good to start with. Initially, this expansion was driven by what was described as 'the worst resurgence of colonialism since the time of slavery', as both the big agri-tech companies and land-hungry countries like China and Saudi Arabia bought up vast tracts of productive land in Africa. I saw this for myself when I was working in Kenya in 2018–2019, and it was pretty brutal. But all that 'land-grabbing' came to a dramatic end after the Great Famine in 2025, as one African country after another took back control of its own land.

What makes Africa's farming triumph all the more remarkable is that it's been driven primarily by small farmers. Hectare for hectare, they'd always been more productive than industrialized agriculture, and when the science of agro-ecology really kicked in – helping farmers to make the very best of the existing natural conditions, soil types and biodiversity – yields were increased by as much as 70 per cent. Given that we still can't 'manufacture' soil – it takes around a thousand years to lay down one inch of soil – everyone now realizes that what matters most is the amount of good old organic matter in the soil.

In some parts of Africa, food yields were increased by as much as

70%

through applying all the bog-standard basics that are now commonplace around the world:

- internet-based education programmes in the field
- organic and ecological management techniques
- food co-ops (both producer co-ops and consumer co-ops)
- permaculture systems and increased use of perennial crops
- integrated and biological pest control
- water retention schemes and drip irrigation
- proper refrigeration in the supply chain

It's also been a

LOW-CARBON TRIUMPH

using agro-forestry schemes combining tree cover with shade-loving plants and crops.

FOOD PRODUCTION

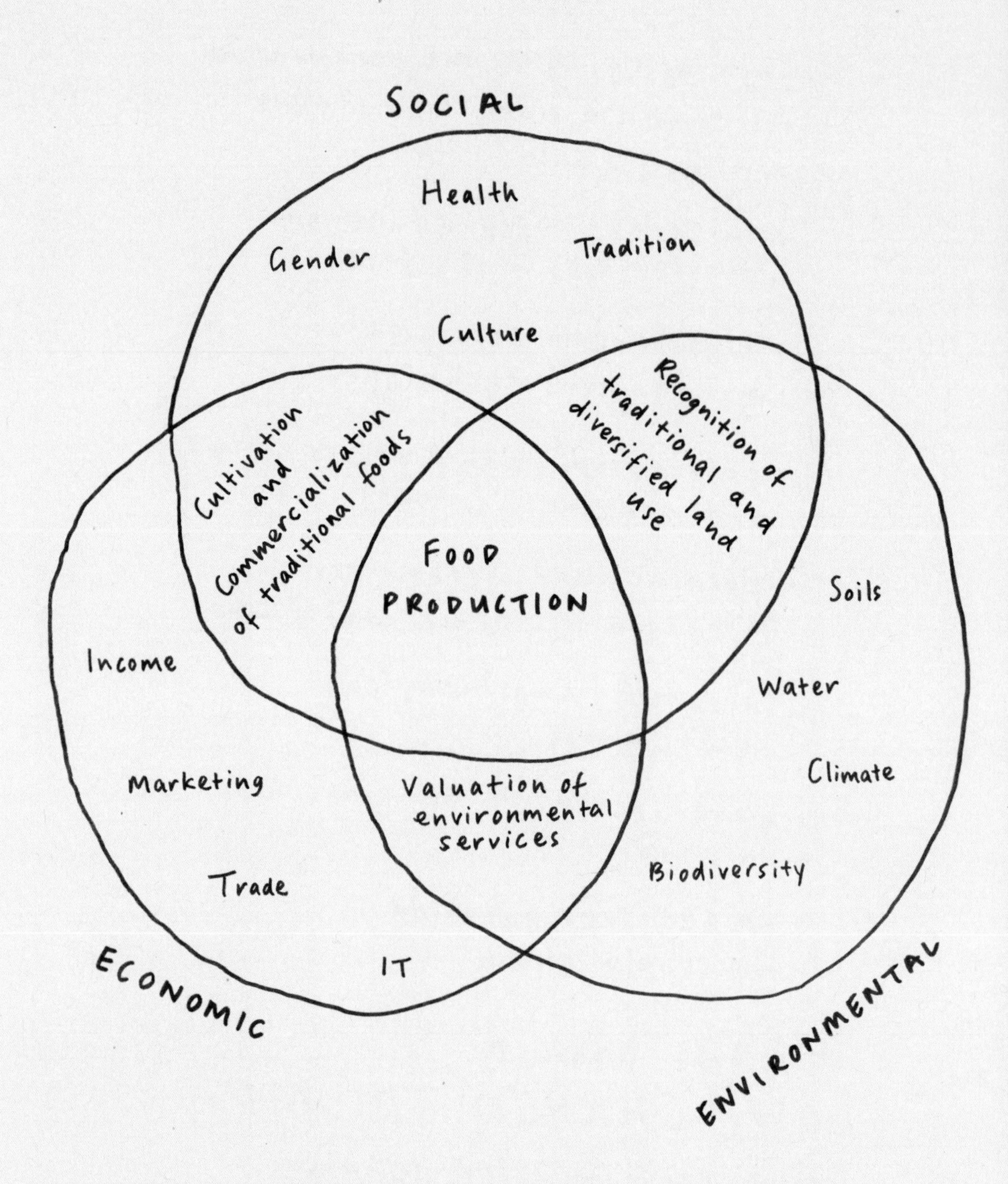

– taking the holistic view!

That productivity revolution had many different elements to it: an IT revolution that transformed farmers' lives and the markets on which they depended; a profusion of renewable energy sources, including the same kind of breakthroughs in advanced anaerobic digestion (AAD) that transformed on-farm energy in Europe and the USA a decade earlier; thousands of miles of new roads (built primarily by the Chinese!); a hugely significant change of heart on the part of big investors in accepting that small really was beautiful as far as African agriculture was concerned; and, finally, optimal crop-breeding based on the open-source genetic sequencing of all key African crops.

And that's where we are today. The cornerstone of Africa's prosperity still lies in its land and its brilliant, resilient, resourceful farmers, with plentiful food, secure livelihoods and billions of tonnes of carbon stored away in the continent's trees and revitalized soils. In other words, sustainable agriculture on a scale the world had never dreamed of before.

From the turn of the century, the Green Belt Movement in Kenya pioneered a continent-wide programme to plant billions of trees, funded in part by carbon credits sold to the World Bank. The only organization in Kenya capable of taking on this kind of organizational challenge then was the Green Belt Movement – which had been set up originally by an amazing woman called Wangari Maathai, who was seen as one of the guiding spirits for the whole EarthCorps initiative (see p.189).

30.07.2050

Incredible Edible Cities

OK, I admit, I'm showing off – but this just happens to be part of our own local Community Farm. Nothing particularly special about it – there are literally millions of such community farms all around the world – but this is the one that we helped make happen. It's where our family gets roughly a third of our food from today, with the rest coming from our local supermarket or from farmers elsewhere in the country, from whom we buy directly.

There's nothing new about urban farming. Even at the start of the century, at the height of industrialized agriculture, there were as many as a billion people engaged in urban agriculture, producing about 15 per cent of the world's food. However, that was mainly in Asia; towns and cities in Europe and the US were pretty much food production deserts, apart from some allotments and food co-ops.

The transformation started soon after that. Food and energy prices were so volatile that more and more people started to get involved in local schemes to protect themselves against constant price rises. Landshare, Communities for Agriculture, Grow On, Urban Harvests, Earthworks, Transition Towns, Harvest of Hope, Slow Food, the worldwide 'Incredible Edible' initiative, Food for All, Plant for Life – it seems like thousands of new movements sprang up around then!

But what swung it for communities like ours were changes in the planning system that forced landowners to put their land into productive use, rather than just sit on it as a speculative asset. The introduction of a new Community Service Volunteers scheme also made a big difference. This makes it possible for municipalities and community councils to certify any local voluntary scheme that provides 'demonstrable and measurable benefits to local citizens'. Any citizen on the electoral roll can then earn credits by committing their time to council-approved schemes, and those credits can then either be set against local taxes or traded through the local currency. Community farms have benefitted massively from this initiative.

There's still a very lively debate about the economic basis for all this. Many urban farms have been set up as conventional food co-ops, or even as profit-making businesses that sell their produce locally (through farmers' markets, direct sales and local shops), rather than giving it away in return for hours worked – or just giving it away regardless! Many towns and cities have witnessed pitched battles between warring producers on different sides of this commerce-versus-cooperation divide.

But that kind of clash is nothing in comparison to the ongoing battle between the 'traditionalists' and 'technos' in terms of food production. From the early 2020s onwards, a lot of our fresh food has been grown without ever seeing the light of day, in totally controlled indoor environments. Depending on each crop's particular absorption spectrum, high-efficiency plasma lighting systems produce just the right combination of blue and red light to promote growth. Water use has been made more and more efficient over the years, so that the only water that ever leaves the building is the water contained in the produce itself.

In between the high-tech and low-tech extremes, we have the 'vertical farmers', growing a wide range of vegetables and crops hydroponically, with just a thin layer of minerals and all the water constantly recirculated – as they first learnt to do at the time of the Second World War in the twentieth century. Special mirrors bounce light around the growing areas, and by keeping everything completely clean (so that pests and diseases can't get in), there's no need for any pesticides, so there's no agricultural run-off. As a rule of thumb, one hectare's worth of floor space produces the equivalent of 12 traditional soil-based hectares – although some of the vertical greenhouses pioneered in Sweden and Japan can do even better than that.

But the traditionalists are still having none of it! On nutritional, health and aesthetic grounds, they believe crops and vegetables should still be produced under real sunshine and rain, just as they believe meat should come from real animals raised in outdoor environments.

Anyone outside Asia who's interested in urban farming still looks to Detroit as the role model. It's a bit of a cliché now, but Detroit's 100 year journey – from industrial powerhouse at the heart of America's car-loving culture to one of the world's most dangerous urban wastelands (with more than a third of the city's land completely abandoned), and on to become 'Green City of the Decade' in the 2020s – remains extraordinarily inspirational.

As part of the response to the city's chronic financial problems, the Detroit Living Blueprint was endorsed in 2015, with plans to create up to 100 square kilometres of productive agriculture. Some of it was very small-scale stuff, like our own community farm. But some of it was truly high-tech: precision agriculture using nano-sensors, smart metering, GPS tracking and computer-assisted drip irrigation – the 'more crop per drop' approach helped achieve yields in Detroit that traditional US farmers are still very envious of.

A vertical greenhouse in 2038. By some calculations, more than 40 per cent of the food we humans consume today is grown – one way or another – in the urban environment: on roofs, derelict land and allotments, in edible 'green corridors', pocket parks, gardens and what were once useless front lawns that just grew grass (and used vast amounts of chemicals) – even in window boxes.

As far as I'm concerned, it seems something of a storm in a teacup – all these different approaches use only renewable energy, they all recycle nutrients from anaerobically digested human and other organic waste, and they all keep water consumption to the minimum. So what's the problem?

On a personal basis, I have to admit that I still prefer the stuff I've helped grow, not least because of the wealth of biodiversity it helps nurture. Our Community Farm recently won a national award for our bee-friendly planting regime, and – like millions of people today – we all get a lot of pleasure from eating our own honey.

I've already touched on the health and educational benefits of this, on top of all the environmental benefits. But perhaps most importantly of all, it now looks as if urban farming has helped us get out of the red in terms of the overall energy balance of global food production. At its most insane level at the start of the century, agriculture in the US and other rich-world economies needed between 5 and 10 calories of fossil fuel energy to deliver 1 calorie of food energy! According to the latest Food and Agricultural Organization report last year, we're just about back to a one-to-one ratio, which has to be the single most important measure of food security for humankind as a whole.

05.08.2050

The Wonders of Modern Medicine

All medical training now relies on the extensive use of virtual learning environments, reducing both costs and the risk to patients. This was one of the first 3D virtual hospital wards for training medical students, pioneered at Keele University in the UK.

The anarchic world of medical wikis has transformed the relationship between doctors and patients – with more and more citizens getting involved in online initiatives, sharing experiences and ideas in ways that sometimes drive doctors mad! 'Every Body on the Net' was already a worldwide phenomenon by 2015, and it has grown and grown since then.

This movement coincided with the realization on the part of politicians that they would never be able to balance the books unless they dramatically changed the model of healthcare. That meant getting away from dependence on hugely expensive acute hospitals – which had the added disadvantage of being very dangerous places for people to be in. Despite everything hospital administrators did to reduce the risk of infection, increasingly resistant superbugs picked up in hospitals killed more and more people every year.

Looking back to the start of the century, one thing jumped out at us while we were doing our research for this whole area: politicians were always prattling on about the importance of preventative healthcare, but almost all public money still went into sorting out people's problems after they got ill! By 2015, 75 per cent of the money spent on healthcare in the rich world went into treating chronic diseases that should never have been allowed to occur in the first place. Much of that was down to the 'medical establishment' at that time, where status was all to do with expensive treatments and specialized surgical interventions – with patients largely treated either as ignorant idiots or as compliant guinea pigs.

To be fair, most of the remote monitoring technology that we take for granted today (and the self-management it makes possible) was only just becoming available then. Apart from all the data continuously transmitted to my doctor about my physical state, I now get a weekly report on my diet and physical activity levels, which is shared with my insurance provider.

A percentage of everyone's annual health insurance premium is paid by the government on a means-tested basis: some people pay 90 per cent, some people just 10 per cent. I'm on 50 per cent at the moment, and strongly incentivized to reduce the percentage I have to pay depending on the amount of exercise I take, my diet, alcohol consumption and so on. Last year, I got my premium right down to below 20 per cent – my best year ever. But I'm way off target this year. Too many 50th birthday parties perhaps!

Diagnosis has also become so much easier and so much more reliable. Even 25 years ago, my mother's breast cancer was picked up remotely via secreted biomarkers in a standard saliva test, followed by instant referral to a specialist in one of this country's four cancer hospitals.

Bio-banking lies at the heart of this. Since it was first pioneered in the UK and China more than 35 years ago, millions of volunteers around the world have allowed their medical data (provided on a strictly anonymous basis) to be correlated against all sorts of lifestyle and behavioural factors. I think that's when people finally woke up to the massive benefits of Big Data, and what it meant to them personally.

Given all this self-managed data being shared on such a wide basis, privacy has been a big issue for the last 30 years or more – especially in genomic medicine. I think it's something like 95 per cent of people globally have now had their genomes sequenced, and most of those who haven't are much older people who just don't like the idea. From time to time, all their worst fears are confirmed by dreadful scandals involving the unauthorized use of personal health data. But on the whole, the impact of genomics on standard healthcare systems has been both positive and dramatic.

In the old days, the only way of testing new drugs was to carry out clinical trials on large numbers of people to see what level of efficacy was achieved. Too bad if the side effects for some people were really serious, just so long as the population-wide impact was more or less benign, then into production those drugs would go.

It was a crazy business model. As the regulatory hurdles got higher, with billions of dollars needing to be spent on every new drug, the pharmaceutical companies would spend even more billions on marketing to make sure that the sales revenue covered the costs of development.

In 2020, mental health costs were also at an all-time high, pretty much across the world. Despite endless shock-horror reports and documentaries about the dangers of tranquillizers and so-called 'stress busters', doctors just kept on writing out the prescriptions. They had all the evidence they needed, even then, that a mix of physical activity, stimulation, good diets, company and community was so much more effective in 'managing' stress, depression and other mental health problems. But it was only the need to slash the drugs budget that got all that sorted.

The science of pharmaco-genomics has also made a huge difference – using genetic information to help develop new drugs. Almost all drug treatments are now tailored to each individual's unique genome and medical history. God knows what would have happened to healthcare costs without that! In 2015, for example, mass medical treatment on a population-wide basis was the norm. Various polypills made up of aspirin, statins, folic acid and other drugs were prescribed, almost as a matter of course, to people at a younger and younger age. Costs were high, but efficacy was questionable – some benefitted, but many didn't.

Once we'd got used to the idea that each individual was truly unique, pretty much everything changed. Drugs were formulated for very specific genetic groups, particularly in relation to high-risk genetic mutations linked to particular cancers. Surgical procedures have become the 'interventions of last resort'. Doctors, genetic councillors, insurance providers and we ourselves – as citizens, not patients – now all pitch in to minimize our exposure to medical treatment. Indeed, the latest remuneration formula for all qualified medics is now based on keeping people in good health rather than paying them for sorting out their ill health.

The higher the level of risk for any particular individual, the wider the range of diagnostics that can be called on. I know my mother pretends to hate it, but the nano-sensors patrolling her arteries give her a high level of reassurance that her cancer won't return – that would have been unimaginable even a decade ago. This is also true in terms of treatments: today's cancerbots only release the relevant chemotherapy once they've come into contact with the target cancer cells, so the treatment is optimally effective with minimal side-effects.

All of this means that people live longer and healthier lives – which has its own challenges (see p.262)!

Almost everybody today (except for a few privacy fanatics) depends on a variety of miniature, high-res devices (I think they were once described as the 'lab on a chip') that remotely monitor all our vital signs:

blood pressure
heartbeat
temperature
respiratory performance
concentrations of glucose and oxygen in the blood
levels of antioxidants
cancer-specific antigen levels
cortisol levels
cholesterol (different kinds)
the calories we're burning
our levels of physical and mental activity
serotonin balances
sleep cycles
body mass index / body composition

- in fact, everything about our physical wellbeing that can be measured!

All this data is shared with our doctors in real time, and any deviations from the normal patterns automatically trigger an alert that the medics can then choose how best to respond to.

The malaria story is just one of the many battles against nature that we've been involved in throughout the last two centuries – and the ethical debates are as lively today as at any point during that time.

For instance, the Research Team was rather taken aback by the trenchantly pro-pathogen tone of this campaigning website from the mid-2020s!

CAIB: CAMPAIGN AGAINST INDISCRIMINATE BIOCIDE

Malaria is obviously horrible. But is it right that we are trying to destroy a unique form of life – the malaria parasite – simply to protect ourselves?

Is that really morally defensible?

We are already making good progress in reducing the numbers of people killed or harmed by malaria. So do we really need to cause the extinction of this life form?

And the malaria parasite is just the start!

There are more than 1400 pathogens out there that can kill people, and an unknown number of bugs, bacteria, weeds, fungi, viruses and other pathogens that threaten both our health and our food supplies.

Don't they have rights too?

11.08.2050
Malaria Tamed

Sometimes you have to stand back and celebrate the sheer genius of people in making this a better world for millions of people. Just take a glance at the table below. 1.7 million deaths in 2005, down to 350,000 in 2020, a few hundred five years ago, and now zero, as far as we know. This success story represents years of endeavour by untold numbers of people (in the field, in the hospital and in the lab) – and around $60 billion of expenditure since 2000.

I had to explain to my young researchers why this was so important – for them, malaria is already history! When I was growing up, my mother (who came from a part of India particularly affected by malaria) was always going on about the horrendous impact of malaria on millions of people, particularly children. Of the 1.2 million killed by malaria in 2010, 60 per cent were under the age of five.

INCIDENCE OF MALARIA FATALITIES

million

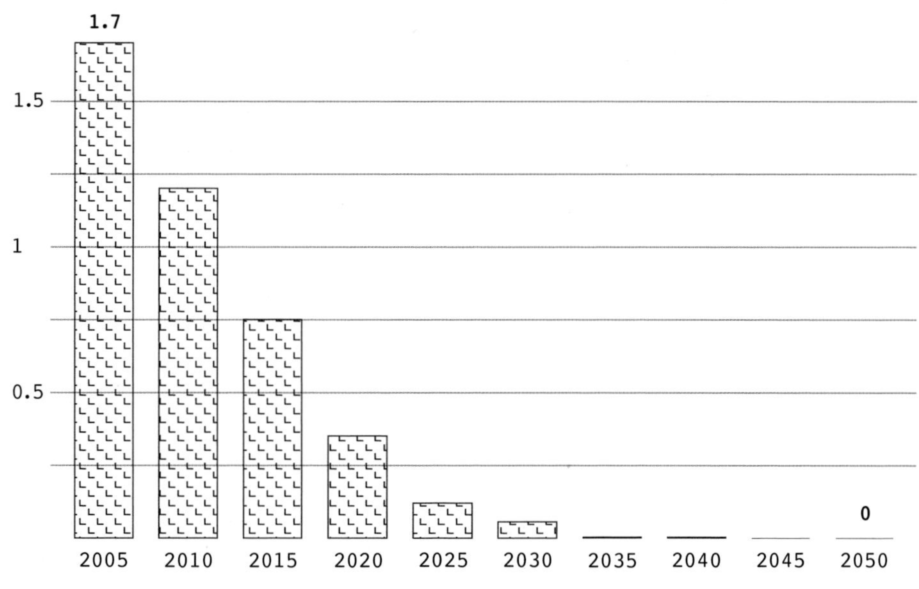

This is another of those stories where you have to give a good deal of credit to the Bill and Melinda Gates Foundation. The Foundation not only put in a fair proportion of all those billions during the time they were involved in malaria management, but in the process they encouraged, cajoled and shamed politicians and other agencies into doing much more than they might otherwise have done.

The Foundation's official archivist (not many foundations have one of those!) wrote an excellent paper on the history of all this in 2037, shortly after the Foundation ceased funding malaria and dengue fever programmes to enable it to move on to other challenges. She described it as a story of four overlapping interventions.

The first was made up of all those things that could be done in the name of public health: reducing and, where possible, eliminating the conditions in which mosquitos breed by draining stagnant pools and waterways; spraying the inside walls of houses and shacks with insecticides; and then the mass distribution of mosquito nets treated with long-lasting insecticides.

Next were the anti-malarial drugs that everyone took when travelling to affected areas. The combinations at that time (both to prevent transmission and to treat people who had already contracted malaria) seemed to be pretty effective. This persuaded key organizations working on malaria to set incredibly ambitious targets of reducing malaria deaths to 'near zero' by 2015.

For the first 20 years of this century, across the whole of India, groups of children used to form anti-malaria 'police', and toured the community, encouraging awareness of anti-malarial precautions such as mosquito nets.

Over-ambitious targets! Although the level of international funding was ramped up enormously during that time, resistance to the most commonly used malarial drugs was also increasing steadily. Even the artemisinin-based combination drugs became less and less effective as the mosquito-borne parasites responsible for malaria inevitably developed resistance. Which meant that more had to be done – in the form of two very different approaches: vaccines and genetic modification.

Once it became clear that drugs alone would never do it, however good the drugs companies got at developing new compounds, the race was on to find a vaccine to help control malaria – the third key strategy. This was done either by preventing the malaria parasite from completing its life cycle within the human body, or by blocking the invasive process right at the point of contact between mosquito and victim. The first vaccine was available by 2015, but it didn't stay active for very long and only reduced cases by around 50 per cent. Other vaccines followed, achieving somewhat higher success levels – but never the 'final victory' in the form of complete eradication of the disease.

The first GM mosquito to be released, 2029.

And that's when the war with the mosquito got really dirty! By the early 2020s, scientists had learned how to modify the mosquito's genome, by adding either a gene that disrupted the development of the offspring or one that prevented the female mosquito from flying.

All very controversial, but as scientists pointed out at the time, it wasn't all that different from the sterile male technique already widely used to control populations of pests like the tsetse fly or the screw-worm fly. Here, large numbers of the male of the species are bred artificially, zapped with radiation to make them sterile and then released into the wild to mate with females – whose eggs then fail to hatch.

Genetic engineering – the fourth strategy – was just the next step in that process. All sorts of potential problems were raised by campaigners (unintended consequences, knock-on effects on other organisms and so on), but in the end the continuing toll on humans was seen to justify this escalation in the war against the malaria parasite and its mosquito host. And as you can see from the data (see p.179), the impacts were soon felt when the first GM mosquitos were released in 2029. There were all sorts of further genetic modifications, but by 2035 the scourge of malaria had been almost eliminated.

So it's only fair that scientists today notch up the reality of a malaria-free world as another victory against all those organisms that threaten our health and wellbeing, just as previous generations did with smallpox, polio and so on. But we make those claims today with rather more humility than we did before; our species isn't the only one on this planet with moral rights.

20.08.2050

China Shows the Way

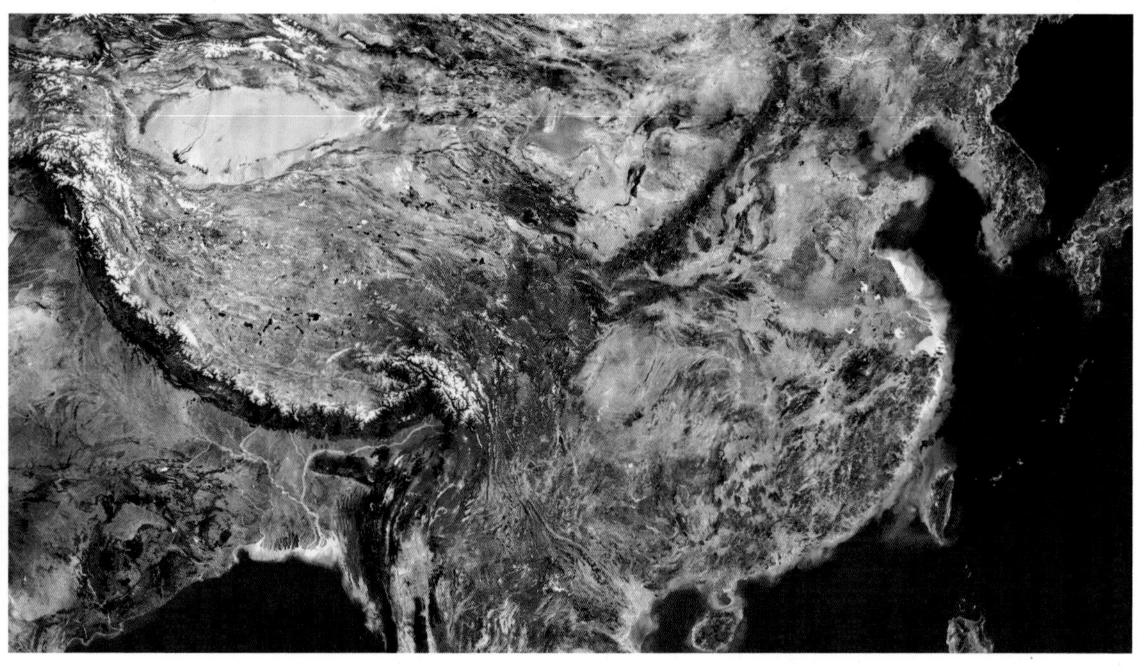

By 2035, the effects of China's massive reforestation scheme along the eastern edge of the Gobi desert, the Great Green Wall, could be seen from space.

So many books have been written over the last few decades about China and the United States that I was loathe to recommend another to our Research Team. But Liu Baojin's 'How America Gifted the Twenty-First Century to China', published in 2045, provides just the most brilliant summary. And it starts with one of those telling 'cross-over moments', as he calls them.

In 2012, China pledged to phase out the one billion incandescent light bulbs in use in the country at that time, because their energy efficiency was so poor. Lighting in China at that time accounted for no less than 12 per cent of their total electricity consumption – twice as much electricity as they got from the hugely controversial Three Gorges Dam, the biggest dam in the world. The change-over saved nearly 50 million tonnes of CO_2 a year from 2016 onwards!

At the same time, the Republicans in the United States were doing the opposite – passing laws to protect the incandescent light bulb to ensure that people should always have a choice of bulb, if that's what they wanted. This was deeply symbolic of what happened over the next 40 years: the Americans got their 'green economy' in the end (see p.48), but they lost more than a decade – at precisely the time that China was working out in great detail what it would mean for their country to thrive in the low-carbon world of the future.

Interestingly, few commentators saw what was going on at that time. With a population of around 1.3 billion and average rates of economic growth of around 10 per cent a year, China used to top the league tables of every single pollution indicator you can imagine. The air was foul, most of the rivers and lakes were horribly polluted, and huge amounts of land were lost to both industrial development and soil erosion. But – and it's a very big but – all that dirty growth enabled the China's rulers to bring more than half a billion people out of extreme poverty in an extraordinarily short period of time, producing a better anti-poverty success story than any other country has achieved at any time in history.

At the same time that China was phasing out incandescent lightbulbs, it was still playing hardball in international climate change negotiations. But back home, change was already underway – first, with improvements in energy efficiency across the economy (a 27 per cent improvement was achieved between 2010 and 2020), and then with further dramatic reductions in greenhouse gas emissions by switching to renewables. Massive investments were made in wind power (both onshore and offshore), and in solar, biomass and small-scale hydro – as well as nuclear, until the Kiev Treaty in 2022 put an end to that (see p.60).

The 'x4' was one of the first EVs on the market to pioneer putting an integrated electric motor, suspension and brakes in each of the wheels – hence the 'x4'! I rented one of this model while I was in China in 2020.

Ambitious grant programmes incentivized the purchase of hydrogen scooters and electric vehicles, while at the same time Chinese companies made great advances in battery technology. The result was that sales of hybrid and fully electric vehicles in China rose from 10 per cent (of the 21 million vehicles sold) in 2015 to 40 per cent in 2031 – which was also the year in which purchases of private vehicles peaked in China, at 40 million. And once they'd cracked the horrors of urban air pollution, Chinese citizens rediscovered their love of electric bicycles – of which there are now more than 350 million on the roads.

Despite such measures, there was always going to be a price to be paid for all that environmental damage. Chinese scientists recognized that they were going to be clobbered very hard by accelerating climate change – and so it proved to be. The Shanghai Inundation in 2024 (see p.117) was just one amongst many disasters.

The poster reads 'Late marriage, late childbearing, single births, more planned births' (Wanhun wanyu dusheng yousheng), China, 1986. For China, it has always been about trade-offs. Earlier this century, the environment was trashed to secure rapid economic development, and political freedoms were ruthlessly curtailed to maintain social stability. By the same token, the one-child family policy (introduced way back in the 1970s and promoted through constant propaganda campaigns) undoubtedly rode roughshod over women's rights – but it worked. As the Chinese kept asking their critics at that time: would you prefer our population today to be 400 million more than it already is? That figure was the number of births 'averted' between 1975 and 2005, as a direct result of the one-child family policy.

In addition to all the anti-pollution measures, schemes to physically protect people and the land had to be put in place. Countless billions were spent on complex sea defences along a vast stretch of China's eastern seaboard.

And tree-planting programmes were massively increased, so that China's 'Great Green Wall' now covers more than 300 million hectares, providing at least some measure of protection against encroaching deserts.

At the same time, water shortages became chronic as 'occasional' droughts dragged on for year after year. By 2020, China was spending more than $50 billion a year on water conservation and efficiency schemes. Farmers, industrialists and increasingly rebellious Chinese citizens had to make dramatic reductions in water consumption, and water rationing was commonplace in many parts of China, as it was in many other countries. Even so, by 2030 nearly 70 per cent of Mongolia's population of three million people had been displaced by drought, overgrazing and unprecedentedly harsh winters. The refugee camps around Ulan Bator told a tragic story of the death of an entire way of life.

When it came to the low-carbon economy, China always had a dual game plan in mind: grow the market domestically; dominate the market globally. And that's what happened: it had just 15 per cent of the world market for low-carbon goods and services in 2015; the last figures I saw showed it at 30 per cent. At the same time as China phased out those one billion incandescent light bulbs, it was actually selling 2.85 billion of them to the rest of the world, including the United States. But that soon changed as China ramped up production of low-energy alternatives: compact fluorescents, then light-emitting diodes (LEDs) and finally high-efficiency plasma lamps, which had already revolutionized certain lighting markets by the 2020s. Always one step ahead: planning, planning, planning.

As I've mentioned before, it helped that so many Chinese politicians were engineers and scientists, and were capable of thinking very long-term. There was always a lot of interest in China's new 'eco-civilization', its 'harmonious' or 'circular' economy, its 'green growth', and so on. We know now that they really meant it, and have encouraged a lot of countries to follow along in their footsteps.

26.08.2050

Putting the World to Rights

I'm not sure that everyone would include EarthCorps in their portfolio of things that changed the world, but I'm just a bit biased about this one as I was an EarthCorps volunteer in 2018–2019!

In his inaugural address after the 1960 US presidential election, John F. Kennedy promised that he would help set up a programme that became known as the Peace Corps. That was the context for his still resonant exhortation: 'And so, my fellow Americans: ask not what your country can do for you – ask what you can do for your country'. Over half a century later, a couple of years after his success in the 2012 US presidential election, Barack Obama promised to help set up a programme that became known as the EarthCorps. Never one to miss a good rhetorical opportunity, his words on that occasion were: 'And so, my fellow Americans: ask not what the Earth can do for you – ask what you can do for the Earth'.

Barack Obama founded EarthCorps soon after his re-election in 2012.

Frustrated by his continuing inability to advance the climate change agenda at that time, and in danger of going down in history as the US president who did even less on the environment than his predecessor, George W. Bush, Barack Obama went for broke with this idea. Joining forces with former Soviet leader, Mikhail Gorbachev, and his Green Cross International (which was active at that time in more than 30 countries), they persuaded many others to join in, including the legendary Warren Buffett, the Apple Foundation (which was still working out what to do with some of its billions after the death of Steve Jobs, its founder and charismatic leader) and the Lebedev Foundation. They created an endowment of $100 billion to ensure the long-term success of the EarthCorps. It all went live on 1 January 2016, and within a short period of time it became a badge of honour to be an alumnus of the EarthCorps programme.

A photo from my EarthCorps experience, Kenya, 2018. This is a pretty personal story for me. The day after my father died in the water riots in the West Bank in 2017, I signed up to EarthCorps. I knew I had to do something as soon as I left school, to turn grief into action. I'd been hoping to go to India, but I got assigned to Kenya instead. It was, as they say, life-changing. I spent weeks potting up tree seedlings in some of their nurseries, and then driving out to remote villages to help with the planting. Even then, Kenya was a model for the rest of the world in terms of reforestation schemes.

It was truly global right from the start: kids from Burkina Faso were just as likely to end up as part of the EarthCorps in Russia or Mexico as kids from the US signing up for the Philippines or Bangladesh. There are now more than 250,000 EarthCorps alumni, and I would say it's one of the most influential networks anywhere in the world.

The money side of it remains demanding. Over and above their travelling expenses, every EarthCorps volunteer gets paid a living wage, depending on their country of origin and their destination.

The EarthCorps still covers that living wage and travelling expenses, but all other in-country expenses are covered either by the host country itself or by corporate sponsorship helping less well-off countries. Host families provide both food and accommodation for free – the whole idea being to make it as much of a privilege for the hosts as for the volunteers themselves. By the early 2020s it was already a huge success, and numbers had to be capped at 10,000 a year.

That's what persuaded a lot of countries to go one step further and set up their own EarthCorps equivalent. A few went further still – turning voluntary schemes into compulsory 'national service' schemes. Including the UK.

It was a hugely controversial development, and I fell out with a lot of my friends by coming out so strongly in favour of this compulsory proposal in 2025. But by then, although I'd only been teaching for a few years, I'd already seen so many young people leaving school ready and keen for work but instantly hitting that wall of indifference from employers. It was the same in so many other countries, with youth unemployment at anywhere between 15 and 30 per cent. Something had to be done about it.

Even against that backdrop, establishing a compulsory scheme was quite a challenge. Eventually a government came into power that made a real priority of this issue, and after a tempestuous debate, the National and Community Service Act was passed in 2027. Since then, every young person between the ages of 16 and 20, without exception, has to do a year's service working for an accredited organization in either the public or the voluntary sector. Those who refuse are assigned to more demanding roles – in the prison service, for instance, to work as volunteers looking after prison gardens.

It's been so interesting sharing all this with the Research Team – and they kind of wonder what all the fuss was about! But looking back to the 2020s, the truth of it is that we were still struggling with the balance between rights and responsibilities, between entitlements and obligations. The second half of the twentieth century was big on rights and entitlements, and all but ignored the other side of the contract. It's taken us the best part of 50 years to put that right.

01.09.2050

Redesigning the Building Blocks of Life

Not being a scientist, there are times when I've struggled to see the significance of some of the things that my students have insisted we should include – but the more I thought about this particular transition, the more remarkable it seemed. At the start of the century, we depended on fossil fuels for almost all our chemicals. These days, almost all the raw materials we use in industry come from the biological world. Back then, the so-called 'bioeconomy' was tiny; now it's all-encompassing.

For instance, we take it for granted today that all carpets, anywhere in the world, are zero-carbon, 100 per cent natural and totally recyclable. But that's only possible because more than 30 years ago pioneers in the field of 'green chemistry' discovered how to make every part of a carpet out of natural, recyclable materials – including the adhesives needed. Before that, recycling carpets cost-effectively was extremely difficult. At the same time, other chemists were taking all the left-overs of the food industry (things like orange peel, cashew nut shells, rice husks, potato and vegetable peelings and so on) and turning them into all sorts of bio-solvents, catalysts, enzymes and other speciality chemicals, producing next-to-zero waste and no toxics.

Avoid waste; get rid of toxics and harmful solvents; use renewable feedstocks; minimize energy use: those have been the hallmarks of 'green chemistry' from those pioneering early days.

These things didn't seem to have much impact on our lives at the time – because nobody saw any difference in what they were buying! The story that people really did notice back in the 2020s was all about plastic. Plastics derived from oil had pretty much defined what progress was all about in the second half of the twentieth century. Production increased from just over one million tonnes in 1950 to around 250 million tonnes by 2000, providing my parents' generation with every conceivable kind of new product and packaging. But from an environmental point of view, it was a horror story.

When I was just 11 years old, my mother stuck this photo on the kitchen notice board, showing the plastic leftovers found in the stomach of a young albatross in the Southern Ocean. Our world then was awash with almost indestructible and often toxic plastic waste. Happily, the stomachs of young albatrosses today are full of fish rather than plastic gunk.

Research into so-called bio-plastics (derived from plants, algae or bacteria) was slow to get going, but we gradually got better at processing them in increasingly efficient bio-refineries. By the early 2020s, no fossil fuels were used at all in the production of 'commodity chemicals' (like polyethylene, polypropylene and polyurethane) for use in industry and consumer goods.

Better yet, all the packaging materials we use today are either reused (time after time), recycled back into the same products, composted – or pyrolyzed. Pyrolysis was one of those technologies that only the boffins talked about earlier in the century. At one level, it's simple: pyrolysis means breaking down different materials (including plastic waste and sewage sludge) using heat in an air-tight, oxygen-free vessel called a pyrolyzer. The stuff doesn't burn, as it does in an incinerator; it decomposes. At another level, the technology is fiendishly complicated in terms of getting the right temperature, the right moisture level, and the right mix of feedstocks.

And that's where algae came up trumps again! As well as being used in bio-reactors to produce liquid fuels (as substitutes for fossil fuels) and other chemicals for use in manufacturing, algal biomass also turned out to have advantages as a feedstock for pyrolysis. Umpteen different varieties were developed over the years, to be grown and used in pyrolyzers, either on their own or combined with other feedstocks, producing energy – and, of course, biochar for incorporating back into the soil (see p.193).

But not all today's bioeconomy has been as uncontroversial as that. Take synbio, or synthetic biology – a topic that is still beset with every kind of scientific, political and philosophical debate that you can imagine. That's not so surprising: in synthesizing DNA, we ended up doing countless things that nature, on her own, could never have done. We've re-ordered genetic material from different species; we've sliced it, diced it and spliced it. We've enabled plants both to photosynthesize more efficiently (harvesting light from different parts of the light spectrum) and to capture nitrogen directly from the air. And we've created a number of new species, including an army of modified microbes that eat and degrade pollutants.

But as with every technology that came before synthetic biology, there's been a dark side to synbio, as we saw on p.94. I don't want to belittle the impact of that dark side, but focusing only on the bad stuff does rather obscure all the advances made through our astonishingly rapid transition to a bio-based economy.

The bioeconomy embraces many different sectors, and industrial biotechnology has literally transformed the way we make so many of the day-to-day things in our lives. Not least beer!

Given the huge increase in the consumption of beer over the last couple of decades, it's a good thing that sophisticated new fermentation processes have now been scaled up in breweries all around the world. My friends in Uganda sent me this photo of one of the biggest breweries in Africa, which makes beer using specially bred drought-resistant grains grown for them by hundreds of smallholder farmers. The farmers use minimal amounts of chemicals and fertilizers – including the recycled urine from all the bars and restaurants they deliver their beer to! The brewery uses an advanced anaerobic digestion system that's super-efficient, making use of all the spent grains left over from the brewing process to produce heat and electricity for their own use, as well as a high-quality biogas to run all their own delivery vehicles and local buses. It's the most water-efficient brewery in the world, using just one litre of water for every litre of beer! What's more, it makes a lot of money, and the company returns more than 5 per cent of profits back to the local communities.

THE CIRCULAR ECONOMY IN PRACTICE

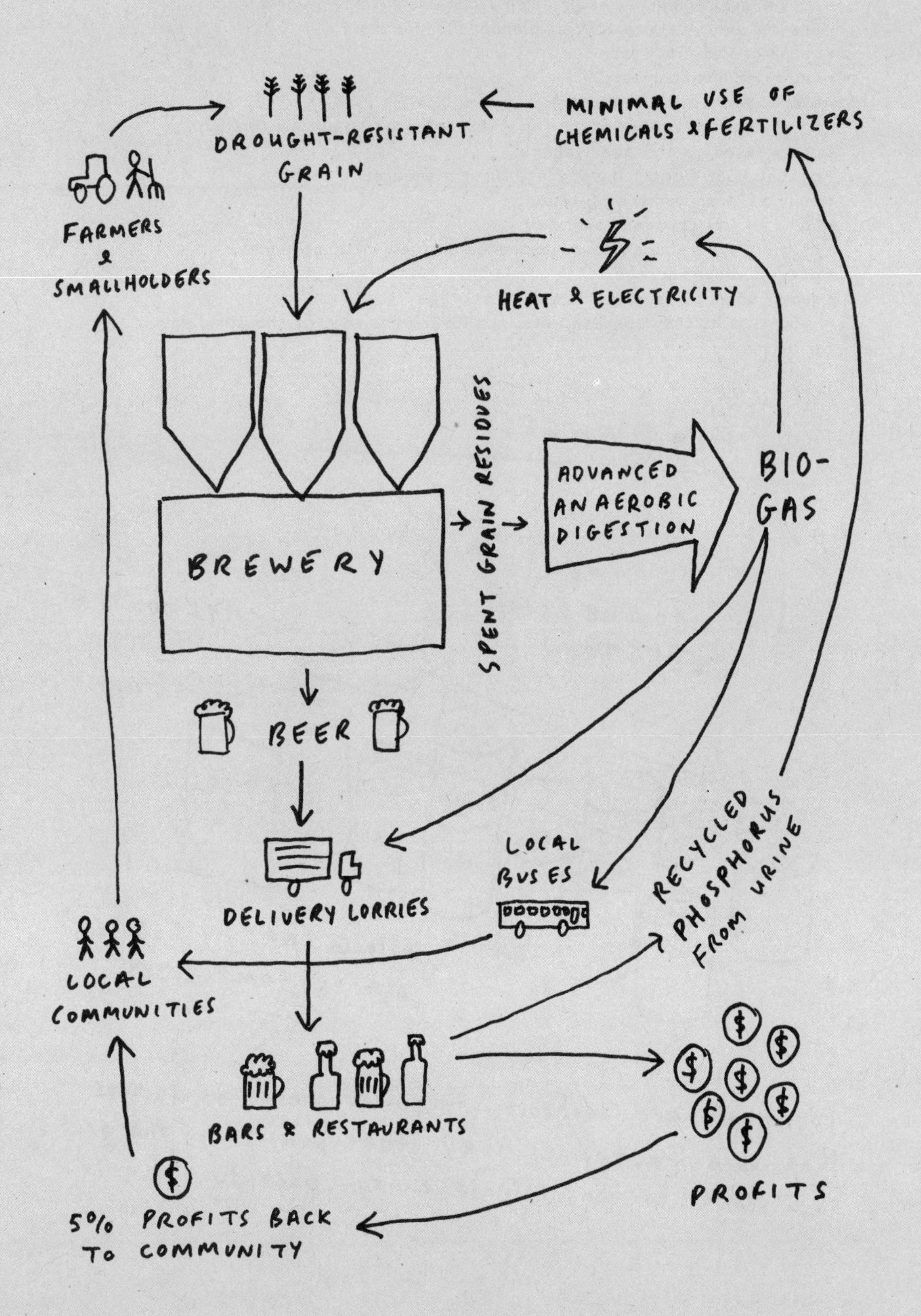

Energy Storage Technologies

By 2020, Japan was involved in every storage technology available. And my Research Team were amazed at just how many they found:

- sodium-sulphur batteries (in which Japan was already a world leader);
- thermal energy storage (first pioneered in Norway);
- rechargeable flow batteries;
- liquid metal batteries;
- molten salt storage systems;
- freshwater/saltwater batteries – still referred to as Blue Energy;
- compressed air storage systems;
- pumped heat electricity storage (first pioneered in the UK);
- many different kinds of flywheel;
- liquid air (or 'cryogen') systems;
- thin-film super-capacitors integrated directly into appliances;
- pumped water storage;
- super-conducting magnetic energy storage

– you name it, the Japanese were into it! And the rest of the world wasn't far behind.

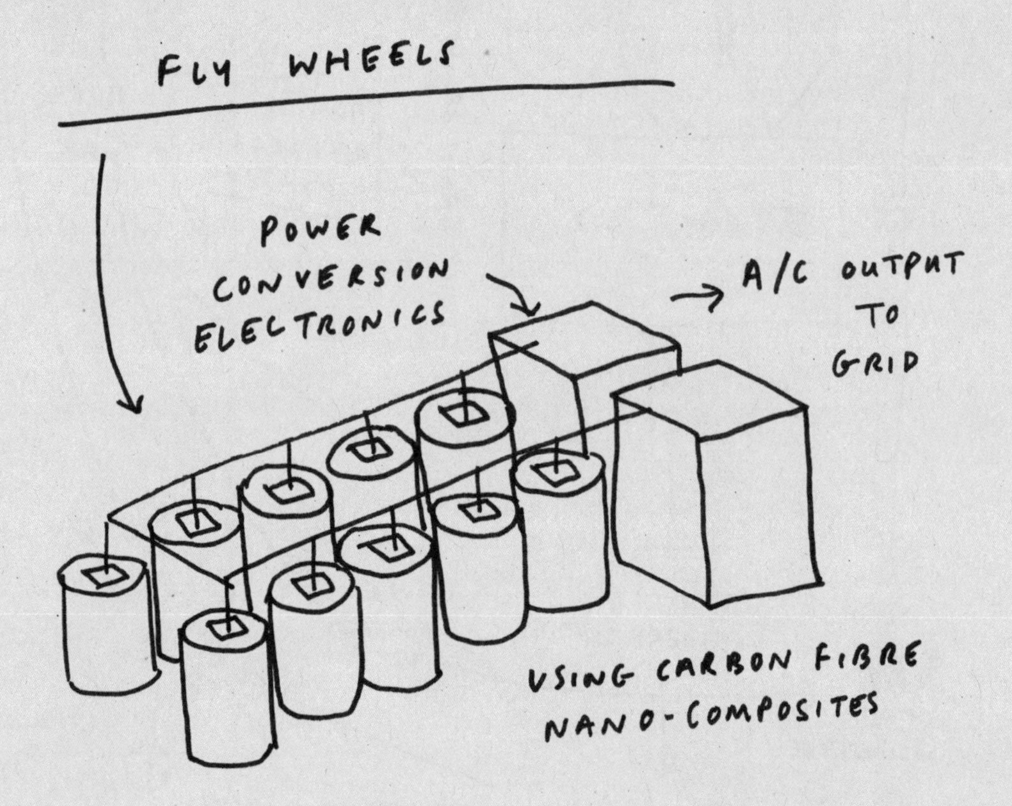

Flywheels are connected to power conversion devices that spin faster as they take power from the grid and slower as they release energy back to the grid.

08.09.2050
The Energy Internet

Here's something to celebrate: almost 20 years on from the completion of Europe's SuperGrid, 94 per cent of the electricity pulsing around that system today is either zero-carbon or very low-carbon – undoubtedly one of the most successful examples of the EU working together to achieve a common goal.

What's gradually emerged is a fully-fledged energy internet, with electrons moving around as seamlessly as bits of information through the internet itself. This had as much to do with IT and computing developments as with energy technologies themselves: 'smart grids' only got smart because IT and communications companies piled in and made them smart.

This transformed the entire energy economy. The principal commercial driver for energy companies had always been to find ways of selling more energy: the more you sold, the higher the reward for your shareholders. Although the concept of 'negawatts' (with profit geared to selling less energy rather than more) was much talked about at that time, it was only in a few US states that regulators ever gave it a real chance. But the arrival of cheap smart meters and IT-based monitoring and management systems made a completely different approach to energy efficiency available. Even the relatively simple technology of voltage optimization (levelling out the amount of electricity needed) led to considerable reductions in the energy use of individual appliances and whole buildings.

Two further developments made this possible: high voltage direct current (HVDC) transmission, and massive investment in storage technologies. Over very long distances, HVDC allows the transmission of electricity with much lower energy losses compared to alternating current systems. HVDC is still expensive, but without it schemes like Desertec (see p.16) would never have got off the ground. The actual amount of land required for large-scale solar energy installations in North Africa is really quite small, set against the vast expanse of its deserts. But without the means to get all that electricity into the EU grid, the necessary investments would never have been forthcoming.

But without a revolution in storage techologies, none of this could have happened. One of the great advantages of fossil fuels was that they were just so easy to store: coal sits in a heap, oil in a tanker and so on. By comparison, storing electricity is not quite so easy. At the turn of the century, electricity storage was basically all about batteries; multi-megawatt battery storage systems started coming online (particularly in the USA) from around 2015 onwards. But that was never going to be enough to allow us to make the most of all those intermittent sources of renewable energy, which are only able to deliver the electrons when the sun is shining, or the wind is blowing, or tidal currents are flowing.

Perhaps not surprisingly, it was Japan that made the running here, together with the USA and China. Japan suffered a dreadful earthquake back in 2011, followed by a devastating tsunami that took out a number of nuclear reactors at a place called Fukushima. For a while, all of Japan's 50 or so nuclear reactors were closed down for safety checks, and even when some of them were fired up again, it wasn't for very long: Japanese people had had it with nuclear.

So although Japan was already one of the most energy efficient economies in the world, with some of the strictest standards under its Energy Conservation Laws, it suddenly had to redouble its efforts in that area and at the same time significantly increase its investment in renewables. Building systems that integrated energy efficiency and renewables from the start gave the Japanese a strong lead in smart grids and advanced storage.

It took the rest of the world quite a while to catch up. Consumers often failed to use the information available to them to reduce their energy bills, and savings in one area were promptly gobbled up by increased consumption on something else – the well-known rebound effect. Thankfully, governments persevered, and the investments started to flow on a city-by-city basis. In Europe, the SuperGrid came together alongside local 'smart grids' and area networks. New sources of supply came on stream, both 'big green' renewable schemes and 'small green' distributed generation from PV and radically improved micro-wind turbines. New storage technologies, such as V2G (vehicle to grid, see p.146) and what were called 'virtual power plants', involving hundreds of individual households, provided the necessary flexibility in managing supply and demand.

The net result? In Europe today, we're using 40 per cent less energy than we did back in 2015, with no reduction in the kind of energy services available to us all – and with huge economic benefits.

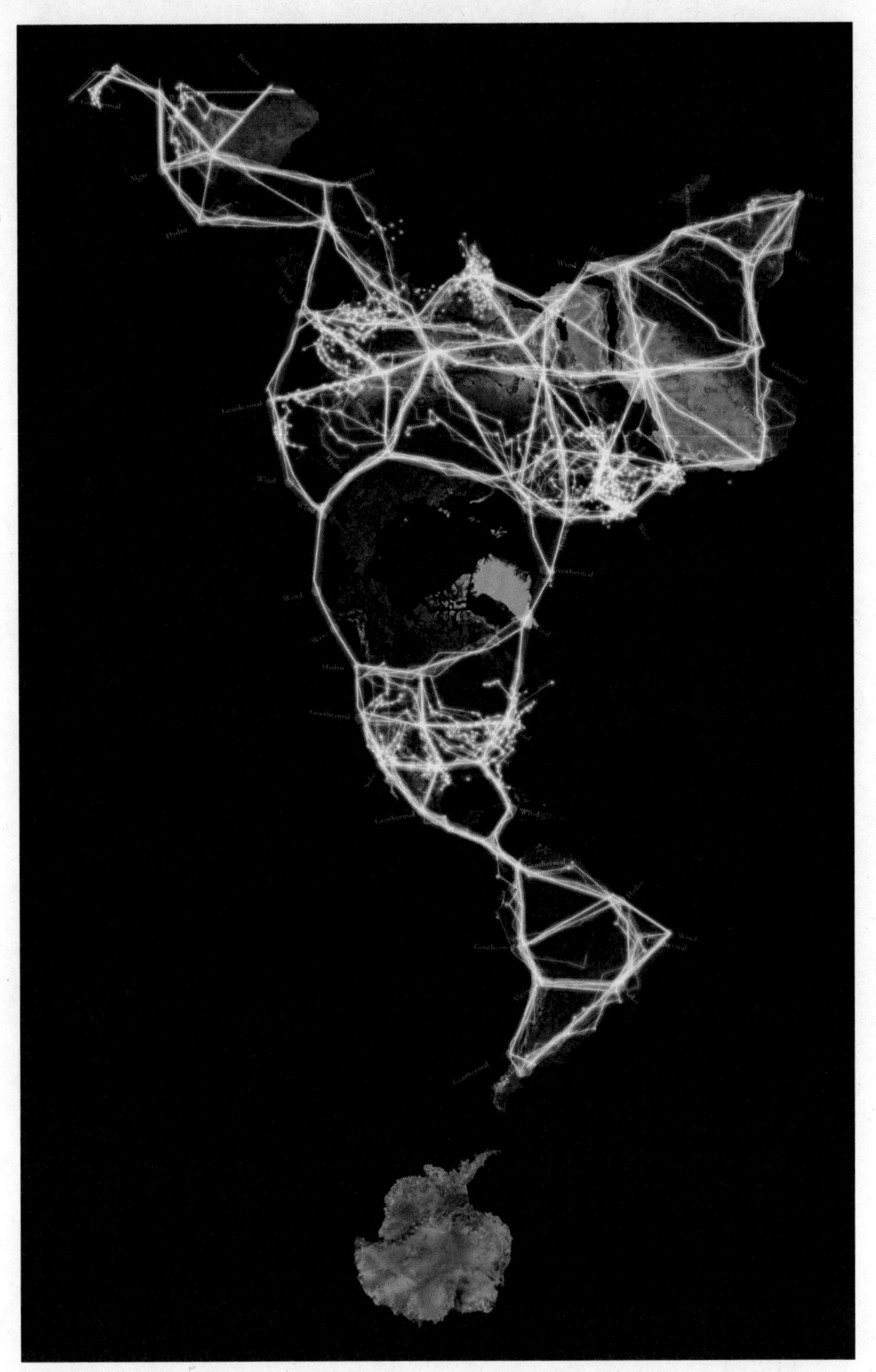

A thing of beauty, isn't it? This diagram from 2011 was one of the very first visual representations of the human species connected up across the entire globe by electricity grids. I can remember my Dad constantly going on about it: he was still hopeful I'd want to be an engineer like him!

15.09.2050

Still Flying High!

When BoeingAir's C2050 was first launched in 2028, the aviation industry was still on the back foot after a dire decade of rising prices, carbon rationing, and the usual security meltdowns. Indeed, BoeingAir was the only remaining global manufacturer of civilian aircraft at that time, after the painful merger at the start of the decade between Boeing and Airbus.

People wanted to fly as much as ever, but something had to be done about the fact that this industry just kept on growing. By 2028, aviation was contributing an astonishing six per cent of total greenhouse gas emissions – a doubling in just 20 years! But governments all around the world had found it practically impossible to come between people and our 'right' to fly.

A critical part of the answer to that dilemma has come in the form of more eco-friendly fuels. Since the C2050 set the benchmark with a 50/50 biofuel/kerosene split, some are now much closer to 70/30 biofuel/kerosene. (It probably won't get much better than that as biofuels aren't as dense as kerosene, a litre of which still gets you further than a litre of bio-butanol.)

All-electric planes are also getting more and more competitive. Superconducting motors are both more powerful and much lighter than even the most efficient conventional engines, and most smaller planes have been either all-electric or hybrids for the last 15 years or so. Super-efficient solar cells are now standard across the industry.

But that's only one reason why total aviation emissions today are down to less than 40 per cent of where they were in 2025. Many other innovations started to come good around 2020, including complex processes to turn waste gases (from steel mills or waste incinerators) into aircraft fuels. And what were once seen as crazy dreams about making fuel from CO_2 (captured directly from the air) and hydrogen (through electrolyzing water more efficiently using renewable energy) had come of age by 2025 – with a significant impact on aviation's total carbon footprint.

But even now, in 2050, aviation is still the biggest user of fossil fuels – in fact, apart from some specialist feedstocks for the chemical industry, it's practically the only user of fossil fuels. As that veteran airline entrepreneur

Some friends of ours took this photo looking out over Hong Kong from the window of a Virgin Zeppelin, back in 2026. 'Slow travel' was already a big thing by then, and more and more people felt perfectly comfortable taking a couple of days to get to special places rather than hours. The air cruiser business was flourishing by the end of the 2020s. Huge numbers of specially adapted airships have been widely used for freight transport for many years now, and most airships today use a significant amount of integrated solar power.

Richard Branson once put it, 'It's no good getting all worked up about this: people just like getting off the ground and going places – whether it's in planes, rockets, airships, blimps or helium bloons. And who'd have thought we'd ever be able to enjoy zero-carbon space tourism!'

Significant advances in air-traffic control systems have also helped. Right up until the early 2020s, air-traffic control systems were so inefficient in the way they regulated take-offs and landings that they were responsible for up to 10 per cent of aviation's total carbon footprint. From that point on, new communications satellites allowed air traffic controllers to pick up signals from transmitters on planes, allowing them to pack planes close together along optimal flight paths.

My researchers find it difficult to believe the hype that surrounded the launch of BoeingAir's C2050 (Concept 2050) in 2028.

It was seen as a real game-changer: the first commercial hybrid electric plane, combining conventional turbofan jet propulsion with electric power. The fuel was a 50/50 biofuel/kerosene blend; the Rolls Royce engines were 30 per cent more efficient than the earlier TrentPlus engines; ultra-light-weighted nano-composite materials (considerably stronger than either steel or aluminium),

with many of the components put together much more cheaply using direct digital manufacturing – in fact, everything you'd expect from a plane that had been on multiple drawing boards for the best part of 15 years!

The C2050 is still flying, 22 years on – and it's still impressive. But it's now rapidly losing market share to smaller, quieter, more efficient, even more climate-friendly competitors – including BoeingAir's own fixed-wing C2080.

India also made a huge contribution on air-traffic control systems with its incomparable software expertise. In 2019, it was the first country in the world to have 100 per cent of its flights taking off and landing using 'optimized glide path' technology. No stacking, no queuing on the apron, straight in and straight out – as fuel-efficiently as possible.

And last but not least, this is one area where politicians eventually got it right. The EU led the way with its emissions trading scheme for aviation, which first went live in a storm of controversy in 2012. This resulted in five years of bitter trade wars with the US, China and other countries, but the Emergency Report from the Intergovernmental Panel on Climate Change in 2016 put an end to all that. By 2023, after three years of wrangling through a special initiative under the Houston Concord, all nations reluctantly signed up to the Global Aviation Carbon Cap (GACC) – which operated as a separate 'bubble' outside all other carbon trading schemes.

Global Aviation Carbon Cap

Once the GACC had been introduced, each nation received its GACC quota of carbon emissions, weighted by population and per capita income. Each nation was then permitted to find its own way of allocating its overall quota amongst its businesses and citizens.

Germany is widely perceived to have developed the fairest system. 60 per cent of Germany's annual GACC quota is distributed, for free, on a strict per capita basis amongst all German citizens. These Personal Aviation Allowances, as they're called, can either be used for one's own purposes, gifted to friends, relatives or charities, or sold on (at home or abroad) through Germany's central GACC register. The remaining 40 per cent is then sold to businesses and all-comers via a quarterly reverse auction – with all the proceeds used to fund further improvements in Germany's transport networks.

Many other countries have now followed suit. Those who fly a lot absolutely hate it, as they inevitably end up paying a lot of money for the privilege. Those who don't fly at all love it, as they end up with quite a lot of extra cash in their pockets! To me, that seems only fair, and there are certainly no complaints in our family. We're still flying, after all – if only occasionally. And globally, there are far fewer passenger miles flown today than there were back in 2028, which is absolutely what had to happen.

23.09.2050

Work, Wealth and Wellbeing

The 'quiet revolution' in the way we work has had far more to do with gradual social change than with technological innovation – though that's played its part too. And it's funny how apparently boring numbers can sometimes tell you so much – as with the graphic below, which provides some important insights into how our working lives in Europe have been transformed during the twenty-first century. The EU's Maximum Working Time Directive was introduced around 2020 – and you can see the impact it has had since then.

AVERAGE WORKING HOURS PER WEEK
→ European Union

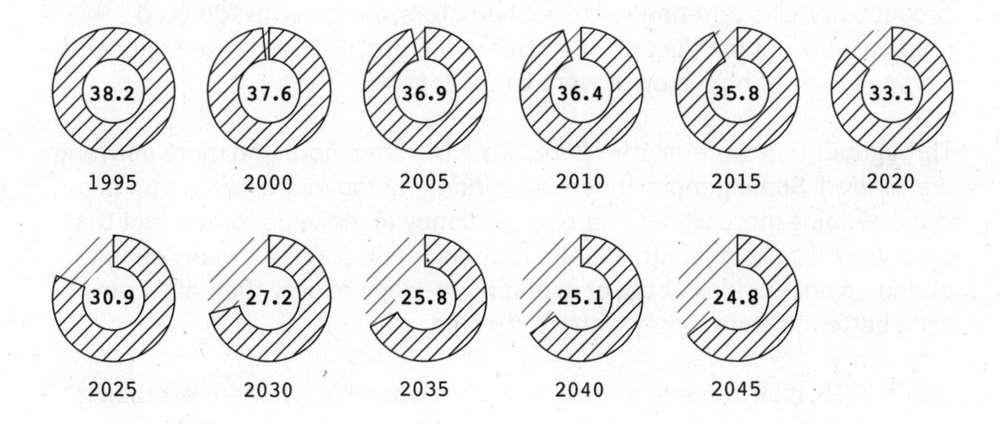

Around the turn of the century, economic policy couldn't have been simpler: maximize growth, as measured by GDP (Gross Domestic Product); stay as competitive as possible in the global economy; and let 'trickle-down' and the market sort out everything else.

Then came the crash of 2008, and it all began to get very flakey. Austerity kicked in; we could no longer borrow our way back to growth, purchasing power collapsed, unemployment remained stubbornly high, and the myth of Europe still being able to compete (on an economy-wide basis) with a country like China was revealed as the absurdity it had always been. People felt completely trapped: they could see that the proverbial Emperor of Growth at All Costs had no clothes, but for 50 years GDP had been the only indicator of success that really counted. It didn't matter how much damage was being done in securing that growth – worsening inequality, runaway climate change, deteriorating public health, impact on the natural world, resource shortages, etc – it was all seen as a price worth paying.

But our research also identified lots of interest in the idea of 'wellbeing' at that time: money is important (especially if you haven't got much of it), but not as important as family, friends, a safe home, supportive communities, financial security, a sense of purpose in life and the opportunity to do useful, rewarding work. Psychologists can dress it up any way they like, but being happy and doing good work just seem to go hand in hand for the vast majority of human beings. Make it difficult for people to find any satisfactory way of working, and the entire social contract (between the state and its citizens) is put at risk. I saw this time after time with the kids we were teaching – full of energy and ideas, but with nowhere to go.

Politicians may have talked about wellbeing, but nothing ever happened! Most EU countries spent the decade after 2008 working their socks off to get back to high growth, global competitiveness and a increased productivity. Like adrenaline-driven hamsters, our growth-addicted political elite couldn't get off their treadmill. But, as you can see opposite, Europe's days of high growth were gone for good.

Throughout that decade after 2008, work became more and more unevenly distributed. Some people ended up working far too much, caught up in a cycle of doing more work to earn more money to make up for the fact that their work was so miserable in the first place! By contrast, many people ended up not working at all, or in minimum-wage misery that left them little better off than if they weren't working.

But in 2018, it all came to a head, with the Enough! movement exploding into action (see p.32). Levels of unemployment (particularly youth unemployment) were extremely high, and the redistribution of paid work became the new rallying cry. The EU finally decided to act, and a number of new directives were introduced one after another – despite fierce opposition from countries like the UK and Poland. The two most important of these directives (the Maximum Working Time Directive) banned overtime work outright and then set a trajectory for all countries to reduce the average working week to no more than 25 hours by 2035.

By 2030 there were further signs of change. Some countries (led by the Scandinavians, Spanish and Dutch) had passed new legislation imposing a duty on their governments to guarantee a minimum amount of 'adequately

EUROPEAN GROWTH RATES 2000 - 2029

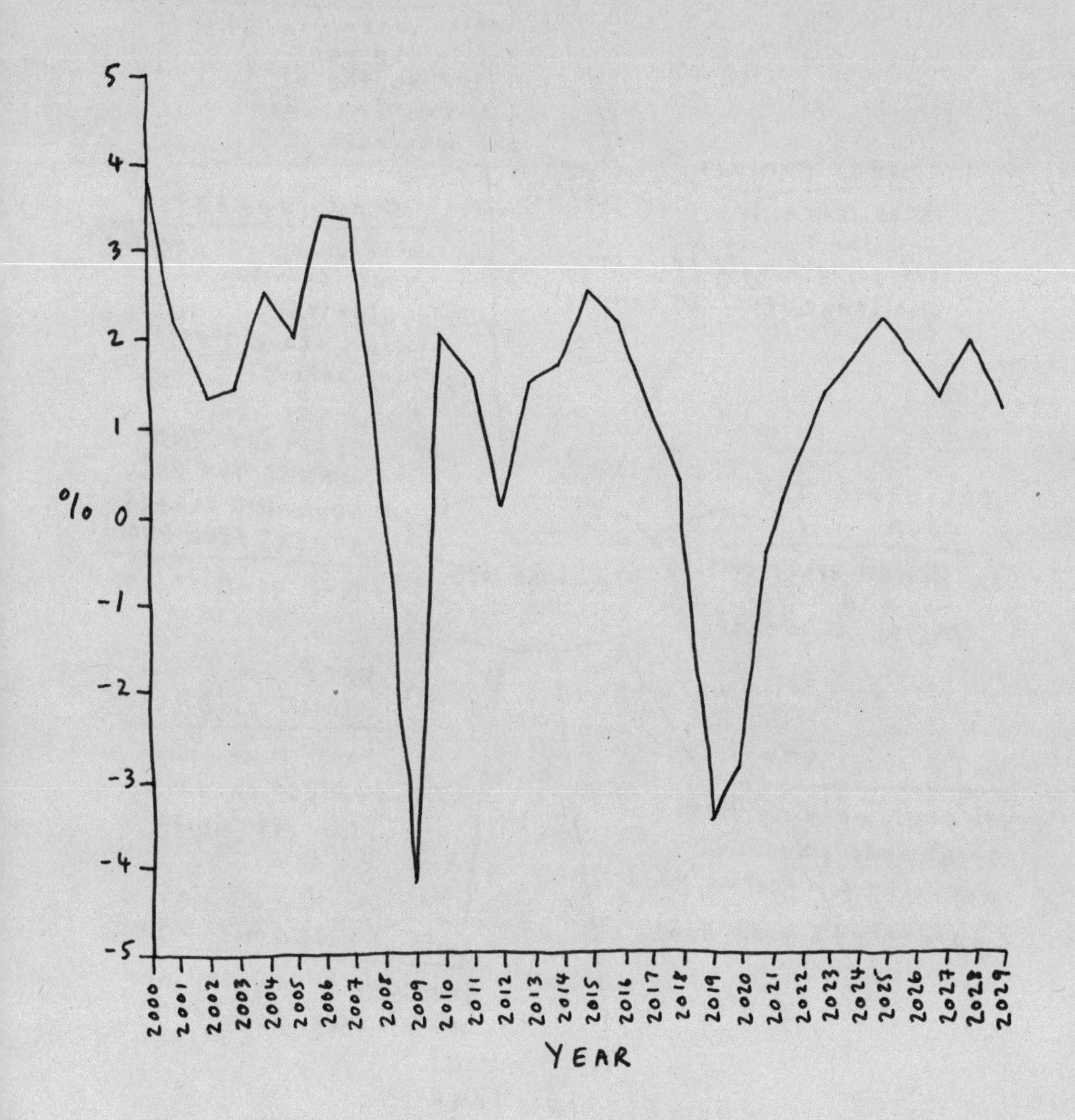

GDP was formally replaced in 2029 by a new global measure: The Index of Sustainable Economic Wellbeing

WELLBEING

GET OUT MORE
- walk when you can
- sit in the park
- listen to the birds
- stop moaning about the weather!

STAY CURIOUS
- keep learning
- try something new
- try something difficult
- challenge received opinions

STAY CONNECTED
- play an active part in your community
- volunteer
- don't leave things to others

CELEBRATE THE EVERY DAY
- in shared experiences and special moments

DO STUFF THAT MAKES YOU FEEL GOOD AND MAKES OTHERS FEEL GOOD
- live your values

KEEP TIME ON YOUR SIDE
- take time out
- reflect on things
- slow it down

GET SWEATY
- there's nothing like strenuous physical activity for feeling good
- gardening's good too!

BE GENEROUS
in what you say and what you give away

INVEST IN YOUR RELATIONSHIPS
with family, friends, work colleagues, neighbours

remunerated work' to any citizen unable to find work near to where he or she lived. Communities took the lead on this, identifying priorities for improving people's lives at the local level – co-housing projects (see p.232), for instance, or maintenance of infrastructure and environmental work – and mixing and matching these to an extraordinary diversity of public/private/community schemes. All so much more valuable to everybody involved than simply paying out billions every year on unemployment benefits.

Some countries went in the opposite direction, introducing the equivalent of a Citizens' Income, where each citizen receives an untaxed minimum income as of right (i.e. without means-testing). The aim has been to get rid of the poverty trap once and for all – and that has indeed proved to be the case, although this requires very high levels of both personal and carbon taxes for the better-off.

As it got easier for people to work flexibly from home or local i-hubs, 'time banking' became an increasingly important phenomenon. Time banking had sprung up in the USA in the late twentieth century as a simple way of exchanging time – giving and receiving it – to get individuals involved in community projects and useful work. By 2010, time banking was already established in more than 40 countries; there are now 125 countries involved, the biggest of which have thousands of different initiatives.

Which brings us to where we are now, in 2050. I guess I'm fairly typical of how this all works out in practice: I do 25 hours of paid work each week as a teacher, another 5 hours or so (unpaid) as a governor of another school, and then about 10 hours a week on different activities – co-ordinated through our very active local TimeBank and paid in local pounds – including working on our Community Farm. It suits me down to the ground – quite literally!

Indeed, nearly 30 years on, most voters seem fairly comfortable with the results of this quiet revolution. Many people have ended up with less money as such, and therefore less purchasing power. But most things that people care about are so much more affordable than they used to be: as we got good at dematerializing the economy, we also reduced costs at every turn.

Moreover, people have more time, a higher quality of life and many more opportunities to do the things that really interest them. I think that's probably what they meant by 'wellbeing' all those years ago!

30.09.2050
Manufacturing Reborn

I made this tricycle for Marika when she was 5 years old at our Fabrication Centre. It has lasted a lot longer than I thought it would!

The 'maker revolution' has been a 40-year journey that has seen the way we make things put onto a completely different footing through developments in 3D printing, biomimicry and nanotechnology.

Early on in the century, manufacturing was all about what economists called 'economies of scale', with great big factories taking in huge volumes of raw materials, using vast amounts of energy and water, heating, beating and treating them to create a profusion of products of varying quality and limited durability. This was the very opposite of today's additive manufacturing, where we use only what we need.

After the shocks and shortages of the 2010s and 2020s, resource efficiency became the operating code for the economy as a whole – right down to the local level. But something else changed too. Looking back over my Dad's project diaries, it's clear that even engineers like him didn't actually make anything themselves.

All the kit he used was made by somebody else, somewhere else in the world, and then installed by people like him at work or in the field. It wasn't like that in countries like India, where roadside 'fixers' still seemed able to make practically anything out of practically any raw materials! But the rich world had lost those skills decades before.

Then, almost imperceptibly, people started experimenting with making things, getting involved in a crazy proliferation of online initiatives. These days, almost all of us end up making stuff in one way or another. In our community, for instance, we have our own fabrication centre with a number of different 3D printers and fabricators that can be programmed with bought-in software to make a wide range of the things we need. Using basic printing materials, corn-based polymers like powdered nylon, purpose-built moulds, increasingly sophisticated nozzles and applicators, and brilliant designs, it's so easy to produce a wider and wider range of items.

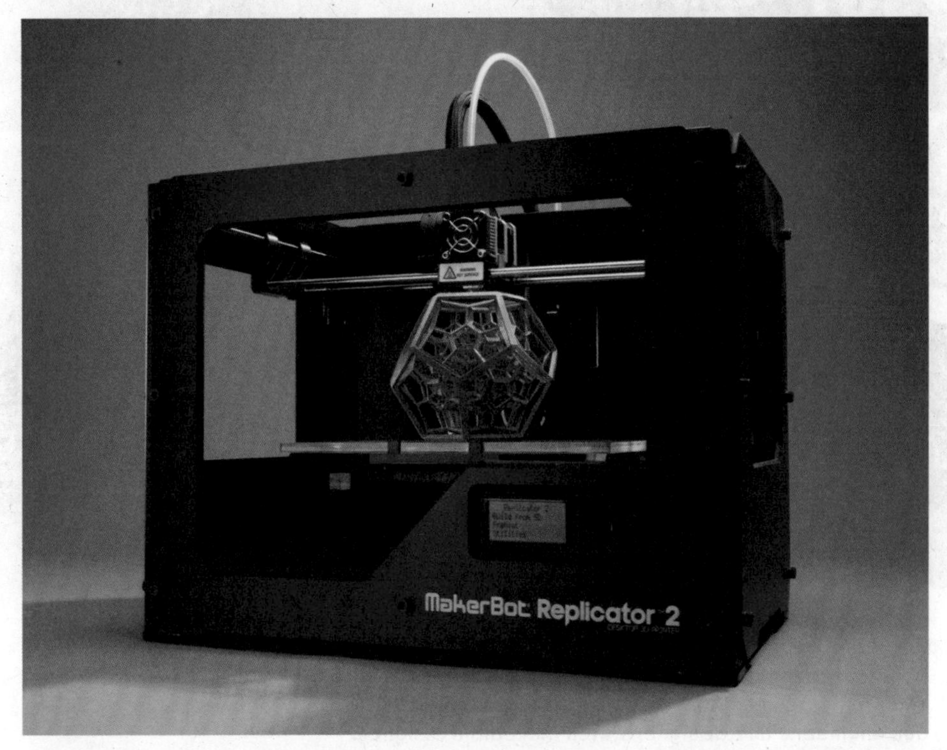

I discovered the other day that the very first 3D printers can be traced right back to the Massachusetts Institute of Technology in 1997! But outside of the early Fab Labs at MIT, a few design schools and universities, nothing much happened until around 2012, when the first home-scale 3D printers (like the one above) started retailing at no more than the cost of an expensive meal out for two people. Many people at that time believed that this would lead inevitably to the end of any mass-market manufacturing, but that just hasn't happened. Current 3D printers still gobble up a lot of energy, and even now, direct digital manufacturing is still more cost effective on the large scale.

Biomimicry draws primarily on the genius of nature – taking ideas from the natural world and applying them to our own lives. It makes sense because nature, in all its astonishing diversity, has had 3.8 billion years to experiment with what works and what doesn't. The resulting treasure chest of ideas continues to provide our engineers and designers with incredible insights.

Inspired by the water-harvesting habits of the Namibian fog-basking beetle (see p.215), Sahara Forest Projects (like the one above in Qatar) provide one of the best practical examples of biomimicry. There are now thousands of these Sahara Forest Projects all over the world. The CSP plant (concentrated solar power, see p.17) powers both the greenhouses and local housing schemes. The greenhouses are cooled by seawater piped in from the sea; as the seawater evaporates, the incoming hot, dry air is cooled and humidified. This produces a much better environment for plants, which suffer less thermal stress and need far less water

as the humid conditions mean they transpire less. Food plants grow both in the greenhouses and under the solar installations, using some of the desalinated water produced on site. Surplus water helps regenerate the surrounding area – you can see some of the new trees planted up over the last 15 years.

Just last week I was reading up on the latest breakthroughs using synthetic silk – another example of biomimicry in practice. Even though we can't quite match the qualities of the stuff that silkworms and spiders make, we're now pretty damn close. Weight for weight, silk is 20 times stronger than steel, incredibly flexible, with its own 'phase-change' properties – sticky one moment and unsticky the next. This synthetic silk is highly resilient (in coping with temperature extremes, for instance) and has no impact on our immune systems. It's now being widely used for in manufacturing, as well as all sorts of vaccine and drug-delivery systems, as well as orthopaedic interventions.

It's been fascinating to reflect on the implications of all this for the kids going through the College today. They spend as much time in the workshop as they do in the classroom – and they're encouraged to get good enough at computer programming, material science and industrial design to use these skills for themselves. It's challenging, fun, cheap – and, because we've got so good at recycling and closed-loop manufacturing (see p.70), nothing much ever goes to waste.

Nanotechnology has proved to be one of the most startling manifestations of the genius of humankind. We discovered early in the century that molecules behave rather differently at the very, very small scale (one billionth of a metre, to be more precise) than they do at their normal size. For instance, carbon atoms bonded together into tiny, latticed structures (or nanotubes) are over 100 times stronger than steel. And then there's graphene, again made just from a single layer of carbon atoms, which conducts heat and electricity better than copper, and is stronger than diamonds and as flexible as clingfilm! And nanocrystalline cellulose – a natural, renewable version of carbon nanotubes, made from forestry waste – is now widely used in construction, electronics and so on.

For family reasons (thinking back to the water riots of 2017), I've always been particularly interested in the impact of nanotechnology on the whole water environment. By 2020, there were dozens of new filters and membrane devices based on nanotechnology: these could filter out not just parasites and fungi, but also bacteria, viruses, heavy metals and every conceivable toxic material – including pesticide residues and arsenic. It's impossible to calculate the number of lives that have been saved and improved by these technologies.

We discovered in our research that there were serious concerns earlier in the century about potential threats to human health from nanotechnology, as well as various nightmarish scenarios in which we somehow lost control of the way in which we manufactured particular devices – nanoscale robots and so on. Happily, people's worst fears never actually materialized. In fact, I can't actually recall when I last heard anyone talking about 'nanotechnology' as such. It's now just another facet of modern manufacturing.

We now know exactly what things are made of and where those materials come from, so we can celebrate, rather than abuse, nature's abundance. And somehow, we live in our world differently because of that.

And here's the little creature that first inspired the Sahara Forest Project:

The Namibian fog-basking beetle!
It thrives in the hottest deserts by capturing moisture from the early morning breeze as it blows in off the sea. Droplets of water are harvested on its back, until it tips up its shell just before sunrise to glug it back. Brilliant!

THE POOR ARE STILL WITH US, BUT...

	TOTAL POPULATION	URBAN POOR
2015:	7.5 billion	2.5 billion
2050:	8.6 billion	2.7 billion

So: more people are experiencing urban poverty in 2050 than in 2015 (in terms of actual numbers). BUT that's still a lower percentage of total world population than in 2015.

AND their lives really have improved too.

07.10.2050

Slumdog Billionaires

Our research has shown us that there were more than 2.5 billion people living in what were called slums in 2015. That means around 45 per cent of the urban population was living crammed together in makeshift dwellings, often illegally, with few – if any – public services. By any standards, life was 'poor, nasty, brutish and short' – as I saw for myself in 2018, when I first worked in the township of Kibera (just outside Nairobi in Kenya) as part of my work as an EarthCorps volunteer.

According to the latest figures from the UN last year, there are now more than three billion urban poor. On the face of it that's an increase, but the lives they lead today are very much more comfortable than 30 years ago, and fewer than half a billion are now living in absolute poverty.

Earlier this year, people were celebrating the 35th anniversary of one of the most extraordinary philanthro-capitalist enterprises of the twenty-first century, which played a big part in this change: the Pro-Poor Alliance. Launched in 2015, the Alliance was initially made up of just a dozen super-rich individuals; there are now more than 200 of them, helping to revolutionize the lives of urban people all around the world. They are now held in correspondingly high regard – which certainly wasn't the case in 2015, when many people were very suspicious of their motives. But with the support of influential NGOs, such as Cities for People (originally known as Slum/Shack Dwellers International) and the International Institute for Environment and Development, they stuck to their guns – and even came to celebrate their nickname: the Slumdog Billionaires.

What they've done is to find ways of working closely with communities, making the best use of the extensive knowledge that people within those communities have. Instead of treating the urban poor as a massive problem, as governments tend to do, the Slumdog Billionaires were able to see them as some of the most resourceful and resilient people in the world – and to persuade city administrations to do the same. By tearing up the rule book, granting legal tenure on both the land and the dwellings involved, and empowering women's groups through community savings and micro-credit schemes, more and more cities found it was possible to turn chronic problems into workable solutions.

Solar Salvation is a huge, integrated scheme in one of the largest slums on the outskirts of Lagos, Nigeria, in 2023. The scheme provides both solar thermal water heaters and basic PV arrays (at a fraction of their full commercial cost) to any shanty owner with a reasonable prospect of securing legal tenure. Finance is usually provided via official community savings schemes, authorized and coordinated by organizations like the Nigerian Federation of Cities for People.

By any standards, this has been an extraordinarily generous commitment – but it was also one very much in line with China's foreign policy at that time. In 2033, the Lagos Women's Cooperative was awarded the Nobel Peace Prize for its extraordinary work through the 2020s, bringing healthcare, education, jobs and sustainable energy to this and many other communities. Their work has inspired millions since.

One of the biggest challenges with illegal settlements in the early twenty-first century was the lack of basic services, particularly electricity, water and waste disposal. The high prices charged (often much higher than wealthier citizens had to pay) resulted in widespread pirating of both electricity and water. This was both dangerous and a permanent source of conflict. Lots of initiatives were tried to address the problem, one of which was started by a bunch of Chinese philanthro-capitalists in the sprawling slums of African cities such as Lagos – as featured on the preceding pages.

What astonished people in those days was the step change that this kind of development stimulated. For all the talk in the rich Northern Hemisphere about the potential for an energy internet (where producers and consumers of energy trade electricity through local grids), the real business of peer-to-peer power sharing first became established in the poorer Southern Hemisphere. Although bigger urban areas were of course connected to the grid, completely decentralized, off-grid energy systems rapidly became the norm, and (ironically) proved to be much more reliable than central grid systems subject to constant breakdowns.

Cheap, clean and green electricity was just the start. In 2015, more than two billion people still had no toilet – and this provided one of the biggest opportunities for the Slumdog Billionaires. The Bill and Melinda Gates Foundation got things moving with its 'Reinvent the Toilet' initiative. This challenged engineers to come up with simple, readily available technologies that would change a source of disease and indignity into a useful resource in its own right.

Solutions ranged from biodegradable 'Peepoo' bags (using urea to neutralize bacteria, viruses and parasites) to sophisticated bio-latrines, waterless toilets and advanced anaerobic digestion (AAD) systems, which provided valuable biogas – or 'poo power' – for both domestic use and energy production, plus fertilizer for local food production. By 2030, the sanitation in many of the world's worst slums had been transformed. With the support of some of the biggest multinationals, organizations like Water and Sanitation for the Urban Poor installed integrated hygiene systems in many slums, providing communal toilet facilities combined with an anaerobic digester to harvest the biogas.

This is one of those areas where the rich world has learned from innovation elsewhere. Being a water engineer, my Dad was pretty earthy in the way he talked about human excrement, but many of my friends at school – let alone their parents – were unbelievably squeamish. 'Out of sight, out of mind'. But the increased sophistication of composting toilets (which now separate out our urine to ensure that all the phosphorous in it can be recycled) and the development of mini-anaerobic digesters for household use has changed all that, in the rich world as much as in the poor world.

Integrated sanitation centre, Kibera, Kenya, 2030.

I certainly don't want to glamorize this. Life in places like Kibera is still hard. Construction techniques are still of the cheap and cheerful variety, with people sharing their building skills and local materials being constantly reused and recycled. There's still not much money around, although the Kibera Shilling is one of the world's most successful local currencies. The impact of accelerating climate change has dramatically altered the availability of water, and per capita water consumption in many parts of the world is still at very low levels, with many smaller urban areas still having no mains supply.

But overall, life in such areas has really improved. With most IT and comms no more expensive in places like Kibera or Mumbai than they are in rich countries, entrepreneurs and cooperatives flourish, healthcare is getting better, and educational courses and materials are provided as cost-effectively via the internet in the urban communities of Pune, Lagos and Mexico City as they are in Paris, Tokyo and Montreal.

13.10.2050

Taming Our Capital Markets

I can't vouch for this one, but the Research Team has dug up a somewhat improbable story (going back to the early years of this century) that an outgoing Finance Minister in the UK government left a note on the desk for his successor, simply saying 'there's no money left' – or words to that effect!

In truth, that was indeed the case for most of the rich-world countries at the time. Much of the economic growth that they had enjoyed from the 1960s onwards had only been possible by building up vast debts – both national and personal. In 2008, that toxic time bomb exploded and governments had to bail out their banks, massively extending their own levels of debt. Hence the Age of Austerity and its deficit reduction programmes, public expenditure cutbacks and so on. I was too young then to really understand the impact of what was happening, but for a lot of people it was a very grim time.

Meanwhile, most of the biggest economies today, particularly China, India and Brazil, were just beginning to flex their economic muscles. From a political point of view, I still think this was the single most important reason why governments eventually approved a tax on financial transactions: the EU and the US simply had to find some additional source of tax revenues to be able to hold their own in the global economy.

It was a long, hard fight. France introduced its own Financial Transaction Tax (FTT) in 2012, and the EU wasn't far behind with a Eurozone Financial Transaction Tax coming in 2014. By 2020 the Eurozone's FTT was generating the equivalent of around €40 billion a year.

But everyone knew that this kind of tax would work best if it could be rolled out across all the world's financial centres, so it needed the shock of the Enough! campaigns to get all the key countries on board, particularly the US and the UK.

INTERNATIONAL FINANCIAL TRANSACTION TAX

	2022–2027 OECD only	2027–2037 All Countries	2037–2047 All Countries
IFTT Rate	0.08%	0.1%	0.15%
ALLOCATION OF IFTT REVENUES			
Average Annual Revenues	$145 billion	$211 billion	$255 billion
Deficit Reduction + Infrastructure	45%	30%	20%
Education, Health + Family Planning	20%	25%	20%
Climate Adaptation	15%	25%	40%
Biodiversity + Conservation	20%	20%	20%

The IFTT is a tax on the vast majority of financial transactions: stocks, bonds, derivatives and foreign exchange. It was first introduced in 2022 at a rate of 0.08 per cent on each transaction. The tax has to be levied at the same rate everywhere in the world, but the revenues can be allocated according to national priorities.

To start with, around 50 per cent of revenues went into deficit reduction strategies of one kind or another – replenishing the empty coffers that so many governments were still trying to deal with. But that began to change from around 2030 onwards.

THE GLOBAL RECOVERY PROGRAMME

(FUNDED BY THE INTERNATIONAL FINANCIAL TRANSACTION TAX)

Having sorted out some of its own problems, the USA then persuaded the rest of the world to set up a Global Recovery Programme - explicitly referring back to that time after the Second World War when the USA got Europe back on its feet through the Marshall Plan.

UNESCO becomes the principal beneficiary

↓

from the mid-2020s UNESCO got around $4 billion a year from the Global Recovery Programme

↓

By 2035, every child on earth is attending primary school!

↓

With 70% staying on for secondary education!

A new international convention was signed in 2020, to come into force on 1 January 2022, with some exemptions. There were just five International Financial Transaction Tax (IFTT) hubs to start with: the US, the EU, UK, Japan and Australia. Three more – China, India and Brazil – came on board in 2027, and everywhere else in 2030.

Once all nations with big financial sectors had the tax, there was little opportunity for tax havens. In addition, any companies found guilty of avoiding their IFTT payments were heavily fined, and many were actually put out of business.

The impact of the IFTT in both the rich world and the poor world was impressive. All the predictions about the collapse of the banking sector and millions out of work came to nothing. Indeed, having fought harder than any other nation to block the tax, the US promptly put those revenues to the best possible use – not just paying down some of its mind-boggling mountains of debt, but also investing in new infrastructure. In around 2020, the US was often compared with 'third world' countries, in that its infrastructure was literally falling to pieces – roads, bridges, sewers, water works, transmission lines, railways and so on. But as the US president said back in 2025, the IFTT was 'like a transfusion of blood running through our sclerotic arteries'.

There had been nothing like it since President Roosevelt's New Deal in the 1930s, nearly a century before. The Rebuild America campaign (which had been launched a few years earlier, taking advantage of early revenues from the Cap and Prosper legislation – see p.50) gained additional momentum. New partnerships were forged with the private sector, and millions of new jobs were created, particularly for young people. Everything was done with a view to minimizing dependence on fossil fuels and reducing emissions of CO_2 – including the biggest housing retrofit programme the world had ever seen.

And guess what? As ordinary people's incomes in the US picked up, tax revenues started growing again, and spending on education and health was restored to something like OECD averages – for the first time for many, many years.

19.10.2050

The Law Steps Up

This is the Tree of Life, a beautiful sculpture made of wood and copper that stood at the heart of the Earth Summit's Global Forum in the middle of Rio in 1992. The Tree of Life raised more than a million pledges at the time to encourage politicians to get on and make something special happen at the Earth Summit – which, to be fair, they sort of did. But it took a long time for those pledges to come good!

As our research confirmed, a lot of things kicked off at the Earth Summit in Rio de Janeiro in 1992, including treaties, conventions, declarations – and a huge, sprawling document called Agenda 21. Among other things, this included a whole section on the legal profession and why it should look at its own role in creating a more sustainable world.

Not much happened at first. Endless meetings, another session in Rio in 2012 followed by yet more meetings, but still nothing tangible. It all came together, at long last, between 2015 and 2018, when more than 4,500 senior lawyers from around the world (including 73 Chief Justices) signed up to a global campaign to start putting pressure on the political system. They called themselves 'Lawyers for Life' – and they already had a lot of excellent raw material to work with.

For more than 20 years, proposals for an International Court for the Environment (ICE) had been quietly moving forward, together with an even more radical idea of establishing the crime of ecocide in international law. I won't bore you with the legal definition, but ecocide basically covers 'the killing of the environment' – and over the years it has been applied to things that cause large-scale or potentially irreversible damage to the 'global commons' on which we all depend: the oceans, the climate, biodiversity and so on.

The plan was to bring in a new crime of ecocide as a criminal act under the remit of the International Criminal Court (ICC). Ecocide campaigners were only too aware of the fact that it had taken 50 years to establish the ICC itself, and were anticipating a long, hard slog. But that's when Lawyers for Life weighed in, supporting the campaigners, taking out class actions against some of the worst corporate offenders, filing injunctions and challenging government decisions through the courts – alongside some publicity-grabbing direct action.

By 2020, an unstoppable momentum had built up around the ICE itself (which now deals with all international disputes concerning the environment) and the specific crime of ecocide. The campaign eventually gained the support of more than 70 countries, including a particularly influential group of countries from South and Central America called the Alba nations – which had already called for a Universal Declaration on the Rights of Mother Earth at the United Nations. Both the ICE and the crime of ecocide were 'done deals' by 2025.

But things didn't change much overnight. There were a few legal skirmishes, none of which went very far. Then, in 2028, the infamous Kara Sea blow-out happened on a huge oil rig operated by a consortium of oil and gas companies in the Russian Arctic. Over a period of more than 11 months, the rig spilled more than 500 million gallons of oil into one of the most sensitive environments in the world. This disaster made both the Exxon Valdez spill in Alaska (in 1989) and the Deepwater Horizon blow-out in the Gulf of Mexico (in 2010) look like small-scale incidents.

The Kara Sea disaster was the beginning of the end for every single one of the big companies involved in the consortium. They were all found guilty of ecocide in the ICE in 2032 – a decision that is still being contested 18 years later! Not that it really matters: before the end of the decade, every company involved had been forced into bankruptcy.

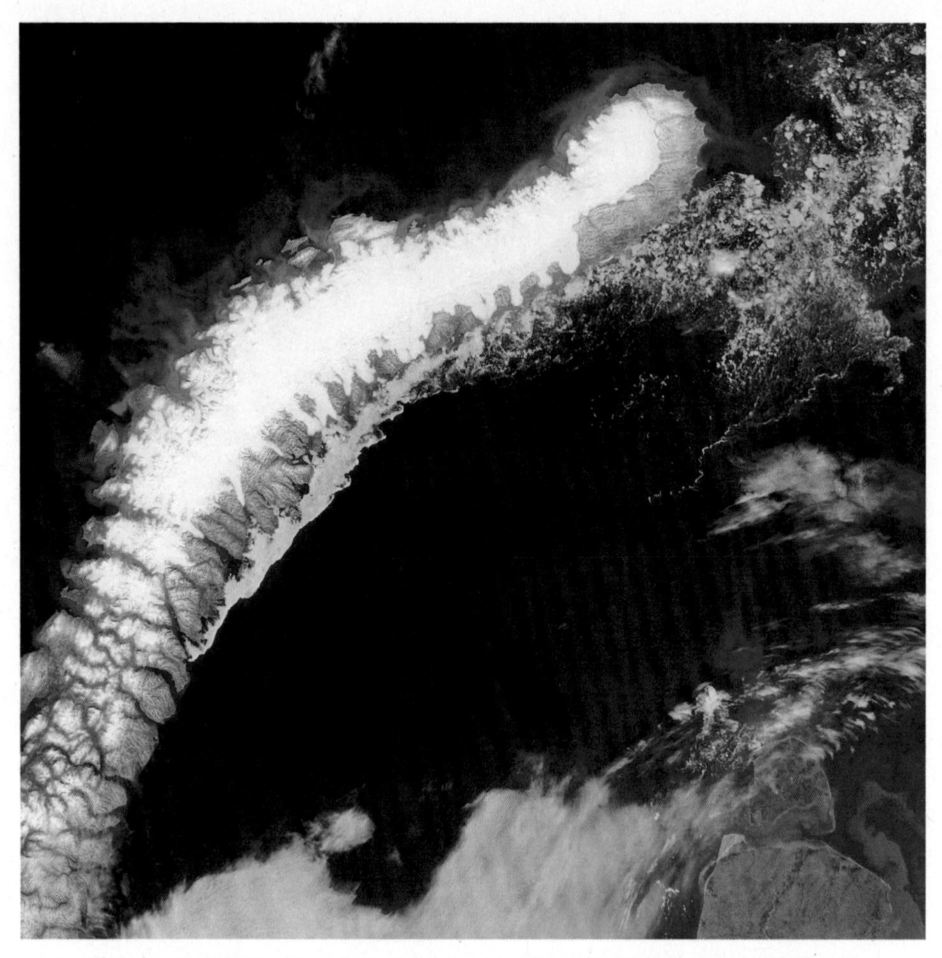

A satellite image of the Kara Sea, one month after the blow-out in 2028. Although the subsequent clean-up has been reasonably effective, scientists reckon it will be another 50 years before the entire eco-system is restored to its previous state.

Whistleblowing: the Kara Sea story

I really want to include the stories of two whistleblowers here, Yevgeny Shokolov and Joe Nathaniel, as a lot of the progress that's been made over the last few decades has depended on people like them – people we just don't hear enough about. And both were involved with the Kara Sea case, in different ways.

When the case came to the ICE, the defence offered by the consortium of companies was – predictably – that they couldn't possibly have foreseen the consequences of such a 'statistically improbable' event as a blow-out. But this was flatly contradicted by a detailed internal report written between 2019 and 2021, when Yevgeny Shokolov was the Director of Operations at the consortium (dealing with all the safely assessments) and Joe Nathaniel was the principal Legal Counsel. Shortly after the blow-out, they felt compelled to put the report into the public domain. It stated categorically that the operators would not be able to cap the well quickly enough in the harsh operating conditions of the Arctic to avoid a disaster. Without the release of that report, the case for the prosecution would have been much weaker.

27.10.2050

Older and Wiser

My mother's now 78, and remarkably sprightly now that she's got her two perma-hips in place. With a bit of luck, she could easily get to be 100. And that's no big deal these days. The number of centenarians just keeps on growing, as you can see from the data below from the UK. These days, you don't get your congratulatory telemail from King Wills until you reach 110! And it's the same sort of story all over the world.

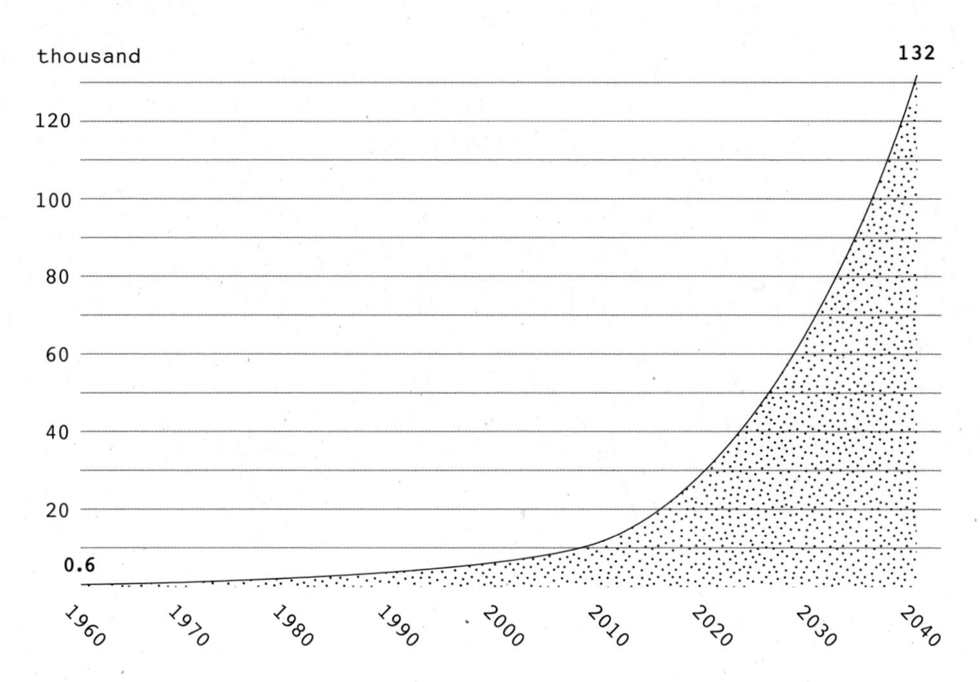

Last year, the number of global centenarians topped three million for the first time, and 22 per cent of today's global population of 8.6 billion people are over the age of 80. This longevity revolution is undoubtedly one of humankind's greatest achievements, but it's also proved to be a massive challenge for our politicians, either just in the background as a cause of constant problems or occasionally exploding into outright intergenerational conflict.

What historians now sometimes describe as the 'war of ages' is not an easy phenomenon to pin down. Most people refer to the Rimini Riots in 2023 as its starting point, when Italians – young and old – confronted each other on the streets of one of Italy's favourite holiday resorts.

Youth unemployment in Italy was then at 38 per cent; 60 per cent of young Italians between the ages of 25 and 35 were still living at home because they couldn't support themselves; and Italy's political gerontocracy (nearly two thirds of the country's business and political leaders were over the age of 65) had failed to grasp the problems.

For the next 15 years, clashes of this kind became commonplace, particularly in Europe, Japan, the US, Australia and China. Young people felt more and more aggrieved at the 'rise of the wrinklies' as the so-called dependency ratio worsened – with fewer and fewer tax-paying workers to help support people over the age of 70 – this became the average retirement age in Europe from around 2030.

Older people didn't feel any happier about it either. Having 'paid their dues' throughout their working lives, they quite understandably expected their governments to provide for a proper retirement on the basis of the payments they'd already made. Millions of older people mobilized politically in a way that had never been seen before, and they gained a growing influence in many legislatures. But almost all governments had failed to put aside adequate resources for the future, even during the 'good times' at the end of the twentieth century.

The truth of it is that everybody's expectations had to change dramatically during that time. People in work had to save more and retire later. Taxes on capital gains and inherited income were substantially increased, and tax avoidance by the rich became less and less acceptable. Slowly and very painfully, budgets began to balance. Happily, lots of other things were changing for the better. After the horrendous price rises earlier on in the century, the basics of life just kept on getting cheaper from about 2030 onwards. The price of food, energy, water and even travel all benefitted enormously from new technology and efficiency gains, and there were the same 'value for money' improvements in web-based technology and social media – almost as vital as food and water.

Today, half of all people aged 75 and over still live alone, and many do (sadly) still feel isolated. But the kind of chronic loneliness that characterized the first couple of decades of this century has largely gone. Older people today are nearly as connected via the online world as young people are. For instance, more than 70 per cent of people over the age of 75 are actively involved in online gaming of one kind or another.

Planning for age-friendly physical environments is now routine all around the world, because independence is still the thing that older people value more than anything else. Digital healthcare, remote sensors, tele-monitoring, purpose-built furniture and appliances, and cheap and cheerful HomeBots (see p.124) have all made life a lot easier – as has the licensing and widespread use of new cognitive enhancing drugs.

The robots are fine, but there's also much more community nursing support available these days – for good old-fashioned financial reasons. Keeping older people fit and well at home represents far better value for taxpayers' money than having to take them into hospital. This was also the principal rationale behind the huge growth in co-housing schemes during the 2020s and 2030s – new or refurbished buildings providing small flats for individual residents, but with a lot of shared facilities, particularly around IT, media and entertainment, gardening and food production, cooking and eating (see over). Co-housing schemes have even made a big difference to the way people suffering from Alzheimer's are looked after.

Back in 2010, more than 35 million people around the world had Alzheimer's, and it was feared at the time that numbers could rise to more than 150 million by 2050. But that hasn't happened: numbers peaked at 100 million, and are now back down to around 45 million. There are several reasons for this: increasing use of smart imaging technologies combined with genome mapping has led to the development of drugs that can slow the onset of Alzheimer's for many years, and also reduce its severity. The vaccines that first came to the market in the early 2020s are now making a huge difference, and once we understood the links between dementia and poor diets (some doctors still refer to Alzheimer's as 'type 3 diabetes') lifestyle changes proved to be as important as any medical intervention. Many people believe that this is another health challenge that will soon be sorted.

But in the end, death still comes to all of us – even if many of us are living longer. And in a way that I think would astonish my grandparents, we seem to enjoy talking about death these days. On a lot of popular chat sites for old people, they love to compare different forms of burial, and the recent controversies about recycling old graves (most cities ran out of 'dead space' a long time ago) have caused a great deal of interest. Cryomation (freeze-drying using liquid nitrogen) seems to be the technology of choice at the moment, but is despised by the traditionalists – including my mother! She has already ordered a beautiful woollen coffin and chosen her plot – and her tree – in a nearby memorial grove that's part of the National Forest. 'Embrace the worms' is now her favourite wind-up line for her grandchildren!

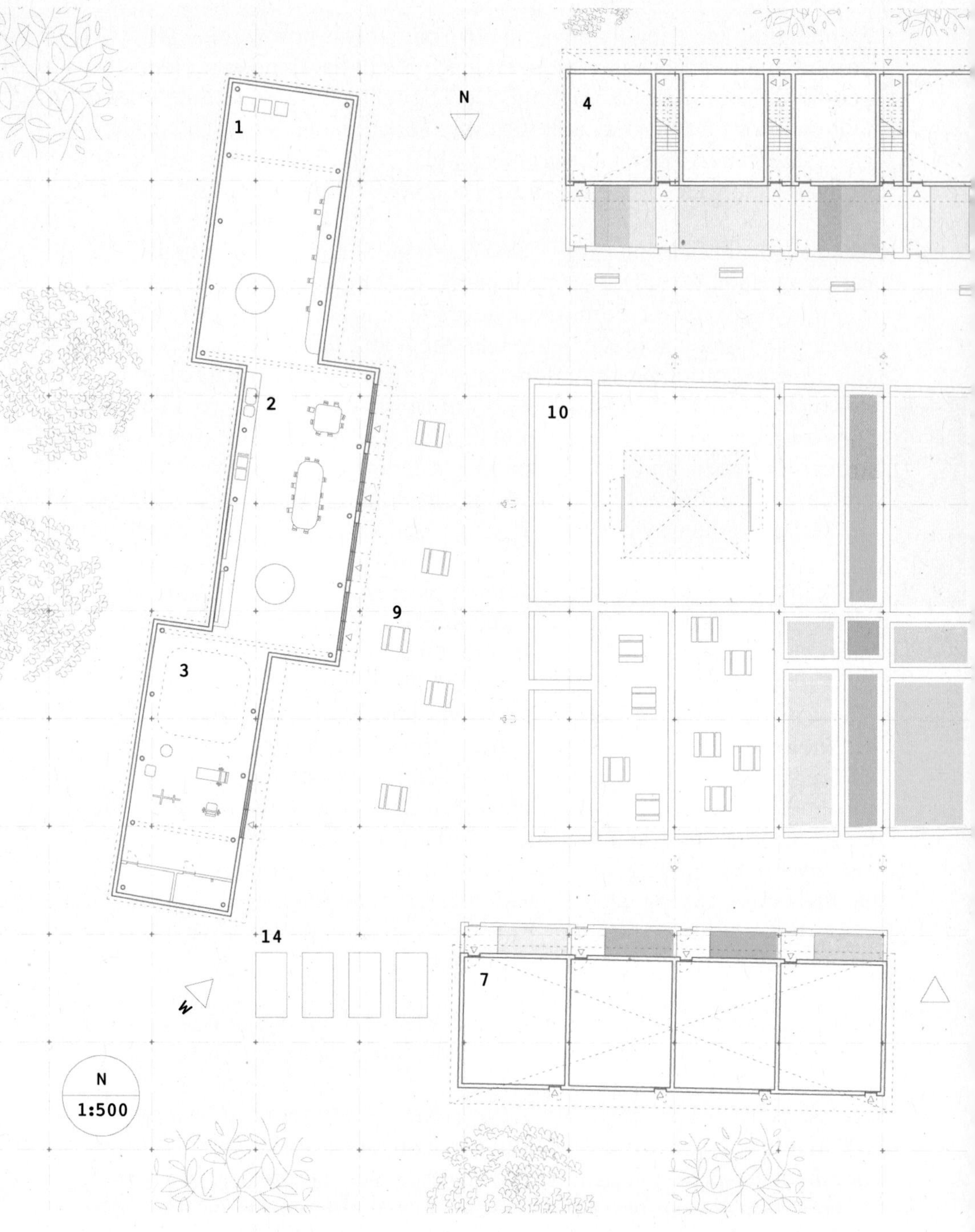

CO-HOUSING SCHEME, BIRMINGHAM, UK

01. Communal building: technology hub, IT centre, robot maintenance and laundry
02. Shared space: kitchen, dining, food processing. Opens out onto the communal garden
03. Shared open space: gym, aerobics, yoga, classes and children's play area
04. Young professionals' apartments, 16 units @ 50m^2/unit (two storey)
05. Four bed family houses, 2 units @ 100m^2 (two storey)
06. Family houses, 4 units @ 80m^2 (two storey)

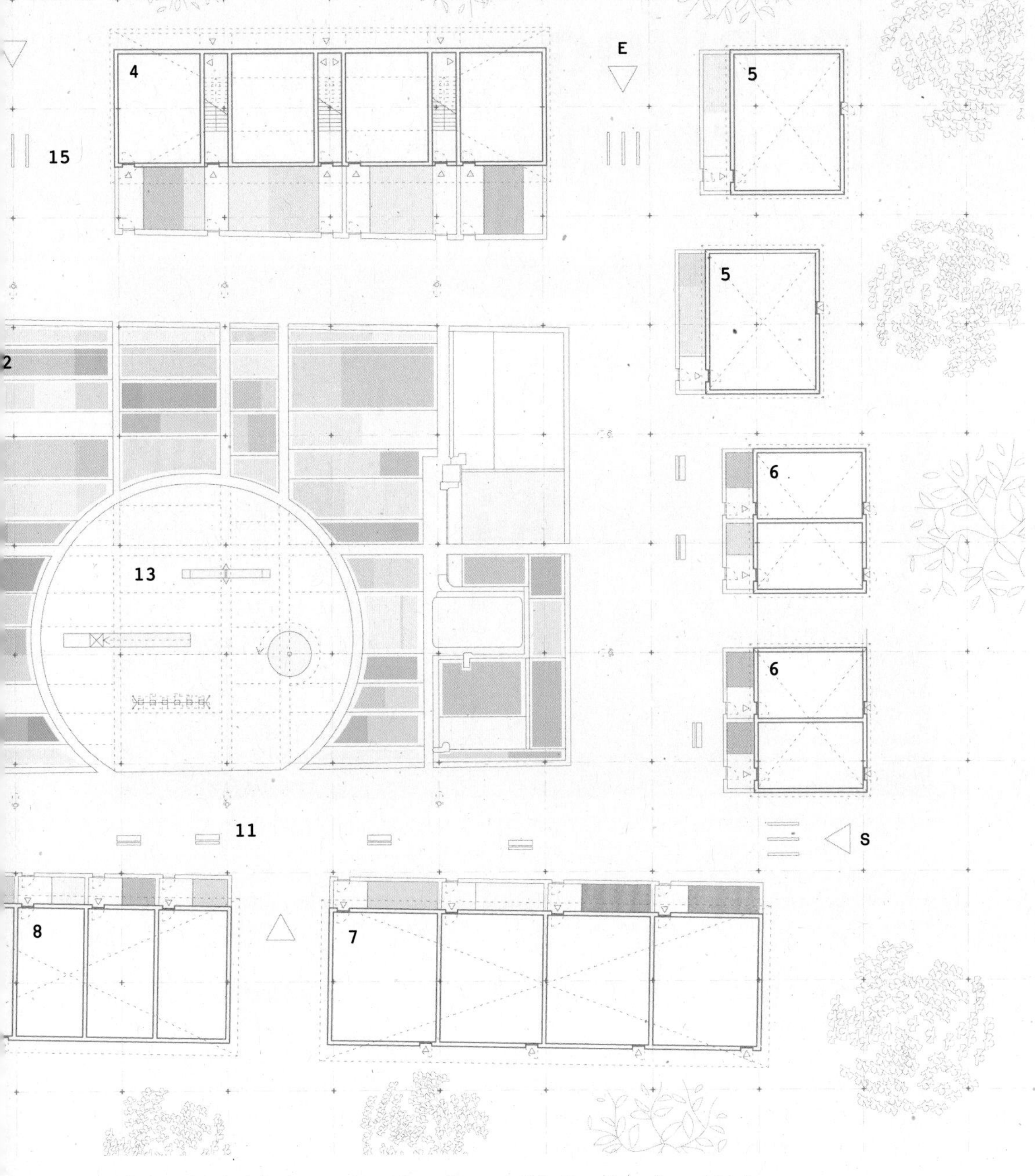

07. Two bed elderly persons' housing, 9 units @ 76m^2 (1 storey), level access
08. One bed elderly persons' housing, integrated smaller units, 3 units @ 50m^2 (1 storey), level access
09. Picnic and BBQ area with easy access to kitchen
10. Open play/sports space
11. Benches for elderly
12. Tapestry of allotments, paths and flowerbeds
13. Therapeutic garden with herbs and aromatic plants
14. Carpool for shared car scheme
15. Bike racks

03.11.2050

Travelling Differently

One of my own photos which I took on our visit to Tibet in 2044. We were lucky enough to spend a bit of time trekking on the Chang Tang, where nomadic people still maintain their traditional way of life. Even the young people (who are as digitally connected to the rest of the world as any other young people) feel little inclination to move to Lhasa or other big towns.

Some of our friends haven't taken a real holiday abroad for over 30 years. Somewhere along the line, they just got hooked on the world of virtual travel and have never looked back. Others still pretend to despise any travel experience that isn't real. And some people (including ourselves) just can't believe their luck to have access to the best of both worlds: virtual and real travel.

But there are a lot more restrictions on real travel these days than when I was growing up. That's what made 2044 so special for us: we'd been in the Tibet lottery (one of the most popular of today's Destination Lotteries, or DLs) since 2030. In 2041 our number finally came up, and then it took a further three years of planning to get us out there.

People initially hated the idea of these DLs, but with the amount of foreign travel increasing all the time (from less than one billion journeys worldwide in 2010 to more than two billion in 2025, with huge numbers of new travellers from China, India and so on), there was really no alternative. Access to many, many places had to be carefully managed.

It was all very elitist to start with: there was no point putting your name into a DL if you didn't have the money to go. But the price of many holidays remained very reasonable (staying with people in their homes rather than in fancy hotels makes such a difference), and a lot of travel firms started cross-subsidizing, providing some very expensive experiences for those who could afford them as well as bargain packages for the rest of us. And even the mega-rich (with their own private airships and yachts) can't bypass the Destination Lotteries – of which there are now more than 12,000.

Modern airships also help to keep costs down: business people may still want to get from A to B as fast as they can, but most recreational travel these days is by airship, boat, train, bus and bike. The time involved isn't usually a problem – with the average working week now at around 25 hours, it's possible for anybody to accumulate a lot of official leave. And today's rail services, pretty much the world over, are so fast, comfortable and reliable that you wonder why anybody choses any other form of travel.

As keen travellers, we go on holiday to far-flung places every three or four years – with the very occasional 'spectacular' like Tibet. We also travel fairly regularly in the UK and Europe – we just love it. But I have to admit that most of my colleagues don't. In their eyes, real travel takes so much time, so much planning, so much hassle – and things often seem to go wrong, unlike in their virtual holiday sphere.

One of my colleagues at Ashton Vale, Annie Lomas, happens to be a historian specializing in the origins of the internet, and she's just done a big study on the way in which a handful of companies offering virtual holidays and travelling experiences at the start of the century have now grown into a $500 billion industry. Some of the best early ideas were aimed at those unable to travel because of age, illness or disability. Uptake was low, but it made a huge difference to people stuck at home or too ill to travel on their own.

Many of the next generation of VITES (virtual travel experiences) were designed to protect special places – such as the Great Mosque of Cordoba, China's Forbidden City, nature reserves and Machu Picchu – by enabling people to enjoy them from afar. Some VITES were embedded in versions of Second Life to add the holiday dimension.

A 'slow travel' air cruiser over Incheon Bridge, South Korea, 2041.

Google's Total-Immersion was launched in 2023, along with all sorts of rival spin-offs stemming from the defence and medical industries. These still struggled to replicate the immediacy and authenticity of real travel across all the senses – and the amount of computer power they needed to provide these 'substitute experiences' was immense.

But, 20 years on, even I have to admit that these technologies are now pretty amazing, with even tactile and olfactory senses fully engaged. Our 'trip' to Las Vegas was truly mind-boggling, while Annie and her partner did the whole of the Santiago de Compostela pilgrimage over a period of three years, without ever once getting off their walking machines in the living room. And before we went to Tibet for real, we 'visited' dozens of places (including the Potala Palace) with some of our best friends, and on one occasion with the Dalai Lama himself as our guide! Brilliant stuff – and it just made the real experience all the more astonishing.

From Annie's historical archive, it's clear that a lot of people earlier in the century felt that foreign travel would become impossible (primarily because of the effects on climate change) for all but the very rich – and that the world would become a narrow, more inward-looking place as a result. Thankfully, that just hasn't happened. The travel and tourism industry really cleaned up its act on both environmental and social issues, and tourism still plays a crucial part in the economies of a large number of countries.

For one thing, all the different carbon offset schemes set up early in the century allowed people to compensate for their emissions of CO_2 by investing in CO_2 reduction schemes. By 2020, these were making a big difference in terms of paying for the protection of the natural environment in the places that people were visiting. But with CO_2 emissions charged at nearly $140 per tonne (see p.240), near-zero CO_2 holidays are understandably popular, particularly with students and young people.

Cheap travel is certainly not seen as a 'god-given right', as it once was, and nobody takes it for granted. But the great thing is that total revenue from travel and tourism, real and virtual, is still increasing, with a far higher percentage of it staying in the countries (and the communities) that people are visiting – in real life or online, through the licenses that people pay. So the world is still out there for those who want to explore it!

10.11.2050
Climate Challenges

WORLD ENERGY SUPPLY BY SOURCE

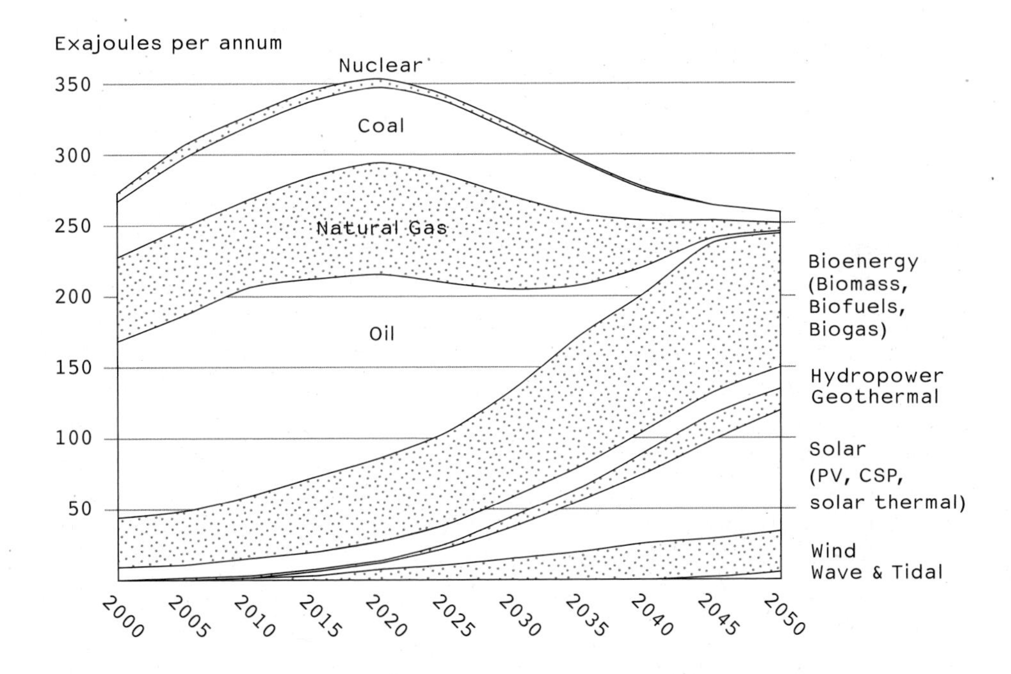

It's five years ago now, but all our friends are still talking about 2045 as if it were yesterday. Quite simply, it was the worst year ever from the point of view of climate change.

These are the statistics: 338,000 deaths, $410 billion of economic damage and more than 1.2 million people displaced. And this is what happened: the Caribbean and the Gulf of Mexico were devastated by two of the worst hurricanes in recorded history; there were droughts across Africa and much of South America; wildfires burned out of control for weeks on end in Australia, Russia and Canada; and terrible flooding spread across Europe, Pakistan and India.

The irony is that we all thought we were doing so well at that stage. We hadn't had 'a bad year' for a long time. Emissions of greenhouse gases had been slashed, and investments in energy efficiency and renewables (creating tens of millions of jobs all around the world) were still running at an all-time high – not least because of all the revenues from the Universal Carbon Tax (UCT). With the exception of Russia and North Korea, all nations had signed up to the principle of a UCT as part of the Houston Concord in 2020 (see p.48) – but the usual political shenanigans meant that it didn't really get going until 2028. The price was very low to begin with (at $30 per tonne of CO_2), but the annual UCT 'escalator' had raised that to $110 by 2045.

The plan had been to cap it indefinitely at that level, but after an emergency meeting in New York in February 2046, in response to the events of 2045, the price was increased to $140 – and some say it will need to go to at least $200 per tonne to squeeze the remaining carbon out of the economy. (The income that governments get from the UCT peaked long ago, given that so much less CO_2 is now being emitted.)

And here's some more bad news: over the course of the century, we're not going to be able to restrict the average temperature increase to below 2°C – a target first set by dithering politicians more than 40 years ago, even as they declared climate change to be 'the greatest challenge humankind has ever faced'. (Such a shame they didn't really mean it.)

So what's the good news? It may sound naive, but the world today really is united in combating climate change. All that rhetoric about 'one human family' doesn't sound as hypocritical as it once did – and that's rubbed off on all sorts of other issues, which I'll return to on p.266.

No doubt there will be more bad years to come, but scientists believe we may be over the worst. As a result, the prospects of staying below an increase of 3°C before the end of the century are excellent, and it may just be that we peg it right back to no more than 2.5°C. The spectre of runaway irreversible climate change appears to have been averted.

If you put me on the spot, I'd put that success down to four huge shifts that have taken place over the last 40 years.

1. We put energy efficiency at the heart of every economic decision

Horribly late in the day, politicians finally got the message: energy is precious, and we should maximize the value we get from every unit of it, whatever its source. That old idea that 'negawatts' (i.e. energy not generated because of increased efficiency) matter a lot more than 'megawatts' is now at the heart of our energy politics, and a combination of rising prices on CO_2, generous incentive schemes and massive retrofit programmes all around the world (see p.126) eventually did the job.

2. We notched up some really important Quick Big Wins

For instance, my Research Team were incredibly struck by the measures taken between 2010 and 2025 to get rid of the pollution caused by soot from inefficient cooking stoves. Led by United Nations Environment Programme (UNEP) and funded primarily by the US, this made a huge difference to people in Africa and other developing countries – averting the premature deaths of more than 2.5 million people every year.

3. We focused on CO_2 in our forests and in the soil

This has been relatively simple: stop cutting down the rainforests; ensure as much carbon as possible is taken up in soils, wetlands, bogs and so on, simply by intelligent and sensitive land management. It sounds mundane, but things like zero tillage (where farmers plant and harvest without ploughing up the soil) and agro-ecology (where trees and shrubs are planted in and around food crops to help prevent erosion and build up organic matter in the soil) have had as big an impact as all the high-tech stuff with renewables.

An aerial shot of typical high-yield farming in the Democratic Republic of Congo in 2045, demonstrating best practice in agro-ecology.

4. We learned how to power the world renewably

Forty years' worth of full-on innovation has seen nation after nation reduce its use of fossil fuels and take full advantage of the potential of renewable energy – as the latest figures from the World Environment Organization (at the start of this entry) demonstrate so clearly.

There's still some oil, coal and gas in the mix, but all on a downward curve. The pace and scale of innovation in renewables (and storage technologies) has been astonishing. Without exception, everything has kept on getting both cheaper and more efficient, particularly with solar, wind and biomass. Geothermal power is also huge, particularly in Africa and parts of Southeast Asia.

Both tidal stream and wave power technologies (determinedly pioneered in Scotland when nowhere else seemed interested – and now a hugely important export for the Scots) have also achieved real scale, though not quite in the same league as the amazing Severn Barrage, which for the last 25 years has been quietly generating around seven per cent of the UK's total electricity demand. And it will be doing the same for at least another 100 years!

Wave power on the west coast of Scotland, 2042. Small, highly efficient wave power facilities of this kind are now commonplace in many different countries.

But it's solar that has really done it. As I explained before, the price of solar came crashing down very early on in the century, but it was harder to maintain the same kind of efficiency gains. It wasn't until researchers made a whole series of critical breakthroughs in thermoelectric materials (including some really cool thermoelectric paints that anybody can apply) that things really began to change in the early 2030s.

Soon after this came the first commercially viable roll-out of artificial photosynthesis, co-ventured by US universities and a number of big Indian companies. Using silicon and nickel-based catalysts, the latest artificial 'leaves' use sunlight to power chemical changes to split water into its constituent hydrogen and oxygen atoms. This technology is already used in more than 40 countries, often in quite remote rural areas, and I suspect that this is going to be huge in the not too distant future.

So we're absolutely on track to a 100 per cent renewables world, with poorer countries benefiting just as much as the rich world. And, hopefully, not too late.

I happened to keep this issue of 'Green Futures' – published way back in 2033. At that time there were just four main variations of AP (artificial photosynthesis) – there are more than 20 today. But even now, they all depend on nature's trick of using the sun's energy to split water into hydrogen and oxygen – these days using various metal-oxide semi-conductors to produce the hydrogen.

17.11.2050

Democracy By Demand

The InterJust logo, 2031.

I grew up in an age of intense political cynicism and mistrust, and though it's much better now, in most countries, there's one thing that politicians have always been rubbish at: thinking long term to protect the interests of future generations.

Interestingly, that unfortunate reality persuaded a lot of environmental activists over the years that democracy and sustainability were simply incompatible: you could have one but not the other. Indeed, there was a time when all people could talk about was 'sustainability China-style'. With no voters to worry about, it's true that China got more done on sustainability issues in the decade between 2010 and 2020 than Western democracies had managed over many decades before that. It's all very different today, of course, now that China is having to manage the same democracy dilemmas as the rest of us.

And it's not just in China that a more democratic world has been unfolding – despite all the economic shocks to the system and the impacts of climate change. In Africa (which was dismissed at the start of the century as a corrupt basket-case) citizens of one country after another got their crooked and venal politicians under control, empowered by new technology and social media just as in the rest of the world.

It's not such a good picture in Bangladesh, where the near-impossibility of protecting tens of millions of people from rising sea levels in the Bay of Bengal means that the military is still in control through maintaining a State of Emergency more than 20 years on from the coup in 2029. Or in Pakistan, where the combination of staggering levels of corruption, an insanely high fertility rate, constant floods and droughts of shocking severity have left tens of millions trapped in chronic poverty.

It's only fair to point out that one of the biggest blows struck for democracy over the last 40 years took place in the United States. The story began in 2010 when, in a deeply unpopular decision, the Supreme Court allowed unlimited and anonymous corporate funding for election campaigns. Corporate lobbying had always been a big problem in the United States, but from that point on big business and wealthy elites pretty much bought out the entire political system through the financial contributions they made to parties and individual candidates.

This came to a head in 2021, when a Supreme Court enquiry found that more than 92 per cent of politicians elected in the 2018 mid-term elections had subsequently provided some direct financial benefit for the people and the companies that had funded them. The campaign for reform of political funding cranked up several gears, resulting eventually in a series of bills restricting personal donations to no more than $5,000 and corporate contributions to no more than $25,000.

Outside the United States, the biggest battleground for most Western democracies has been the age-old conflict between the political power centre on the one hand, and regions, cities and local communities on the other. The overall direction of travel has been clear: a slow but steady move away from central control, with more and more powers (including taxation and spending) passed down to regional legislatures or large city authorities. This in turn has meant more power coming right down to the local level. For instance, most municipalities in Europe now rely heavily on participatory budgeting to determine local spending priorities, with people voting on how they want their money to be used. We've got a particularly active Citizens' Budgeting Network in our city, which I've been somewhat involved in over the years.

Beyond that, it's a crazy patchwork of diverse electoral and democratic systems that has emerged around the world. From the early 2020s, new technology made it easy (as in both cheap and secure) to set up direct consultative and voting systems. Although most countries (interestingly) have opted to stick with representative democratic systems, the levels of engagement and accountability have been transformed as a result. And the InterJust movement has played a major part in that.

InterJust began as a loose global network of high school students that sprang up in the late 2020s. The name stood for 'intergenerational justice' – in other words, what one generation should be doing to protect the interests of future generations. In effect, InterJust was the raw anger of youth online. They'd come to the conclusion that all the momentum achieved by the Enough! movement 10 years earlier had been lost. Things were starting to get better, but it was all far too slow – and even my generation wasn't doing enough as far as InterJust was concerned, let alone my parents' generation.

So InterJust started campaigning for the rights of young people all around the world. To begin with, everything was coordinated and shared online. What they did was to target elected politicians of any and every party. They spoofed, hacked and graffitied their websites, jammed all communications with voters (which was all electronic by then), blocked donations and mass-mailed scurrilous stories and rumours. By using ridicule and humour, they got right under our politicians' thick skins. And then they came out on the streets.

There's no doubt that InterJust had a huge impact – not only at the time, but through the politicization of hundreds of millions of young people since then. They used the latest technologies to hold politicians to account through constantly evolving activist networks. InterJust even put up candidates of their own to campaign tirelessly for reducing the voting age and improving voting systems, and against cyber-censorship. By challenging authoritarianism and mobilizing extraordinary numbers of people on diverse issues across national and religious boundaries, they really have been the 'netizens' of a connected world.

InterJust campaigns in (clockwise from top left) Italy, Spain, Somalia and Algeria. As InterJust grew, kids in schools picked it up and started their own campaigns. On 1 April 2031, it was estimated that 80 per cent of school children all around the world went on 'strike'. And they did it again on 1 May – and then on the first of each and every month that they were in school. In some countries, this went on for more than two years. I'd just started teaching at Ashton Vale then, and can remember just how invigorating it all felt.

25.11.2050

Reefs: Back from the Brink

The Great Barrier Reef in Australia has been under active protection since 1975. The Marine Park Authority increased the scale of no-catch zones from five per cent of the area in the 1980s to 33 per cent by 2010 and more than 75 per cent today. The MPA's water quality plan dramatically reduced the run-off of chemicals earlier on in the century and the problem has been almost eliminated since then. Almost all the remaining fishing rights are managed by Aboriginal communities.

By 2020 more than 135,000 square kilometres of the world's reefs had been either severely damaged or completely lost. It was an environmental disaster on a colossal scale.

To be fair, it's clear that people were worried about this at the time. There were more international conventions, mandates, commissions and initiatives – by both governments and NGOs – than you could throw a stick of dynamite at. Yet all the national and international diplomacy had completely failed, for the simple reason that the vast majority of reefs fall under national jurisdictions rather than under international laws.

It's amazing that any reefs survived – but they did, and from 2020 onwards the alarm bells were ringing so loudly that they could no longer be ignored. Both the United Nations Environment Programme (UNEP) and UNESCO secured massive additional funding both for their own restoration programmes and for NGOs like WWF, Conservation International and the International Coral Reef Initiative. A great deal of repair work had to be done – and there were almost as many views on how best to do this as there are species of coral! Nurseries for different reef species had to be established. Concrete 'reef balls' and biorock technologies of one kind or another (first pioneered in the 1980s) were installed in hundreds of different localities to help regeneration. Artificial reefs made from recycled plastics were also widely used in places like the Red Sea, with some success near Abu Dhabi and Dubai.

A concrete reef ball in the Red Sea, showing encouraging new growth after just a couple of years.

But there's no point in restoring a reef unless you can put an end to what it was that caused the problems in the first place. By working with local communities, educating children and young people, and demonstrating that environmental protection was very much in communities' own interests, more and more reefs had been declared as no-catch zones by the end of the 2020s.

At that time, thousands of organizations and literally millions of people were involved in perhaps the single most significant rescue operation of the twenty-first century. This required an unprecedented level of coordination and shared learning based on UNESCO's Global Ocean Observing System, which connected up every single reef protection and restoration project around the world. This was science at its best, put to good use by local fishermen, tourism managers and marine biologists: a triumph by any standards.

The Research Team pretty quickly got the message on this one.

This was their report:

REEFS ARE THE RAINFOREST OF THE SEAS

What's more, reefs are an economic powerhouse, generating benefits worth tens of billions of dollars through fisheries, tourism etc.

1%

JUST 1% OF THE OCEAN FLOOR

25%

HOME TO MORE THAN 25% OF THE OCEAN'S CREATURES.

Yet by 2020, 135,000 sq km of reefs had either been severely damaged or completely destroyed through:

- **Local fishing communities indiscriminately using both dynamite and poison**
- **Commercial trawlers scraping away the living coral**
- **Agricultural run-off (fertilizers and pesticides)**
- **Soil erosion causing severe sedimentation**
- **Sewage and industrial pollution – at an unbelievable scale!**
- **Mismanagement by tourism agencies – even though the reefs were what their visitors were coming to see!**
- **Inappropriate economic development in sensitive areas**

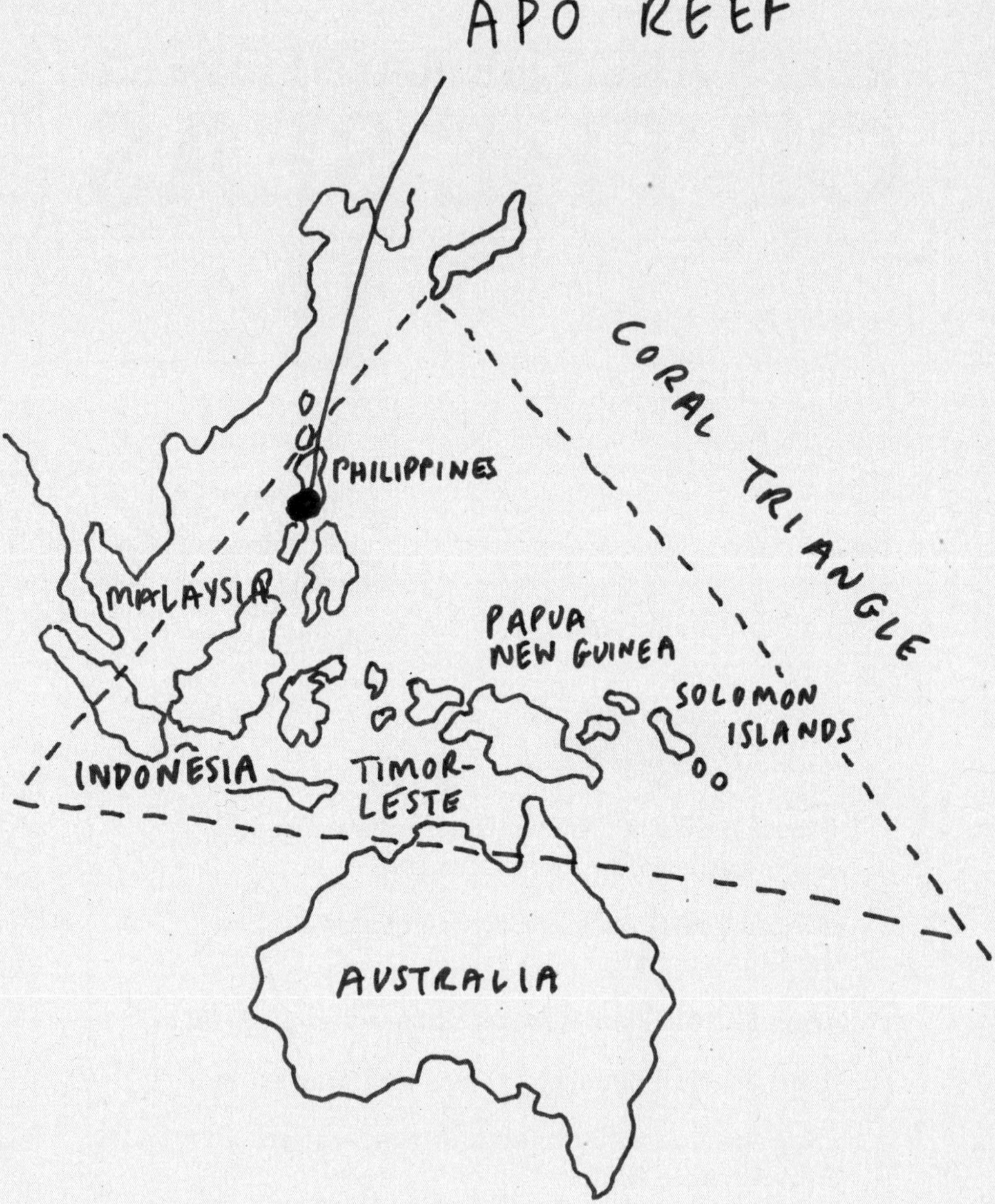

APO REEF

CORAL TRIANGLE

PHILIPPINES

MALAYSIA

PAPUA
NEW GUINEA

SOLOMON
ISLANDS

INDONESIA

TIMOR-
LESTE

AUSTRALIA

But even this mighty effort could do little to counter the damage caused by the twin hammer blows of unchecked global warming and increased acidification. The oceans had started warming up, very slowly, in the twentieth century. By 2010, the average temperature increase over the preceding 100 years amounted to around 1°C, and there has been at least another 0.5°C since then. That may not sound much, but the delicate relationship between corals themselves (small marine creatures called polyps) and the algae that live within their tissue is all too easily undermined by rising temperatures. Many coral reefs have been 'bleached out' by warmer waters as the pigment-producing algae are lost.

Saving the Apo Reef

The Apo Reef is right at the northern tip of the Coral Triangle – an area of around 5.7 million square kilometres, spanning the seas of Indonesia, Malaysia, the Philippines, Papua and New Guinea, the Solomon Islands and Timor-Leste. Back in 2007, it was in such a state of ruin (primarily through criminal over-fishing) that the entire reef had to be closed off.

For the next 20 years, the only way of making this restoration project work was to protect the livelihoods of all the communities involved in fishing by developing alternative fishing grounds – and building up local eco-tourism businesses. This programme was coordinated by WWF and Conservation International – and it's worked a treat.

The Apo reef now has the highest yield of fish biomass per square kilometre in the whole of the Coral Triangle, as well as a thriving (and totally sustainable) trade in reef fish, with sales reaching across the entire region.

Coral bleaching in the Apo Reef, 2007.

The Apo Reef after its restoration, 2048.

But, if anything, the problem of acidification could yet prove to be even more serious than the warming of the oceans. All the CO_2 absorbed by the oceans (comprising 30 per cent of all the human-made emissions) changes the chemistry of the ocean's surface water, building up higher concentrations of carbonic acids. This has a serious impact on the way corals form their skeletons and can even cause the slow dissolving of entire stretches of reef.

Unfortunately, there's little that can be done about this: climate-proofing the world's reefs would be a geoengineering challenge too far. On the Great Barrier Reef and in the Red Sea, marine biologists have been experimenting with applying limestone to counter acidification in some of the worst-affected areas, and it does seem to have had some effect. But it's costly and hugely energy-intensive.

So even as we've had some real success in dealing with some problems (all that pollution and over-fishing), we're still struggling with the really big things – climate change and ocean acidification. And that still leaves our reefs in a pretty bad position: on the mend, but all too vulnerable to further deterioration.

02.12.2050

Shipping Cleans Up

Shipping had always been deeply conservative – slow to move and quick to complain, a bit like farming was in the old days! So it must have been one hell of a shock for shipping companies to wake up to a world of rising energy and commodity prices, disputes about labour conditions and growing concerns about air pollution and accelerating climate change – in 2010, shipping's CO_2 emissions were four per cent of the world's total.

But what a change there's been since then. A neat report from the International Maritime Organization (IMO) in 2048 provided a brilliant summary of the 40 last years (see p.257).

And those CO_2 figures will continue to improve from now on. The thing about ships is that they last a long, long time – at least 30 years. The oldest ships out there today were constructed back in the 2020s, when things were still pretty primitive. So further improvements are in store, and by 2070 it's reckoned that the CO_2 intensity figure will be right down to less than two grammes of CO_2 for every tonne of freight.

But perhaps the most significant piece of data in the table on p.257 is the tonnes carried. For as long as I can remember, there has always been a very vocal movement arguing that we should all go back to complete self-sufficiency – not just communities, but whole nations. Our local Green Party, for instance, used to have a particularly active self-sufficiency group, arguing that this was the only way to avoid the apocalyptic horror story unleashed by the 'heedless globalization' of the twentieth century.

Selfishly, as someone who's got a bit of a thing about coffee, tea and chocolate (and even the odd pineapple or mango!), I'm pretty relieved that this turned out not to be our fate. There are certainly fewer vessels in the global fleet than there used to be, but the actual amount of freight carried is more or less the same as it was back in the 2030s – with more trade now focused on regional rather than global routes. (The economies of West Africa, for instance, have benefitted enormously from huge upgrades in their ports and shipping infrastructure, which was once almost completely derelict.) So we still live in a world that's connected not just virtually, but also physically, through travel and trade.

Shipping is what has made that possible – indeed, shipping has always been the primary engine of world trade. But it was precisely that engine that was causing all the problems at the turn of the century. The huge growth in shipping through the twentieth century was powered by the use of heavy fuel oil – the really cheap and dirty stuff left over from the process of refining oil. This 'bunker fuel' was very high in sulphur and other pollutants (causing big problems in terms of local air pollution and impacts on health), as well as emitting CO_2. The last 40 years has been all about finding alternatives to heavy fuel oil.

Looking at where we are now, a combination of improved ship design, radically improved engines (including fuel cells), cleaner fuels, waste heat recovery systems, slower speeds and much smarter logistics (both at sea and in port) have transformed the performance of the entire industry. To start with, there was a big push on substituting liquefied natural gas (LNG) for heavy fuel oil.

And it worked well in terms of reducing emissions of 'SOx' and 'NOx' – all the pollution from oxides of sulphur and nitrogen that had been causing serious health problems up until then. But retrofitting ships for LNG was a seriously costly business. What's more, it didn't sort out the emissions of CO_2. It did, however, provide a bridge to today's modern ships.

With the big, ocean-going bulk carriers, container ships and liners, everything now runs on either methanol-based fuel cells or dual-fuel hybrid engines, using biogas or algae-based biofuels – with a lot of help from fully automated sky sails or solar panel sails. Interestingly, some of the most pioneering work on biofuels for shipping was done decades ago by the US Navy, which is still the biggest user of marine fuels today. Its Green Fleet initiative provided a steady flow of hundreds of millions of dollars for research into innovative technologies. Several navies were also using small nuclear reactors for some of their large ships until the signing of the Nuclear Decommissioning Treaty in Kiev in 2022 (see p.60).

As regards all the smaller ships that ply coastal shipping lanes, as well as modern leisure craft and ferries, these are now 100 per cent renewably powered, mostly by solar and sail, with a back-up biofuel capability. Reducing the drag on ships as they move through the water has also helped: by pumping streams of bubbles along the hull and, more recently, using a host of new polymer coatings and lubricants that also prevent fouling by barnacles and other marine organisms. The combined effect of just these innovations, steadily improved over the last 20 years, has reduced fuel consumption by around 25 per cent.

INTERNATIONAL SHIPPING DATA

	2010	2050
NUMBER OF OCEAN-GOING SHIPS	103,000	81,000
TONNES OF FREIGHT CARRIED	8.4 BILLION	7.9 BILLION
CO_2 EMISSIONS (TONNES)	870 MILLION	92 MILLION
CO_2 EFFICIENCY* (CONTAINER SHIPS)	15g	3g

* Grammes of CO_2 emitted for each tonne of freight carried for 1 km

After years of debate at the International Maritime Organization, the Ballast Water Convention was finally ratified in 2014 – a full 10 years after it was first agreed. The purpose of the Convention was to end the problems caused by the release of invasive species from ships' ballast water.

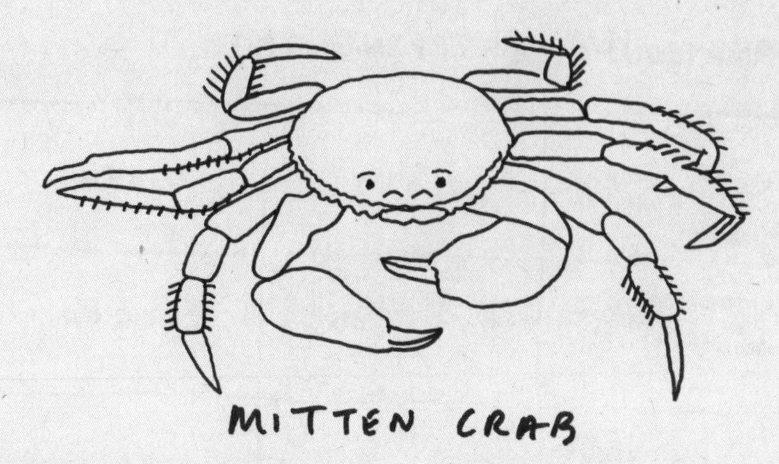

MITTEN CRAB

This little beast, for instance, has caused untold damage as an alien invader from China in dozens of different countries.

The Convention accelerated the drive for innovative pre-discharge treatment systems, including filtration, advanced oxidation, electrolysis, various biocides and other chemical-free water purification technologies – the latest versions of which are now standard on every ocean-going vessel.

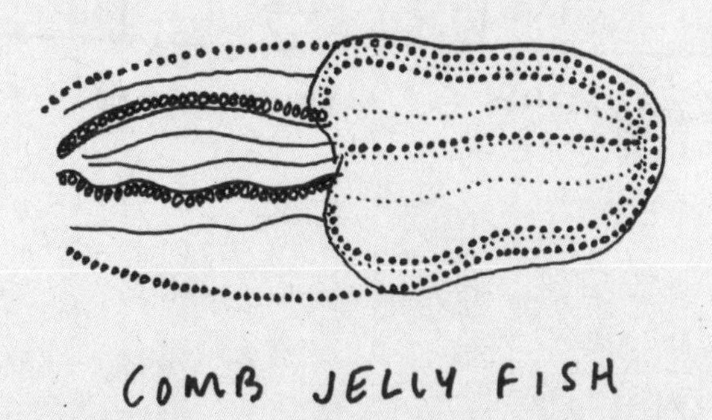

COMB JELLY FISH

And this one (the comb jelly fish) caused havoc in the Black Sea where it was dumped in ballast water from an American ship in 1983. They called it 'the blob that ate the Black Sea', causing a collapse in marine life as it consumed all the different kind of plankton on which that eco-system depended.

Recycling of Ships

Here's another thing we take for granted today. It took 10 years for the Hong Kong Convention of 2009 to come into force, but today all ships (large or small) are now 100 per cent recyclable, with their own cradle-to-cradle passports. That didn't mean much to begin with, as the facilities didn't exist to disassemble ships in a resource-efficient way. Indeed, the ship-breaking industry was still in a shameful state at that time, with appalling working conditions (particularly in Bangladesh and India). It's to the huge credit of the shipping industry, supported by the World Bank, that instead of just closing down those businesses, substantial investments were made in proper ship-breaking facilities to 'close the loop' in terms of all the principal materials used in shipbuilding, providing thousands of highly skilled jobs in far safer conditions.

I guess the shipping industry is just as invisible to most people today as it was at the start of the century. But all these improvements actually did a lot to raise the image of the industry, and that made it possible for companies to recruit more skilled staff and to raise their game dramatically in terms of safety, working conditions and human rights. To the great satisfaction of everybody involved, shipping is now considered a great industry to work in.

This is a conventional bulk carrier, commissioned around 15 years ago, with both the sky sail and the solar panel sails that are now standard kit. It also relies on a state-of-the-art Air Cavity System (ACS) which pumps air out of holes in the hull, providing a carpet of bubbles under the hull, and on the latest anti-drag, water-repelling polymer coating. It is, in effect, self-cleaning – much like the skin of a shark. The principal energy source for ocean-going carriers like this

are bio-based fuels (either gas or algae-based diesel), and the latest model is now capable of harvesting algae as it goes, to provide part of the fuel mix. More often than not, it's operated remotely, with no humans on board (hence the very small bridge for use only in emergencies), and is loaded and discharged fully automatically in port. Like all ocean-going vessels, it can be stripped down in its entirety, enabling closed-loop ship manufacturing over very long periods of time.

13.12.2050
Miracle Cures?

At the grand old age of 50, it's reassuring to think that I'm probably only halfway through my life – all being well!

This life expectancy story is one aspect of the ongoing health revolution that still astonishes my young researchers. Between 1970 and 2020, life expectancy for humankind as a whole increased by an average of three months for every calendar year that passed! Figures published a few months ago show this is now going up even faster, by four months each year.

Much of this improvement is down to narrowing the life expectancy gap between rich and poor. Getting the basics right – sanitation, hygiene, clean water, disease prevention, maternal mortality, HIV/AIDS and so on – across Africa and the rest of the poor world has made all the difference. The widespread use of nanopatches to improve the efficiency of vaccination campaigns is just one of multiple breakthroughs that have really helped.

Tuberculosis

Unfortunately, there's still one horror story we've not made much progress on: tuberculosis (TB). Cases of drug-resistant TB were multiplying as far back as 2010, but despite endless warnings, the over-prescribing of antibiotics (even for coughs and colds) still went on.

Even more irresponsible, in my view, were the US politicians who continued to licence the use of penicillin and other antibiotics to promote growth in farmyard animals. Despite clear evidence that some bacteria could jump from animals to humans, sometimes acquiring resistance along the way, the US Food and Drug Administration didn't impose a total ban on antibiotics for such purposes until 2018.

Cases of TB continued to grow throughout the 2010s – and antibiotics had less and less effect. Multi-drug-resistant TB was commonplace by 2020, and extreme drug-resistant TB (XDR-TB) was by then present in up to 30 countries.

Only then did the politicians finally understand the gravity of the crisis – but far too late to avoid the death of millions of people from a disease that should never have been allowed to re-establish itself, having been almost eradicated in the twentieth century. Now, however, new drug combinations have managed to get on top of the problem again.

TB apart, I'm still massively impressed by all the advances in medicine over the last 35 years. What's become fairly standard for us today, through technology breakthroughs of one kind or another, would have been referred to formerly as miracles. For example, the fact that most people's sight can now be restored by implanting tiny light-sensitive panels (linked to a video camera on a pair of glasses) would have been seen as pure science fiction back then.

As I mentioned before, much of the increase in life expectancy is down to the roll-out of cheap personal genomics. But the parallel introduction of smart-sensing technologies, including super-sensitive imaging and monitoring devices that measure minute changes in electrical fields and other vital signs, has completely revolutionized the business of early diagnosis. The ability to tell almost instantly what virus or bacterium is causing an infection has saved countless lives. Cancers can be picked up within weeks or even days of their formation; clogged arteries are quickly spotted and de-clogged as a standard procedure.

And hardly a day passes without us being regaled with yet another breakthrough in the bionic enhancement of standard human capabilities, both physical and intellectual. Advances in regenerative medicine and stem-cell therapies, allowing the replacement of kidneys, livers, retinas, nerves, muscle tissue and bones, keep on coming. The use of transcranial magnetic stimulation has made a massive difference to stroke victims or people suffering from depression or Alzheimers.

Different countries have dealt with the ethical implications of these medical advances in very different ways. Many have followed California's example in setting up Citizens' Panels – not least to hold scientists and politicians to account on behalf of future generations. Fears that these advances would be used to create a 'super race', or further oppress ethnic minorities, have not been borne out.

But what such advances have done is to divide the world, all over again, into the 'haves' (those who can pay for some of these startlingly expensive interventions) and the 'have-nots' – the vast majority of people, who can't afford them.

In this regard, we're all watching with fascination to see how well the 'Scandinavian model' will work out in practice. In Scandinavian countries, once a particular procedure has been approved that cannot be paid for via ordinary tax-funded health services, then individuals can use their own money to buy that procedure – but only if they are prepared to fund the same procedure for one other person (selected

The man who came to be known as 'Mr Re-gen', running the New York Marathon in 2031. With two new kidneys, a regenerated spinal cord, trachea and pancreas, one prosthetic hand, enhanced vision and both testicles fully regenerated, he was lionized by the media as the world's first truly bionic marathon runner.

via a simple lottery process). As Norway's prime minister said at the end of last year, 'It may be bureaucratic, and even a bit harsh for the individuals involved, but what's the alternative? A world in which a rich elite buy their way into longer, healthier lives, while the rest of us look on in envy? That's not how we do things in Norway.'

And we shouldn't get this out of proportion: it's still only a tiny fraction of people who can extend their lives in this way. And however long we're living, it still matters far more whether we're living with dignity and a good quality of life. So perhaps it's not too surprising that the debate about the right to a good death (in terms of assisted suicide and voluntary euthanasia) became more and more intense throughout the 2020s and 2030s as the difference between 'increased life expectancy' and 'increased healthy life expectancy' became ever sharper. A whole new movement emerged all around the world to advance what they saw as the 'inalienable right for people of sound mind to determine for themselves the timing and the manner of their own death'.

Here in the UK, Dignity in Death recruited more than two million supporters for this campaign over a five-year period between 2021 and 2026. The Church of England and many other religious bodies were split down the middle. Medical opinion was equally divided – as were the media. But by the end of the decade, with public opinion running at more than 75 per cent in favour of voluntary euthanasia, a strictly controlled but definitive right to die was passed into law at the end of 2028.

22.12.2050

The Great Turning

So that's that: a fleeting snapshot of some of the things that have transformed our lives over the last 30 years or so. At many points during the last year, I've kept thinking back to when I was their age, about to leave school in 2018, full of hope at the prospect of becoming a teacher, but also with the deepest apprehension.

So would I rather be 18 today than back in 2018? You bet I would! For all the threats the future still holds – and I've done my level best not to gloss over those – most people seem to think that we're through the worst. In effect, we've witnessed a momentous turning away from a model of progress that threatened to drag us all down with it.

Looking back on the way that people were talking about the prospects for humankind at the turn of the century, anyone suggesting that we'd be where we are now would have been dismissed as totally unrealistic. Almost without exception, commentators at that time assumed that we'd remain at each other's throats, and that nationalism, tribalism and xenophobia would make it impossible for us to work cooperatively as a species – across all the other divides that separate us.

Once we realized that we could only combat the threat of runaway climate change by working together, as one human family, we discovered something extraordinary: we were never 'hard-wired' by our genetic inheritance to kill each other off. 'A war of all against all' is not the natural state of humankind. In fact, we're actually hard-wired to work together, to make better lives for ourselves and our families, for our friends and our 'tribes', and then, when we can, for everyone else. We're every bit as cooperative as we are competitive, every bit as altruistic as we are selfish. If we are predisposed to anything, we're predisposed to empathy.

And science has played its part here too. The last 40 years have seen remarkable advances in our understanding of neurotransmitters like serotonin and the various endorphins. These 'feel-good' chemicals are now proactively managed to help reduce stress or addictive cravings, to enhance our immune systems, and to improve our memory and learning – often in conjunction with oxytocin.

With uncanny timing, after 35 years of learned scientific debate, the Global Union of Science Academies issued its final determination just a month ago that we are now officially living in a different geological epoch. The Holocene has gone. Welcome to the Anthropocene!

Here's how WikIDD (Wiki's Instant Demystification for Dummies) told the story yesterday:

The Holocene epoch (10,000 BCE to 2050) was an extraordinarily stable time from a climate point of view – and the human species prospered accordingly.

From around 15,000 years ago, our Palaeolithic ancestors were already having an impact on the natural world, as the use of fire and primitive tools allowed them to clear significant stretches of forest. But that process speeded up around 8,000 years ago, when tribes stopped moving around and started farming in one place: modern agriculture in the making.

And then, just a couple of thousand years ago, we learned how to dig up all the fossil fuels laid down millions of years before – and that was the beginning of the end for the Holocene.

Whether we like it or not, we've fundamentally transformed the way the world works, and our destiny now lies primarily in our own hands. Nothing else will sort it out. So the Holocene is dead – long live the Anthropocene!

EMPATHY

Empathy is all about recognition and response: being able to identify with what someone else is thinking or feeling, and then to respond to their thoughts and feelings with an appropriate emotion.

It's the power of 'as if', seeing someone else's situation or joy or suffering, as if it were one's own.

This simple understanding lies at the heart of our educational system today: enabling all young people to care about the world they live in — and the people who share it with them.

Well known as a hormone released during childbirth and breastfeeding, oxytocin was gradually synthesized for use as an empathy enhancer, encouraging people to behave more generously and trustingly. Many continue to see it as something that provides the hormonal equivalent of the Golden Rule of morality: 'Do unto others as you would have done unto you'. Its usage became very widespread during the 2020s and 2030s, although there are some commentators who still argue that even this kind of 'virtuous circle' (with oxytocin helping to enhance empathy, which in turn reinforces more moral behaviours, which in turn builds trust, which in turn promotes the release of oxytocin) is just another form of 'chemical manipulation'.

As it happens, we hear rather less about oxytocin these days. Most people get as much of a high from walking in the park, gardening, or just sitting under a tree. Marika told us the other day that Japan's new (and quite amazing) urban woodlands are based on a very old concept of *shinrin-yoku* – which translates literally as 'wood-air-breathing'. Scientists have demonstrated how positively our senses respond to all those subtle compounds 'breathed out' by the trees and breathed in by us – although I tend to see it as more about enriching the human spirit than stimulating chemical pathways in the brain.

But it is indeed science and technology that have opened up the world to allow empathy to flourish. Two things made that possible.

First, <u>the internet</u>: effortless, ubiquitous connectivity for every single one of us – that's what we have today. There are still all those national borders, walls, barriers, no-go-zones and keep-out taboos, but for the students I have shared this project with, they simply don't let those barriers get in the way of what they want to do. They go anywhere, anytime, with anyone, and seem ready to share everything.

The internet is still the greatest destroyer of barriers, and the greatest enemy of dictators. Especially in Africa, where a combination of fibre-optics and satellite broadband transformed the continent, enabling free and fair voting systems, a people's 'war on corruption' and hugely improved education and healthcare systems.

The second thing is the <u>solar revolution</u>. It's not just that solar energy is clean and cheap; it's also <u>ours</u>. Reserves of oil, coal and gas were owned either by governments or by big multinationals. As owners, they exploited those sources of energy for their own national interests and for profit. Sunshine isn't like that: it's 'owned' by the whole of humankind, to be used in the interests of every single citizen on Earth. Which makes solar the greatest ever technological leveller in the history of humankind, bearing down on those divides between the haves and have-nots.

There are many, many other reasons why it's made such good sense to reduce the economic divides between the rich and poor over the last few decades. Empathy doesn't work if everybody is too busy looking after number one at everybody else's expense. The more unequal a country is, the less content, settled and sharing its people are. Injustice corrodes the human spirit; it always has done, and it always will.

Sadly, our world is still full of people arguing the case for privilege and for economic policies which reinforce the divisions between rich and poor. We'll never be rid of such people (that's diversity for you!), but they seem to matter less and less in economies that benefit increasingly from people working together, rather than working against each other.

Kids today just 'get' that. They look back in horror at the way in which we lived earlier in the century. In working on this project with my Research Team, I'm convinced that there's never been a generation more focused on doing the right thing for people today and for people tomorrow. This thought fills me with hope.

When I was training to be a teacher, we had a brilliant psychology professor who was part of a pioneering movement at that time to focus public policy on the early years of a child's life. His words about what children need have stayed with me throughout my life as a teacher: 'Limitless love, total security and lots of fun and games – forget the rest! If it's a better world we're after, just make sure that every child reaches the age of six feeling radiantly happy.'

We're not there yet, I'm sorry to say, but we're making good progress.

This is one of our favourite videowall settings – a beech forest in Japan that Marika knows well. It provides us with a bit of virtual 'wood-air-breathing', as it were.

'The World We Made' is dedicated to all those amazing individuals and organizations already striving to create a sustainable world.

As Samuel Beckett said:
'Ever tried. Ever failed. No matter. Try again. Fail again. Fail better.'

Until we succeed.

Looking Forward

'The World We Made' is written from the future, looking back to today.

Here, we look forward to 2050 and to how we can make a difference today and help achieve a more sustainable world.

Postscript by Jonathon Porritt

So much for the world of Alex McKay. Back to today's reality!

2050 does sometimes seem a very long way away. But the more I've dug down into what actually has to happen (in terms of the practical changes required) to get us to a more or less sustainable world by 2050, the clearer it's become that it won't be possible to make it happen any faster. Even 2050 will seem completely impossible to those who are still stuck in the land of 'business as usual', moving forever at the speed of whichever power broker in the system has the most to lose by moving any faster. By contrast, for many of my colleagues (who sometimes fear that it may already be too late), 2050 is still much too far away.

Picking an arbitrary date like 2050 is somewhat meaningless: it will take as long as it takes, and we really don't have a clue how long that is. The pace of change over the next 40 years will be determined as much by those things it's completely impossible to predict as by those that I've had a crack at predicting. And unfortunately, as history all too gloomily tells us, I suspect that it will be the unpredictable shocks, rather than the more predictable opportunities, that will have the bigger impact on what happens.

For me, writing this book has been a big deal. It has powerfully reinforced my belief that securing a genuinely sustainable world for around nine billion people by 2050 is still possible; I wouldn't be wasting my time, let alone yours, if I didn't believe that.

And, like any parent, I see all this as much through the eyes of my children as through my own eyes. I was born in 1950, so for me personally 2050 is a bit academic – although I guess I'm looking forward to a little bit of that regenerative medicine to keep me going! But it's far from academic for our daughters (who are aged 21 and 24 at the time of writing), let alone for any children they may have.

Surprisingly, perhaps, having been involved in the world of sustainability for 40 years, my own emotional state in relation to how we are doing is still pretty confused. Most of the time, I'm more angry than I dare describe. Seeing this beautiful planet of ours systematically abused, day after day, and seeing the misery of billions of people constantly ignored, day after day, gets harder and harder to bear. How dare we continue to live like this?

But at the same time, I'm more excited about the prospects for us learning to live sustainably on this planet than I've ever been before – and it's technology that's made the difference.

I'm reasonably persuaded that we already have everything we need, technologically, to get the job done – just about. And when you start looking into the 'innovation pipeline' for every single one of the crucial areas (energy, water, raw materials, waste, manufacturing), it's clear that the answers are all there.

Inevitably, however, this makes me pretty frustrated that relatively few people share this excitement – especially those people in places where it would really make a difference, including our politicians. When it comes to working out what a genuinely sustainable future might look like, most of our politicians (whatever their party may be) seem disinclined even to try. They're hopelessly trapped by what's happened over the last few years since the 2008 crash, and disempowered by the 'perfect storm' scenario bearing down upon them. That makes it a wretched time to be trying to get today's political classes to think beyond the next election.

But I've also been very struck by how often people say to me, 'I just can't see what a sustainable world would really look like'. How will we live, work, play, eat, save, sleep, travel, get born, get old, get high in 2050? Will it be better or worse than today? Will it be all sackcloth and ashes or high-tech eco-fixes?

I can't pretend it's been possible to provide enough of an insight on such questions in this one volume, but I hope it might encourage others to do an even better job. Because that's the only way we're likely to make faster progress: yet more tales of doom and gloom are not going to make any difference. It's so much easier, after all, for our politicians to stick with the devils they know.

And those devils often do have all the best tunes – as I've learned to my cost. After 20 years of battling it out with my go-to bête noire, Jeremy Clarkson, I have to admit that I'm somewhat in awe of his ability to keep on selling the delights of a way of life that is so clearly heading for the abyss! It all seems so uncomplicated for Clarkson. He just loves speed, big cars, black-and-white certainties, money and high-octane engineers like Isambard Kingdom Brunel – all based on the assumption that our earth-trashing fantasia can just go on and on forever.

Although I too have huge admiration for engineers like Brunel, I feel much more ambivalent about offering up what is in essence a 'technotopia' – a partial-utopia made available to us primarily because of the extraordinary technological breakthroughs that are now unfolding in our midst. It's not an ideal world I've conjured up in 2050, but it does at least provide a vision of the future that doesn't entail the near-total collapse of everything we hold dear in our lives today.

I hope the balance of ideas in 'The World We Made' makes it abundantly clear that such a technotopia is not a panacea. It doesn't even deliver many of the things I care most passionately about: a world in which today's vicious gaps between the rich and the poor are dramatically reduced; in which our love of nature can be sustained without having to put a monetary value on it; and a world in which every child starts out with at least even odds of getting to the age of six still feeling loved, valued and protected. But what I hope it does deliver is the prospect of some breathing space, to be able to go on working away at those and other precious causes.

If we can't deliver the necessarily limited vision of a better world mapped out in 'The World We Made', then the harsh truth is that no other vision will be available to us anyway, on any terms. That's the 'do it now or else' horror story that I wouldn't want to be forgotten.

If that dystopian side of things is still there in the background, the foreground is very different. It's a vibrant, dynamic, risky, innovation-driven transition that I've tried to capture. It has absolutely nothing to do with sacrifice, settling for second best or seizing the moral high ground – all the better to look down on those perfectly content just to muddle along.

And it takes seriously Ray Kurzweil's Law of Accelerating Returns, first outlined in 1999, which tells us that we already have at our disposal the intellectual and technological fire power to stop thinking in slow, linear, incremental terms. Step changes in practically every area of our life are available to us right now. The bottom line is this: should we so wish, we can still move to address today's converging crises faster than the speed at which those crises threaten to overwhelm us.

I attribute a lot of this residual hopefulness to the work that I and my colleagues are privileged to do through Forum for the Future – which is always challenging, always solution-focused, always seeking out angles that keep at bay the comfortable cynicism of those who've given up anyway. And those attributes are particularly true of 'Green Futures' – Forum for the Future's flagship publication, and its wellspring of hope. Many of the ideas, people and initiatives that I'm encouraging you to get excited about in this book surfaced first in 'Green Futures'. So I defy anyone to give up completely on our prospects for a 'soft sustainability landing' without first having had a look at 'Green Futures'!

Amongst the many reasons to be cheerful about our prospects is the growing readiness of people to do what they can personally to make a difference. This might be a small thing when set against the immensity of the challenge in hand, but it all adds up. Small actions multiplied many, many times over can make a big difference. So for each of the 50 entries I've made a few suggestions, where it's appropriate, about relevant actions, organizations and connections (see p.280).

Of course, even modest hopefulness about the future becomes its own worst enemy if it isn't true to the reality of what's happening on the ground. In that regard, the gap between what is actually happening and what needs to happen remains deeply disturbing. Windows of opportunity don't stay open forever – and this one does seem to be closing fast.

'The World We Made' is just one of many initiatives seeking to keep open that window of opportunity for as long as we can, inspired both by the genius of our species and by the countless individuals already dedicated to making that possible.

About Forum for the Future

Forum for the Future was established in 1996 – specifically to help accelerate our journey towards a more sustainable world. Jonathon Porritt is Forum's Founder Director and a Trustee.

At Forum, we don't just cover the environment: sustainable development is just as much about society, economics and ethics – hence the very wide range of issues covered in 'The World We Made'.

We are a registered charity (or 'non-profit' in US terms) that works globally with business, government and others to help solve some of today's truly 'wicked issues'. We have a particular focus on today's food, energy and finance systems – the problems we face are indeed big and systemic, and can't just be sorted out at the organizational level.

Futures is a big part of the work we do. While we can't predict the future, we can think more about the sort of future we want and how to achieve it.

At Forum, we help organizations understand the systems they operate in and the potential impacts of global trends like climate change, economic transformation, population growth and emerging technology. We use a range of techniques to help them think in a useful and structured way about the future, to challenge their assumptions about the world, to navigate risk and seize opportunity.

We do this through our advisory work, our educational work (including our Masters Programme) and our communications work – particularly 'Green Futures'.

<u>All royalties from the sale of this book go to support the work of Forum for the Future.</u>

To find out more about our work, go to www.forumforthefuture.org

A Sustainable Book

This book is printed on 100 per cent recycled, FSC® recycled certified paper. It is completely recyclable and its carbon footprint is only 1.8kg CO_2 emissions per book.

More than two million titles are published every year globally. That's a hell of a lot of paper, a lot of chemicals, ink, water, energy, and a lot of CO_2 emissions! CO_2 emissions per book can vary enormously depending on the kind of paper used, the printing process, distances involved and so on. The average (for the USA) is around 4kg of CO_2 per book, roughly two thirds of which is attributable to the forestry end of things, and one third to paper production, printing, binding and distribution.

Given that, I'm often asked by a lot of people if I believe that physical books will still be around in 2050 or will everything have been 'dematerialized' for e-readers? As far as I'm concerned, there's nothing like the look, the feel and even the smell of a real book. But it's clear that for some books, going digital makes a lot of sense from a sustainability perspective and, maybe in the future, to reach a wider readership. That said, I'm equally clear that printed books will still have an important place in a sustainable world. We should still aspire to making, and passing down, real books, whose physicality works to enhance their content. So much that's digital is so ephemeral – and sustainability is about making things that are both beautiful and durable.

So it was particularly important to me that this book should reflect the highest sustainability standards. Working with Pureprint Group and Arjowiggins Graphic has made it possible to meet almost all of our ambitions in that regard. These two suppliers really understand sustainability, and have embedded it into their businesses and the products they manufacture. Pureprint received the UK's leading sustainable business award, the Queen's Award for Enterprise: Sustainable Development in 2003, 2008 and 2013, and Arjowiggins is the leading producer of high quality recycled fibre and paper in Europe – rated first in the WWF's Paper Company Environmental Index (Fine Paper).

Paper

Arjowiggins turned waste paper into high-grade pulp and then into the four different papers used in 'The World We Made' in their mills in France. The papers (Cocoon Offset, Cocoon Silk, Cyclus Offset, Cyclus Print) were delivered to Pureprint in East Sussex, UK, where all production took place before despatch to warehouses in the UK, USA and Australia. By printing this book on 100 per cent recycled papers the environmental impact was reduced by 17,120kg of landfill, 371,887 litres of water, 35,013kWh of electricity, 3,105kg of CO_2 and greenhouse gases, and 27,817kg of wood.*

Printing

All inks were made from vegetable-based oils not mineral oils, no isopropyl alcohol was used during printing to reduce ground-level ozone, the papers have high bulk and low weight to reduce resource use and distribution, and the printers and paper mills are audited to ISO 14001, EMAS (printers), EU Ecolabel (paper mills) and FSC® standards.

Carbon footprint

This book has been designed and produced to minimize its carbon footprint. The remaining carbon emissions have been assessed by The CarbonNeutral Company at 29,022kg,* and have been offset through climate and development experts ClimateCare with an investment in the LifeStraw Carbon for Water Project in Kenya's Western Province – a UN-endorsed project that cuts carbon and improves the lives of more than four and a half million people, providing them with safe water, creating jobs and saving them money on fuel bills (for further details visit ClimateCare's website: www.climatecare.org). In producing this book the following carbon emissions were created:

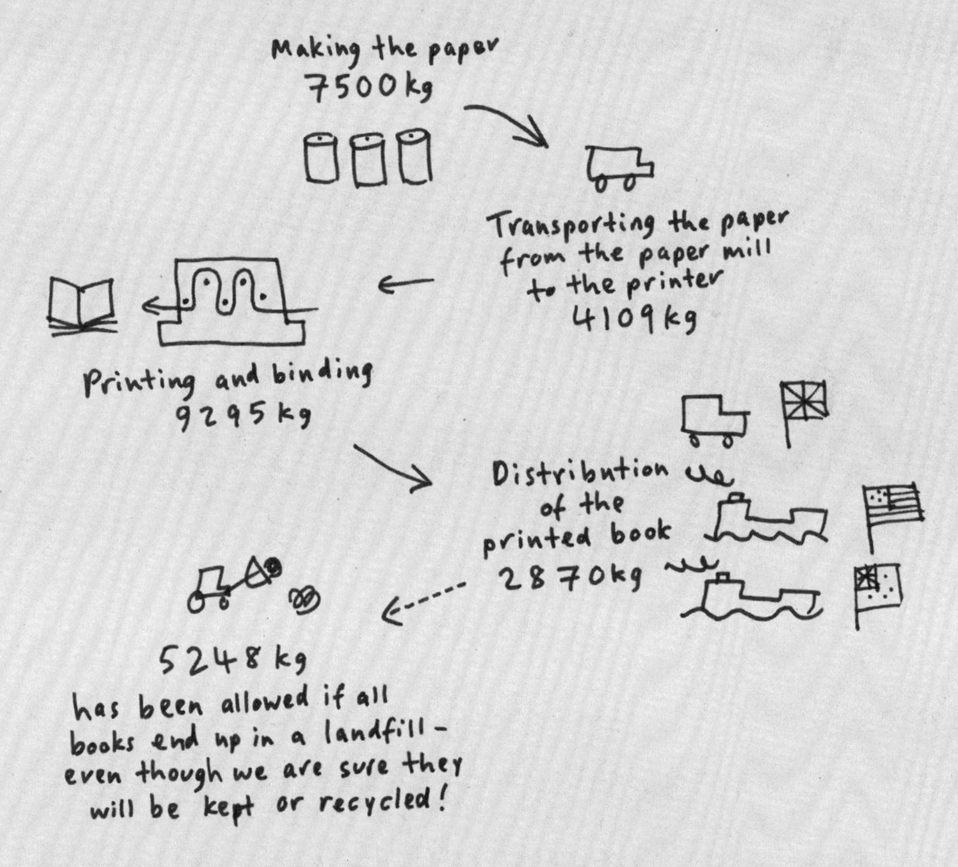

*Source: Carbon footprint data evaluated by FactorX in accordance with the Bilan Carbone® methodology. Reduction of carbon emissions from paper calculations are based on a comparison between the recycled paper used versus a virgin fibre paper according to the latest European BREF data (virgin fibre paper) available

Connections & Inspirations

The issues I've been grappling with in 'The World We Made' are vast and daunting – runaway climate change, the future of capitalism, collapsing eco-systems, unpredictable technology shifts and so on. The sheer scale of these things tends to obscure all the astonishing initiatives already going on out there to help put the world to rights.

So in this section, I'm keen to give the briefest of introductions to some of the organizations and individuals currently 'on the front line' of that worldwide movement for change.

Find out more at www.forumforthefuture.org/theworldwemade

- Organizations
- Books
- Websites
- Films

Introduction

If the idea of a sustainable world means anything to the vast majority of us, it means better lives for people all around the world, in secure, convivial communities providing good education, rewarding work and a clean, green environment.

As Alex points out in the Introduction, there are more and more people who now believe that this kind of simple vision may already be unattainable – primarily because of the damage we've already done to our planet.

The one big idea behind this whole project is that it's not too late: such a vision is still attainable. Obviously governments and business have a role in making that a reality rather than a dream, but a lot of it still comes down to each and every one of us. It's no good urging others to change without doing everything we can to be the change ourselves.

10:10: cutting carbon 10% at a time
www.1010global.org

Global Action Plan
www.globalactionplan.org.uk

The Co-operative (Join the Revolution)
www.co-operative.coop/join-the-revolution

B&Q Street Club
www.streetclub.co.uk/about

KIVA
www.kiva.org

NeighborGoods
www.neighborgoods.net

Ecomodo
www.ecomodo.com

Freecycle
www.freecycle.net

Roo Rogers and Rachel Botsman, 'What's Mine is Yours: The Rise of Collaborative Consumption' (Harper Collins, 2011)

P15 → Solar Revolutions

Solar power is one of the most exciting technologies in the world today – and it works both at the very big scale (as you saw from those visuals) and at the very small scale (on your roof, for instance).

Because there are still no penalty charges for all the CO_2 that today's fossil fuels are putting into the atmosphere, many governments are providing financial support for solar power and other renewables – basically to help level the playing field.

You'd need to check out what support is available in your own country, and then find a reliable source of information if you're thinking about installing some PV or solar water heaters on your roof.

A good starting place for information in the UK is the Solar Trade Association:
www.solar-trade.org.uk

The Renewable Energy Association has lots of useful information as well:
www.r-e-a.net

As does the European Solar Thermal Electricity Association: www.estelasolar.eu

In the USA, check out:
The Business Alliance for Local Living Economies
www.bealocalist.org

American Council on Renewable Energy
www.acore.org

One of the best-known providers of PV products is Solarcentury:
www.solarcentury.co.uk

Solarcentury also set up Solar Aid, a brilliant charity for making PV available to those who need it most in less well-off countries.
www.solar-aid.org

Finally, Desertec is for real! Check out its inspirational website at www.desertec.org

Jeremy Leggett, 'The Solar Century' (Profile Books, 2009)

P22 → Water – a Matter of Life and Death

Droughts and severe water shortages are much more commonplace these days – just think of how it was in both the USA and the UK in 2012! Australia's most recent drought went on for eight years, and much of China's best agricultural land is in a near-permanent state of water shortage.

But all that seems bearable compared with the lives of hundreds of millions of people for whom not having enough water is their daily reality. So at last we're beginning to take water much more seriously – which, hopefully, will help avoid anything quite as awful as is imagined here.

As is so often the case, what we can do as individuals seems small compared with the immensity of this challenge. But it all adds up!

Both the WaterWise website www.waterwise.org.uk and H2house www.h2ouse.org provide all the information you might need to start saving water. There's a rich array of designs and technologies available to help.

There are many organizations doing great work to help people elsewhere in the world to meet their water needs.

H2O for Life
www.h2oforlifeschools.org

Water Aid (an excellent source of up-to-date reports on water and sanitation issues)
www.wateraid.org

Water.org (a highly respected US-based non-profit)
www.water.org

Blue Planet Network
www.blueplanetnetwork.org

Worldwatch Institute
www.worldwatch.org

Fred Pearce, 'Keepers of the Spring'
(Ireland Press, 2004)

Lester R. Brown, 'World on the Edge: How to Prevent Environmental and Economic Collapse'
(W.W. Norton, 2011)

P28 → Internet Wars

The world today is still divided between its 'digital natives', who've lived most or all of their lives immersed in IT and social media, and those for whom these new technologies remain just a little bit strange.

It's impossible to predict where this rolling internet revolution will have taken us by 2050: even forecasts for the next decade sometimes seem outlandish in terms of the scale and intensity of change.

But I imagine some things will still be very familiar even then – not least the constant struggle over the uses to which the technologies are put, by citizens, governments and business. Today's battle over the right to privacy gives us a tiny taste of what's still to come.

Happily, there are a number of organizations that are intent on protecting our digital rights.

Electronic Frontier Foundation (San Francisco)
www.eff.org

American Civil Liberties Union
www.aclu.org

Global Network Initiative
www.globalnetworkinitiative.org

Open Democracy
www.opendemocracy.net

Global Voices
globalvoices.org

Pew Research Centre: The Future of the Internet
www.pewinternet.org

Adbusters
www.adbusters.org

'On the Darknet Project:
www.arstechnica.com/information-technology/2011/11/the-darknet-plan-netroots-activists-dream-of-global-mesh-network/

Clay Shirky, 'Here Comes Everybody'
(Allen Lane, 2008)

Evgeny Morozov, 'The Net Delusion: The Dark Side of Internet Freedom' (Penguin, 2012)

P32 → Enough!

There's a simple enough story here: we'll never get to live in a more sustainable world unless it's also a more fair and equitable world. That may be 'an inconvenient truth' for those who don't want to hear it, but it's the truth for all that. And it's a message that I believe more and more young people are attuned to – in a way that promises much in terms of future political engagement.

There are countless organizations all around the world campaigning for social justice in one form or another. Some will be right up your street; others a bridge too far. Getting stuck in is what matters.

Avaaz is an amazing network for activists, and it's notched up some real triumphs over the years: www.avaaz.org

The Equality Trust
www.equalitytrust.org.uk

World Changing
www.worldchanging.com

One Young World
www.oneyoungworld.com

The Center for a New American Dream
www.newdream.org

Rebuild the Dream
www.rebuildthedream.com

Occupy Wall Street
www.occupywallst.org

Fair Elections Now
www.action.fairelectionsnow.org

If you're are up for some serious reading on the impact of inequality on society in general, 'The Spirit Level' by Richard Wilkinson and Kate Pickett (Penguin, 2010) is an extraordinary book.

Paul Hawken, 'Blessed Unrest' (Penguin, 2008). Even though it's a bit old now, it provides an inspiring snapshot of civil society around the world.

Tim Gee, 'Counterpower'
(New Internationalist, 2011)

'Dare to Change: Environmental Justice, Leadership for Climate Justice, Sustainable Communities and a Deep Green Economy' (Movement Strategy Center, 2010)
www.movementbuilding.movementstrategy.org/resources

P37 → The End of the Age of Oil

Of all of the projections I've used in this book, I suspect it's this one that may cause more eyebrows to be raised than any other. From 76 million barrels of oil a day to just 4 million barrels by 2050: you cannot be serious!

I believe that huge reductions in our use of oil are going to happen – not because we're actually running out of the stuff, but because it gets more and more expensive to get every new barrel out of the ground. Just as it gets more and more risky – as I flagged up in 'The Law Steps Up' (see p.228), where I forecast a disaster in the Russian Arctic. And all that before we begin to think about climate change!

All of which means the alternatives (whether it's biofuels or electric vehicles) are already starting to compete with oil.

350.org
www.350.org

Greenpeace
www.greenpeace.org

Post Carbon Institute
www.postcarbon.org

Association for the Study of Peak Oil and Gas (ASPO)
www.peakoil.net

SymbioCity
www.symbiocity.org

David Strahan, 'The Last Oil Shock' (Murray, 2007)
www.lastoilshock.com

Amory Lovins, 'A Farewell to Fossil Fuels: Answering the Energy Challenge' (Rocky Mountain Institute, 2012) www.rmi.org/Knowledge-Center/Library/2012-01_FarewellToFossilFuels

'Dirty Oil' (Leslie Iwerks, 2009)

P42 → It's All In Our Genes

This is the first of three entries on health – it's such a critical part of what a more sustainable world might look like. Yet in many ways, the health sector today is just about the most conservative and resistant to change of any the different sectors that I've covered.

Many people now believe that personalized genetic data will provide the spur that will change all that, and accelerate a process of change that has been absent until now. It all sounds very high tech, but in the end it all comes down to how we live as individuals – and in particular, how we eat and how we exercise.

When it comes to diet, although deciding whether to eat meat is a personal issue, it's also a massively important global factor when considering climate change, water shortages, land use and so on.

The Personal Genome Project
www.personalgenomes.org

Compassion in World Farming
www.ciwf.org.uk

The In Vitro Meat Consortium
www.invitromeat.org

Diabetes UK
www.diabetes.org.uk

People for the Ethical Treatment of Animals (PETA)
www.peta.org

Eleanor Boyle, 'High Steaks' (New Society Publishers, 2012)
www.highsteaksbook.com

Marion Nestle, 'Food Politics and What to Eat' (North Point Press, 2007)

Robert Lustig, 'Fat Chance: Beating the Odds against Sugar, Processed Food, Obesity, and Disease' (Hudson Street Press, 2012)

Lester R. Brown, 'Full Planet, Empty Plates' (W.W. Norton. 2012)

Jacky Turner and Joyce D'Silva, 'Animals, Ethics and Trade' (Earthscan, 2006)

'Sugar: The Bitter Truth' (Robert Lustig, 2009)
Www.youtube.com

P48 → Houston Concord on Climate Change

The US signing up to a legally binding agreement to reduce emissions of greenhouse gases by 90 per cent by 2050 – does this seem far-fetched? In fact, it really could happen! Two US Senators (Cantwell and Collins) first introduced a version of what I've called the Cap and Prosper Bill back in 2010. A coalition of US environmental organizations said at the time, 'No other proposal does as much to help American families, our economy and our planet'.

As to the projected change of heart on the part of the majority of US citizens, who knows? Once people start linking weather and climate, anything could happen.

Cleantech Group, Princeton University
www.cleantech.com

On the Commons (a 'commons' strategy centre that brings together stakeholders around certain issues). They run the 'cap and dividend' project.
www.onthecommons.org
www.onthecommons.org/cap-and-dividend-solution

Clean Edge Inc (dedicated clean-tech market research firm)
www.cleanedge.com

Environmental Defense Fund
www.edf.org

The Natural Resources Defense Council
www.nrdc.org

On the Commons
www.onthecommons.org

'The Energy Report: 100% renewable energy by 2050', (WWF, 2011)
www.wwf.org.uk

'Low Carbon Environmental Goods & Services 2010', BIS report (2012)
www.gov.uk

P54 → Companies, Cooperatives and Consumption

The business world is an interesting place right now: on the one hand, some important leadership on sustainability issues is emerging from dozens of big global companies; on the other, we still see too many examples of corporate greed and ruthless business practices – and not just in the banking sector. Businesses, large and small, are the lifeblood of our economy, so we need them all to be raising their game on sustainability.

One of the issues we often confront in our work at Forum for the Future is what will happen to multinational companies. Will they even exist in 2050? I'm suggesting that they will, but they'll be playing a very different role from today.

In the meantime, we can look forward to the continuing growth of the global cooperative movement.

B Lab (B corps)
www.bcorporation.net

The New Economy Working Group
www.neweconomyworkinggroup.org

Tellus Institute
www.tellus.org

International Co-operative Alliance
www.2012.coop

Co-operatives UK
www.uk.coop

Tim Mohin, 'Changing Business from the Inside Out' (Greenleaf Publishing, 2012)

Juliet Schor, 'Plenitude: The New Economics of True Wealth' (Penguin Books, 2010)

Richard Branson, 'Screw Business as Usual' (Virgin Books, 2011)

John Elkington, 'The Zeronauts' (Routledge, 2012)

P58 → Nuclear Power's Last Gasp

It sometimes seems as if the debate about nuclear power just goes round and round on the same old circuit – but there's a good reason for that.

If we make the wrong decision on nuclear power – that is, if we give it one last chance – everything we need to do to decarbonize the economy and ensure lasting security of energy supplies will be seriously jeopardized. And whilst I appreciate that the industry never wants to talk about the threat of nuclear terrorism, in one form or another, that threat is real – and many people close to the security issues are astonished that we haven't already had a serious incident.

I am hoping that more and more people will just give up on these nuclear fantasies, so that we know exactly where we stand on energy efficiency, renewables, smart grids and so on.

Friends of the Earth
www.foei.org

Greenpeace
www.greenpeace.org

Campaign for Nuclear Disarmament (CND)
www.cnduk.org

International Campaign to Abolish Nuclear Weapons (ICAN)
www.icanw.org

World Nuclear Association
www.world-nuclear.org

Mycle Schneider, Anthony Froggatt, Julie Hazeman, 'The World Nuclear Industry Status Report 2012' (2012)
www.worldnuclearreport.org

Sean McDonagh, 'Fukushima: the Death Knell for Nuclear Energy?' (Columba Press, 2012)

Amory Lovins, 'The Essential Amory Lovins: Selected Writings', (Earthscan 2011)

P62 → Spiritual Militancy

I am sure some people will question why there's an entry here on faith and religion, but I've learned over the years that the way we see things in the UK is far from typical. The world outside the UK is still predominantly faith-based, and the fact that the major faiths are not really talking a lead on the challenges of sustainability is both a big problem and, from my point of view, an even bigger opportunity.

What's at stake here is the gap between large numbers of committed individuals with a strong faith base and the failure on the part of the leaders of those faiths to show the kind of collective leadership that is now required. Hence the Lhasa Declaration!

ARC (Alliance of Religions and Conservation)
www.arcworld.org

UN/ARC Seven Year Plans for Generational Change
Read about it at www.arcworld.org

A Rocha
www.arocha.org

Operation Noah
www.operationnoah.org

The Conservation Foundation
www.conservationfoundation.co.uk

Interfaith Declaration on Climate Change, 2011
www.interfaithdeclaration.org

Sustainability in Crisis (faith and sustainability)
www.sustainabilityincrisis.wordpress.com/

Assisi Declaration, 1986
www.arcworld.org

'Beyond Belief', WWF/ARC document (WWF/ARC, 2006)
www.arcworld.org

'Moving Mountains' special edition of 'Green Futures' magazine, July 2011
www.forumforthefuture.org/greenfutures/shop/special-edition/moving-mountains

Chris Philpott, 'Green Spirituality' (AuthorHouse, 2011)

Tristram Stuart, 'Waste' (Penguin Books, 2009)

P67 → The Material World

Everywhere you look, new ideas and technologies are beginning to make a huge difference via the idea of a 'circular economy' – where waste is either minimized or eliminated. And I have to admit that this is the sort of thing that has restored my faith in innovation.

The degree to which we either find waste acceptable (as we seem to today) or are appalled by it (as we were for a 20-year period after the Second World War) is shaped by complex cultural and economic factors. I just hope we're now moving into one of those periods where, once again, waste becomes completely unacceptable.

There are now many more possibilities for finding rental alternatives to personal consumption – car clubs, for example. And in the last few years we've also seen an explosion in peer-to-peer exchange and sharing platforms.

Collaborative Consumption
www.collaborativeconsumption.com

Better Cotton Initiative
www.bettercotton.org

M&S Shwopping
www.plana.marksandspencer.com/about/partnerships/oxfam/shwopping

Worn Again
www.wornagain.co.uk

Swapstyle
www.swapstyle.com

B&Q Streetclub
www.streetclub.co.uk

Enough Project (Washington DC)
www.enoughproject.org

FairPhone (Netherlands)
www.fairphone.com

WRAP
www.wrap.org.uk

Michael Braungart and William McDonough, 'Cradle to Cradle: Remaking the Way We Make Things' (Vintage Books, 2009)

'Towards the Circular Economy', Ellen MacArthur Foundation report (Vol. 1, 2012, Vol. 2, 2013)
www.ellenmacarthurfoundation.org/circular-economy

P74 → Restoring the Web of Life

The world is not short of people who really care about nature – people in every country, not just the many millions who support conservation groups and NGOs in the rich world. The growth in concern about the natural world has been one of the defining features of the last 40 years.

But the campaigning challenges around biodiversity are as pressing today as they have ever been, as the parlous state of the honey bee has recently demonstrated. That's why the work of organizations like WWF, Conservation International, Sierra Club, Pesticides Action Network and the Soil Association remains so important.

There's a lot we can do here as individuals, by minimizing our carbon footprint, reducing our paper consumption and thinking carefully about the impact on the natural world of what we buy (with wood products, for example) or where we go on holiday.

WWF
www.wwf.org

Soil Association
www.soilassociation.org

The International Ecotourism Society
www.ecotourism.org

WildLab
www.thewildlab.org

BirdLife International
www.birdlife.org

Conservation International
www.conservation.org

Sierra Club
www.sierraclub.org

Pesticides Action Network UK
www.pan-uk.org

Richard Louv, 'Last Child in the Woods' (Atlantic Books, 2010)

Tony Juniper, 'What has Nature Ever Done for Us?' (Profile Books, 2013)

Alison Benjamin and Brian McCallum, 'A World Without Bees' (Guardian Books, 2008)

P79 → Education Unlimited

In all sorts of ways, today's challenge does indeed come down to education. One of the reasons why my generation of politicians and leaders has made such a mess of reconciling prosperity and sustainability is that the vast majority of them left school and university unaware of the importance of this issue. If we miss another generation, it's game over.

Moreover, there's a lot to be said for the kind of education the kids get at Ashton Vale. Back in the 1970s and 80s, I taught for nearly 10 years at a comprehensive in west London – and the best I managed to do was to sneak a few plants into my classroom! So I'm making up for things here.

UN Decade of Education for Sustainable Development www.unesco.org

UNESCO Education for All initiative www.unesco.org
Teaching and Learning for a Sustainable Future (UNESCO) www.unesco.org/education/tlsf

Think Global
www.think-global.org.uk

CO2nnect
www.co2nnect.org

WWF
www.wwf.org

One Laptop Per Child
www.olpc.com

Schools Global Gardens Network
www.globalgardens.org.uk

Gardensforlife
www.gardensforlife.com

LandShare UK
www.landshare.org

'Food Education for Sustainable Development' (Finland) www.mtt.fi

'From Green Economies to Green Societies', UNESCO document (UNESCO, 2011) www.unesdoc.unesco.org

Ken Webster and Craig Johnson, 'Sense and Sustainability' (TerraPreta, 2009)

P86 → The Great Famine

This is gloomiest entry in the book. But it needs to be there, as the chances of avoiding some kind of food mega-crisis are as close to zero as you can imagine. Not least because we're still in denial that anything quite so horrific could actually happen in the foreseeable future.

The premise here (as with a number of entries) is that only devastating crises of this kind will provide the non-negotiable pretext for change. The temptation otherwise is for world leaders just to muddle along – especially as the alternatives will be so fiercely opposed by all those with vested interests, who are currently making so much money out of undermining genuine, long-term food security.

As for Ug99, many highly respected agronomists believe it's only a matter of time before this causes major problems for wheat production. So it's best not to avert our eyes from this prospect.

But there's still a lot we can do here: buy local where possible, and buy organic or fair trade produce. Check out any local schemes (grow-your-own or veg box deliveries), and avoid fast or processed food if you possibly can.

Oxfam's agriculture campaign
www.oxfam.org/en/campaigns/agriculture

Soil Association
www.soilassociation.org

Food First
www.foodfirst.org

Slow Food
www.slowfood.com

Sustain
www.sustain.co.uk

Earth Policy Institute
www.earth-policy.org

Lester R. Brown, 'Full Planet, Empty Plates: The New Geopolitics of Food Scarcity' (W.W. Norton, 2012)

Raj Patel, 'Stuffed and Starved' (Portobello Books, 2008)

Francis Delpeuch, 'Globesity: A Planet Out of Control?' (Earthscan, 2009)

Colin Tudge, 'Good Food for Everyone Forever' (Pari Publishing, 2011)

P91 → Putting Nature to Work

The current debate about biofuels is so polarized that I know some people will find my pro-biofuels line hard to stomach. But the truth is that new technology of this kind has the potential to deliver real benefits – if we're prepared to make substantial investments.

That's why the idea of 'biofuels done well' is so important. We're not doing biofuels very well at the moment, and we need to move on from today's poor quality biofuels (of which ethanol from US maize is simply the most inadequate) to the next generation of advanced biofuels. To do that, we need today's entrepreneurs and innovators to crank up their innovation efforts – however controversial some of them may be.

Biofuelwatch (the best-informed NGO campaigning against inappropriate biofuels)
www.biofuelwatch.org.uk

Friends of the Earth
www.foei.com

Biofuels Digest
www.biofuelsdigest.com

Roundtable on Sustainable Biofuels (Switzerland)
www.rsb.org

If you're interested in what the cutting edge of biofuels research and development looks like, check out some of these:

Joule Unlimited
www.jouleunlimited.com

Green Biologics Ltd
www.greenbiologics.com

LS9
www.ls9.com

Novozymes
www.novozymes.com

Synthetic Genomics
www.syntheticgenomics.com

Butamax Advanced Biofuels
www.butamax.com

Solazyme
www.solazyme.com

Green Fuels
www.greenfuels.co.uk

P95 → Security in an Insecure World

We're all becoming more aware of the threat of cyber-terrorism: any large-scale plant, installation or system is now vulnerable to attack through its operating software. That's why so many countries are now greatly strengthening their cyber-defences.

But there's a bigger issue I wanted to grapple with here. What chance have we got of investing in those things that our world so urgently needs when we're still diverting trillions of dollars into weapons of war? As many people have pointed out over the last couple of years, we don't have that much time to completely redefine what we mean by 'national security'.

Now that the US has owned up to having used the Stuxnet virus as a deliberate cyber-attack on the Natanz uranium enrichment plant in Iran, things are likely to escalate in a disturbing way over the next few years.

But on the nuclear weapons front generally, I remain somewhat more optimistic – I even go so far as to suggest that both the UK and France will get rid of their own nuclear weapons in the not too distant future. Just wait for that moment when the Campaign for Nuclear Disarmament's most influential supporters are the armed forces themselves!

Campaign for Nuclear Disarmament (CND)
www.cnduk.org

Center for Arms Control and Non-Proliferation
www.armscontrolcenter.org

Stockholm International Peace Research Institute (SIPRI)
www.sipri.org

International Peace Institute (IPI)
www.ipacademy.org

Financial Times Cyberwarfare
www.ft.com/indepth/cyberwarfare

Tobems Cyberwar
www.tobem.com/cyberwar

P100 → Containing the Biotech Genie

We see more and more these days of the impact of the 'law of accelerating returns' – Ray Kurzweil's theory that the rate of technological change increases exponentially. It is now almost impossible to predict just how fast certain technologies will advance.

Whilst there are breathtaking positives that emerge from this speed of change, the darker side of such changes can look breathtakingly negative. Nowhere more so than with biotechnology and the potential abuse of our ability to manipulate the very stuff of life.

So this entry remains pretty ambivalent about the biotech 'genie' right to the end. Will we be able to regulate this industry in such a way as to protect ourselves from abuse – including the threat of bio-terrorism – or will the technology always be several steps ahead of the regulators?

No easy answers here, I can assure you!

ETC Group (Synthetic Biology)
www.etcgroup.org/issues/synthetic-biology

Friends of the Earth (Synthetic Biology)
www.foe.org/projects/food-and-technology/synthetic-biology

Greenpeace
www.greenpeace.org

The Federation of American Scientists
www.fas.org

Ray Kurzweil (The Law of Accelerating Returns)
www.kurzweilai.net/the-law-of-accelerating-returns

P104 → Water For All

Having given voice to both astonishment and anger at how badly we're managing our water environment today in 'Water – A Matter of Life and Death', here I wanted to show just how brilliant our response to that challenge could be.

Water is one of those areas where the innovation pipeline looks particularly hopeful – with major investments coming forward from governments, big businesses and start-up entrepreneurs. From water quality to demand management to desalination, the pace of change is brisk.

Equally, this is one of the areas where technology alone will never crack it. It's about people's mindsets – the way we think about and relate to water – and people's behaviour. The experience from the 2012 drought in Australia was that it's hard, but not impossible, to persuade people to be much more efficient in their use of water.

Oxfam (Agriculture Campaign)
www.oxfam.org

Practical Action
www.practicalaction.org

Water Aid
www.wateraid.org

Solar Spring
www.solarspring.de

Farming Solutions
www.farmingsolutions.org

Driptech
www.driptech.com

Solvatten
www.solvatten.se

P4P Energy
www.p4penergy.com

IBM Smarter Water Management
www.ibm.com/smarterplanet

Siemens: The Crystal
www.thecrystal.org

Hitachi (Intelligent Water System)
www.hitachi.com

Singapore Water Association
www.swa.org.sg

'Making Water: Desalination – option or distraction for a Thirsty World?' (WWF Report, 2007) www.waterwebster.org/documents/desalinationreportjune2007.pdf

P111 → Defusing the Population Time Bomb

I can't deny that population has been a bit of a hobby horse of mine for the last 40 years – ever since I read 'The Ecologist' magazine's 'Blueprint for Survival' in the early 1970s. As David Attenborough so succinctly puts it, 'All environmental problems become harder – and ultimately impossible – to solve with ever more people'.

However, persuading many of my colleagues to share this insight (and to campaign accordingly on the strength of it) has proved to be extraordinarily frustrating!

So I suspect that my somewhat whimsical account of how the next Pope comes to 'see the light' on the subject of artificial contraception won't go down well with a lot of people. But if you don't agree with me, you might like to check out the Royal Society report below.

The overall approach in the Royal Society's report is very well covered by an organization called The International Planned Parenthood Federation: www.ippf.org

In the UK, Population Matters provides an excellent sounding board both internationally and for the UK: www.populationmatters.org

Bill & Melinda Gates Institute for Population and Reproductive Health (John Hopkins Bloomberg School of Public Health)
www.jhsph.edu

Population Action International
www.populationaction.org

Population Council
www.popcouncil.org

The Royal Society's 2012 Report, 'People & Planet' – the product of 18 months of intensive research conducted on a global basis:
www.royalsociety.org/policy/projects

Jorgen Randers, '2052' (Earthscan, 2012)

P116 → A World Without Coal

If decarbonization is the name of the game (reducing emissions of CO_2 as fast as possible), then coal is our enemy. It's the most carbon-intensive of all the fossil fuels, and the source of many other health and environmental problems over and above its contribution to climate change. That's why I'm less worried about an increase in the use of gas, as long as this helps to shut out coal.

And if we learn how to commercialize carbon capture and storage (CCS), then using CCS with gas rather than coal makes a great deal of sense.

But, as the International Energy Agency itself has estimated, we have no more than five years or so to shift investment away from fossil fuels, putting the emphasis ever more purposefully on renewables, energy efficiency and storage. This is going to be one of the defining sustainability battlegrounds of the next decade.

Greenpeace International & UK
www.greenpeace.org

Carbon Tracker
www.carbontracker.org

Munich Re
www.munichre.com/en/group/focus/climate_change

Sierra Club/Beyond Coal
www.sierraclub.org/coal

Rising Tide
www.risingtidenorthamerica.org

Clean Energy Action
www.cleanenergyaction.org

ClimateWorks Foundation
www.climateworks.org

P123 → Minds and Machines

When I started planning this book, I honestly didn't think I'd be reading up on robots, let alone on the fascinating issue of 'augmentation' – how far can we go in adding to both our physical and our intellectual capabilities?

But these things will have a profound impact on the way we live and how we manage our health and social services, as well as on our general quality of life. And that's what makes them as much a part of the wider sustainability agenda as biodiversity or energy efficiency.

The balance between the upside and the downside, regarding both robotics and augmentation, struck me as particularly compelling. In seeking to reflect that balance, I've not gone as far as those who believe that humans and machines will merge ever more intimately over the next few decades, challenging the very notion of what it is to be a human being. And I suspect that debate will not be resolved by 2050!

Envisioning Technology
www.envisioningtech.com

IEEE Spectrum Robotics
www.spectrum.ieee.org

NASA Robotics
www.robotics.nasa.gov

Massachusetts Institute of Technology
www.web.mit.edu/museum/exhibitions/robots

Singularity Hub
www.singularityhub.com

Singularity University
www.singularityu.org

Professor Kevin Warwick
www.kevinwarwick.com

'IBM Debuts Cognitive Computing Chip'
www.roboticstrends.com/research_academics/article/ibm_debuts_cognitive_computing_chips

'Robots and Avatars Health and Wellbeing Report'
www.robotsandavatars.net/documentation/writing/health-and-wellbeing-report

'Mind over matter: will computers enhance or limit our brains in the 21st century?' (NESTA, 2011)
www.nesta.org.uk

P126 → Urban Makeovers

By 2050, at least 75 per cent of the 8.6 billion people with whom we'll be sharing this planet will be living in cities. The more you think about that projection, the more astonishing the prospect becomes. And the challenge is all the greater, given that a very significant proportion of those people will still be living in tomorrow's equivalent of today's shanty towns and urban slums – a reality to which I return later on.

But the focus in this entry is on rich-world cities – both existing and new – and the incredible opportunities now available to us in making those cities genuinely fit for purpose in a low-carbon, resource-efficient world. Many of these changes are already underway, and the scale of ambition from those running our cities increases all the time.

C40 Cities
www.c40cities.org

CISCO/New Songdo International City Development
www.songdo.com

ARUP/Where now for cities?
www.arup.com/Homepage_Archive/Where_now_for_cities

SymbioCity
www.symbiocity.org

RIBA
www.architecture.com/SustainabilityHub

World Green Building Council
www.worldgbc.org

'Guide to Sustainia' (Project Green Light, 2011)
www.sustainia.me/resources

P133 → Of Men and Money

OK – so we might all hate the bankers! But that doesn't get us very far in terms of working out how to get to a world where we can once again trust our financial institutions, and where the get-rich-quick merchants no longer dominate our capital markets.

There's been a huge amount of work done over the last 10 years on developing new initiatives and policy reforms in the area of sustainable finance. But after the economic crash of 2008, decision makers remain so risk-averse that we've barely begun to think through what needs to happen next.

Again, some might see capital market reforms of this kind as being on the margins of the sustainability debate. But you can guarantee we'll not be progressing towards a more sustainable world as fast as we need to without some dramatic changes in this area.

BitCoin (an experimental digital currency)
www.bitcoin.org

Freecycle
www.freecycle.org

Global Alliance for Banking on Values (GABV)
www.gabv.org

Hey, Neighbor!
www.heyneighbor.com

LETSlink (local exchange trading systems)
www.letslinkuk.net

Local exchange and trading systems: Sharehood
www.thesharehood.org

New Economics Foundation (nef)
www.neweconomics.org

New Resource Bank
www.newresourcebank.com

Triodos
www.triodos.co.uk

The Co-operative Bank
www.co-operativebank.co.uk

UK Sustainable Investment and Finance Association (UKSIF)
www.uksif.org

ZOPA
www.zopa.com

P136 → Fixing the Climate

Given that there are as yet no mini-DACs (direct air capture machines) available in your local hardware store, there's nothing much you can actually do about geoengineering – other than get informed and get involved in what is going to be one of the liveliest and most significant debates of the next couple of decades.

However, even getting yourself informed about this topic isn't all that easy. NGOs are so fearful that politicians will prefer to pluck some geoengineering wheeze out of the air, rather than get on with all the really hard work needed to reduce the emissions of greenhouse gases in the first place, they've pretty much limited themselves to rather grim warnings of the 'don't go there' variety.

The exception is Friends of the Earth in the UK, which has produced a very helpful report on geoengineering and why we had better just grit our teeth and get on with research into those options (or 'negative emission technologies') that make the most sense. This was also pretty much the conclusion of a 2009 report from the UK's Royal Society.

For more overtly hostile positions, see the website of ETC: www.etcgroup.org and Greenpeace www.greenpeace.org and for full-on, industry-funded, gung-ho enthusiasm, the Bipartisan Policy Centre (www.bipartisanpolicy.org which isn't really bipartisan at all!) is as good a place to go as any.

Duncan McLaren for Friends of the Earth, 'Negatonnes: an initial assessment of the potential for negative emission techniques to contribute safely and fairly to meeting carbon budgets in the 21st century' (Friends of the Earth, 2011) www.foe.co.uk/resource

'Geoengineering the climate: Science, governance an uncertainty' (Royal Society report, 2009) www.royalsociety.org/policy/publications

Jamais Cascio, 'Hacking the Earth' (www.openthefuture.com, 2009)

Clive Hamilton, 'Earthmasters: The Dawn of the Age of Climate Engineering' (Yale University Press, 2013)

P144 → Electric Motion

At present, there are just a handful of hybrids and electric vehicles (EVs) in amongst all the rest of the traffic on our roads. So the gap between where we are now and where we'll need to be by 2030, with EVs on at least equal terms with petrol and diesel vehicles, is perhaps too great to imagine.

But that's how it's going to be – which may explain why all the big car manufacturers are investing billions in EVs and hybrids. They are also hedging their bets by designing ever more efficient petrol and diesel models – after years of telling us that any possibility of ultra-efficient (100 mpg plus) vehicles was just unrealistic. So who knows who will win out in this pitched battle between EVs and the internal combustion engine? The great thing is that the battle has now begun – with sustainability as the principal driver of change.

There's no end of opportunities for car owners to get involved here, in the choice of vehicle (new or second-hand) or in the way those vehicles are driven and maintained. And why not find out about car share schemes, as more and more people are already doing? What, after all, is the point of paying thousands to have a lump of metal parked outside your house or flat most hours of the day?

Buzzcar
www.buzzcar.com

Carsharing.Net
www.carsharing.net

Zipcar
www.zipcar.com

IBM Battery 500 Project
www.ibm.com/smarterplanet

Zero Carbon World
www.zerocarbonworld.org

Better Place
www.betterplace.com

Ecotricity/EV
www.ecotricity.co.uk

Seth Plether, 'Bottled Lightning: Superbatteries, Electric Cars, and the New Lithium Economy' (Hill and Wang, 2011)

'Who Killed the Electric Car?' (Chris Paine, 2006)

'Revenge of the Electric Car' (Chris Paine, 2011)

P151 → Nature's Balance Sheet

It's more than 10 years now since scientists and NGOs started talking about 'payment for ecological services' (PES), particularly in the context of preventing further losses of the world's rainforests. It's simple enough: keeping the forest standing is worth more economically than cutting it down, but our short-term, smash-and-grab economics has no way of recognizing that.

Today, governments and international agencies such as the World Bank are getting closer to doing some real deals based on PES, but it's still unbelievably tortuous and controversial. This is basically all about re-defining self-interest. Brazil won't adequately protect its rainforests until Brazilians recognize the direct economic benefits of so doing – and, in my opinion, that moment isn't far off. (I suspect, however, that many people won't agree with my prediction that it will be soya farmers that become the ultimate tree-huggers!)

This is another area where consumer power can make a real difference. Some of Greenpeace's most successful campaigns have been based on mobilizing massive consumer-led initiatives to stop big branded companies sourcing their raw materials from countries and regions that are still involved in deforestation. Wherever you can, therefore, buy goods that are certified: 'Rainforest Alliance', or 'Forest Stewardship Council'.

Greenpeace (Protecting forests campaign)
www.greenpeace.org

Rainforest Action Network
www.ran.org

Amazon Watch
www.amazonwatch.org

The Prince's Rainforest Project
www.rainforestsos.org

Global Canopy Programme
www.globalcanopy.org

UN REDD Programme
www.un-redd.org

Mongabay.com
www.mongabay.com

Trucost
www.trucost.com

Rhett A. Butler, 'Rainforests' (Mongabay, 2011) – for kids and adults!

P155 → Fisheries Bounce Back

The idea of managing a fishery sustainably has always been one of the easiest ways of explaining what sustainability means. Catch more fish than are replaced naturally every year, and you're in trouble; catch no more fish than are replaced, and there's no reason why that stock of fish shouldn't go on feeding people into the future. And that, of course, is what we've totally failed to do.

Many fisheries are already either in serious decline or completely fished out. Although aquaculture (which also has its share of sustainability challenges) has filled the gap to some extent, the trend is still pretty clear: if we don't give the oceans and seas a chance to recover, then the outlook is truly grim.

But this 'fish fight' is still winnable. People understand how mad the current situation is, and those who love eating fish hate to think that they are (a small) part of the problem. Hence the success of the Marine Stewardship Council (MSC), brilliant campaigns by Greenpeace and other NGOs, with huge support from retailers all around the world. It seems to me the tide really is turning.

Marine Stewardship Council (look for their label on products!) www.msc.org

Marine Conservation Society
www.mcsuk.org

Blue Marine Foundation
www.bluemarinefoundation.com

Oceana
www.oceana.org

Greenpeace (Oceans campaign)
www.greenpeace.org

WWF (Oceans and Coasts)
www.wwf.org

Blue Climate Coalition
www.sites.google.com/site/blueclimatesolutions

The Good Fish Guide (from the Marine Conservation Society) www.goodfishguide.co.uk

Fish 2 Fork – an international website rating alternative fish restaurants www.fish2fork.com

Charles Clover, 'The End of the Line: How Overfishing is Changing the World and the Way We Eat' (Ebury Press, 2005)

Callum Roberts, 'Ocean of Life' (Allen Lane, 2012)

'The End of the Line' (Rupert Murray, 2009)
www.endoftheline.com

P160 → Feeding the World

As food prices rise all around the world, we're starting to come to terms with the fact that the era of cheap food is over. And given the growth in both populations and incomes, our food security prospects do not look good – as we saw earlier. But, as ever, the answers are there.

There's no single 'silver bullet' that will solve all the problems – rather, a total rethink in the way that we manage land, soil, water, energy and biodiversity is what's needed. And there's so much more to this agenda than today's polarized debate about GM food, not least in terms of the power of the food industry and who makes the decisions on our behalf. So I've tried to get a bit beyond the either/or here – this is one area where we really are going to need a bit of everything.

And that's the starting point for us as consumers. Being mindful is the key challenge here: avoiding the bad stuff, doing what we can to help the good guys, celebrating food and the farmers on whom we depend.

What that means, in practice, boils down to things like eating less meat, buying local, avoiding food waste and buying organic or certified produce (where you can).

Soil Association
www.soilassociation.org

Slow Food
www.slowfood.com

Sustain
www.sustain.co.uk

Pesticide Action Network UK
www.pan-uk.org

Farming and Wildlife Advisory Group (FWAG)
www.fwag.org

AGRA
www.agra.org

If you need any further reminders as to why we need radical change, watch the documentary 'Food Inc' (Robert Kenner, 2008)
www.documentaryaddict.com

P168 → Incredible Edible Cities

People are surprised to discover that around 15 per cent of food people eat today is produced in or on the edge of cities. So I expect they'll be even more surprised by my suggestion that this figure will have risen to 40 per cent by 2050!

But there are so many advantages to promoting urban agriculture – in terms of reduced environmental impacts, community engagement, livelihoods, skills, better health (physical and mental) and so on. Things are already moving in this direction, but they need a real push. And this won't all be low-tech, dig-it-yourself stuff. Some of the most exciting innovations today are in the field of 'vertical farming', as food entrepreneurs find ways around the lack of land and water. Hydroponics is already a burgeoning technology.

In essence, this is about reconnection with the land and with the business of food production at a very personal level. The advice offered for the previous entry also applies here – but why not also find out whether there are ways you can get involved in local schemes or farmers' markets?

Farmers Market Coalition US
www.farmersmarketcoalition.org

Transition Towns Network UK
www.transitionnetwork.org

Landshare
www.landshare.net

Incredible Edible Todmorden
www.incredible-edible-todmorden.co.uk

PlantLab
www.plantlab.nl/4.0

Plantagon
www.plantagon.com

Earthworks Detroit
www.cskdetroit.org

Capital Growth
www.capitalgrowth.org

Guerrilla Gardening
www.guerrillagardening.org

'Feeding the City' series (Grist)
www.grist.org/series/food-feeding-the-city

Rob Hopkins, 'The Transition Handbook: From Oil Dependency to Local Resilience' (Green Books, 2008)

'How We Can Eat Our Landscapes', Pam Warhurst, Incredible Edible Todmorden (2012) www.ted.com

P174 → The Wonders of Modern Medicine

One of the best things about life today is that we're living longer – but the real trick is to be healthier too! And technology is going to have a huge impact here.

A lot of people believe that the one big area of our lives that has not yet been revolutionized by information technology is medicine – or healthcare more generally. As I mentioned before, most healthcare systems around the world are incredibly conservative and slow-moving, but we're just beginning to see how rapidly this might now change.

For all the fancy technology that I've flagged up in this entry, there's still a great deal to be worked out here between the providers of healthcare services and ourselves. There's a lot of talk today about 'personalized healthcare' and 'self-management', but most people still seem to be stuck in that old patient/doctor dependency. That's clearly going to have to change.

PatientsLikeMe
www.patientslikeme.com

CureTogether
www.curetogether.com

Eric Topol, 'The Creative Destruction of Medicine: How the Digital Revolution Will Create Better Health Care' (Basic Books, 2012)

'The Wisdom of Prevention', report by nef (2012)
www.neweconomics.org/publications

Nigel Crisp, 'Turning the World Upside Down: the Search for Global Health in the 21st Century' (RSM Press, 2010)

P178 → Malaria Tamed

Malaria remains one of the cruellest killers in those countries where it is still endemic – and 60 per cent of those who die are under the age of five.

The amount of research that is currently underway to address this is extraordinary, inspired in no small part by the Bill and Melinda Gates Foundation. But many experts remain convinced that there will never be a complete solution through public health interventions and anti-malarial drugs, because the malaria parasite (and its mosquito carriers) have proved to be incredibly resilient. So I think we can guarantee some very lively debate about the ethics of genetically manipulating mosquitoes, which is where the focus is now shifting.

And then there's still dengue fever to address – an affliction for which there are currently no drugs or treatment. As the climate changes, so too does the prevalence of dengue fever, with cases recently recorded in Florida and Southern Europe. So we can expect to hear a lot more about efforts to combat this disease too.

Bill & Melinda Gates Foundation
www.gatesfoundation.org

Stop Malaria Now!
www.stopmalarianow.org

Malaria No More
www.malarianomore.org

Nothing But Nets
www.nothingbutnets.net

Roll Back Malaria Partnership
www.rollbackmalaria.org

P183 → China Shows the Way

There's no such thing as a sustainable world without a sustainable China! For some people, who can only see the dark side of what's happening in China, that leaves them bordering on despair. But it's about time they woke up to the bright side as well.

The problems that China faces are indeed daunting, but there's a prevailing 'engineer's mind set' there that makes the Chinese more purposeful about the solutions than most other countries in the world today. What's more, they think about the long term in a way that no other country does – 'thinking like a civilization' as one expert put it, rather than fire-fighting their way from one short-term crisis to another.

Anything to do with China and the environment is obviously very controversial – just as it was when China introduced its One Child Family policy in the 1970s. But we all have reason to be thankful that they did, and that they are now beginning to show real leadership on today's sustainability challenges.

chinadialogue
www.chinadialogue.net

JUCCCE
(Joint US-China Collaboration on Clean Energy)
www.juccce.org

IPE (Institute of Public and Environmental Affairs) – one of the most highly-respected NGOs in and beyond China, focused on the water environment and the responsibilities of multinational companies
www.ipe.org.cn

P189 → Putting the World to Rights

We've done such damage to the natural world over the last 50 years that we'll need at least another 50 years to help put things right. And that kind of long-term restoration and healing will inevitably come at a price.

I'm sure I'll be accused of extreme naivety by projecting my vision for such an initiative as the EarthCorps onto President Obama. But the vast majority of US environmentalists reckon he's got a thing or two to prove before he leaves the White House in 2016, and I thought I'd just give him a bit of encouragement!

Behind all this is the deeper challenge of how best to harness young people's energy to enable them to play their part in building a better world. The type of national service I'm envisaging here won't be everybody's cup of tea, but the dramatic circumstances in which we now find ourselves will inevitably require some equally dramatic responses.

Part of my inspiration for this idea came from the existing EarthCorps, based in Seattle, Washington, and set up in 1993 by a returned Peace Corps volunteer, Dwight Wilson. His vision was to extend the Peace Corps' original mission to enable young people to work on environmental projects in the Cascades bioregion. It's still doing great work.

A lot of young people are already involved in working with organizations in other countries, and this kind of volunteering on ecological or community projects can be a life-changing experience. However, caution is advisable. Some programmes can cause more harm than good to the environment, and can also perpetuate elitist, patronizing attitudes of rich kids 'helping out the poor Third World'.

VSO (Voluntary Service Oversees)
www.vso.org.uk

EarthCorps
www.earthcorps.org

Green Cross International
www.gcint.org

Green Belt Movement
www.greenbeltmovement.org

Stanley Meisler, 'When the World Calls: The Story of the Peace Corps and its First Fifty Years' (Beacon Press, 2012)

P192 → Redesigning the Building Blocks of Life

Just stand back for a moment and try and imagine what life would be like without any plastic materials whatsoever. A minority of people believe that's exactly what we should be trying to achieve, but the impact on our overall quality of life would be massive. So if we want to continue to benefit from the use of plastics, we're going to have to make and use them in very different ways – in the first instance, by using natural feedstocks rather than fossil fuels, and then by reusing or recycling them.

Personally, I don't think that sort of position is particularly controversial. Synthetic biology, on the other hand, is probably less controversial than it should be! It seems improbable to me that our current regulatory arrangements are fit for purpose, and the pace of change here is breathtaking – worryingly so.

Which means we're back to that double-edged sword of innovation: huge potential benefits from breakthroughs in this and many other areas, but the dark side of synthetic biology could cost us very dear indeed.

Center for Green Chemistry and Green Engineering (Yale University)
www.greenchemistry.yale.edu

Green Chemistry Network
www.greenchemistrynetwork.org

Industrial Biotechnology Leadership Forum
connect.innovateuk.org/web/industrial-biotechnology

Interface
www.interfaceglobal.com

SABMiller
www.sabmiller.com

ETC Group (Synthetic biology)
www.etcgroup.org

P196 → The Energy Internet

Frankly, today's endlessly recycled debates about energy policy are very unhelpful. From a technology perspective, there's little doubt that a combination of renewables and storage technologies (within an economy that's ruthlessly prioritizing energy efficiency) could meet almost all our needs (and the needs of almost all countries) by 2050 – and probably a great deal earlier if we put our minds to it.

Geothermal power also has a critical role to play in some parts of the world – including Africa – but I haven't been able to cover that in any detail.

But the real issues are storage and grids – which are perceived to be too boring, I fear, for most politicians to get very excited about. At long last, however, the innovation story on storage is moving ahead in leaps and bounds, and everybody I talk to about this is convinced that we can now crack many of the challenges in this area within the next decade.

Upgrading our antiquated grids is a rather different matter. Hundreds of billions of dollars will be required to get this challenge sorted – and while politicians go on obsessing about nuclear power or fracking gas, the pace of progress here is glacial. All this as the glaciers melt away in front of our eyes.

Institute of Mechanical Engineers
www.imeche.org

Highview Power Storage
www.highview-power.com

FierceSmartGrid
www.fiercesmartgrid.com

Desertec
www.desertec.org

P200 → Still Flying High!

Long ago, I once had to give evidence to a Parliamentary Committee where I was told by its chair that cheap air travel was 'a God-given right'! I've never quite forgotten that – and it's still true that it takes a brave politician to come between voters and their love of flying.

Some people worry a lot more about this than others, but here are my few words of advice in terms of getting on top of one's 'flying footprint', in the form of a quick and easy check list.

1. For work, fly only when you have to. Otherwise, use Skype or teleconferencing.

2. For personal travel, avoid air travel if you possibly can.

3. If you can't, try and limit yourself to one long-haul or two short-haul flights a year.

4. Get serious about offsetting – and pay a realistic price for every tonne of CO_2 that your flights cause to be emitted.

5. Treat flying as a rare and special privilege, not as a commonplace commodity.

Offsetting remains controversial, but there are some very good offset providers out there who will provide you with an excellent introduction. For example:

ClimateCare
www.climatecare.org

CarbonNeutral Company
www.carbonneutral.com

BP Target Neutral
www.bptargetneutral.com

If you want to know more about what the aviation industry is up to on sustainability, check out Sustainable Aviation
www.sustainableaviation.co.uk

Air Fuel Synthesis
www.airfuelsynthesis.com

'Offset Positive: Buying Change – the Case for Carbon Offsets', (Forum for the Future, 2010)
In 2010, 'Green Futures' produced this special supplement on offsetting, where we looked at all the pros and cons.
www.forumforthefuture.org/greenfutures/shop/special-edition/offset-positive

P205 → Work, Wealth and Wellbeing

It often seems as if economic growth is the only thing that matters to politicians today. Yet I suspect, deep down, that most of us in the UK know we're never going to see high levels of economic growth again. Those days are gone.

So how can we improve things for people today (and in the future) with permanently low growth? That remains quite a challenge!

For me, it means putting the focus on wellbeing and on equity, ensuring at the very least that everyone has access to rewarding work, both paid and unpaid.

And a very different world begins to emerge if one follows through on that kind of logic.

New Economics Foundation (nef)
www.neweconomics.org
(Have a look at their projects: Five Ways to Well-being and Towards 21 Hours)

Business in the Community/Workwell campaign
www.bitc.org.uk

The Art of Living Foundation
www.artofliving.org

Action for Happiness
www.actionforhappiness.org

The Equality Trust
www.equalitytrust.org.uk

Time banking (do check to see if there's a timebank operating anywhere near you!)

TimeBanks (US & International)
www.timebanks.org

Timebanking (UK)
www.timebanking.org

Sustainable Society Index (SSI) from the Sustainable Society Foundation www.ssfindex.com

Richard Wilkinson and Kate Pickett, 'The Spirit Level: Why Equality is Better for Everyone' (Penguin, 2010)

Richard Layard, 'Happiness: Lessons from a New Science' (Penguin, 2006)

P210 → Manufacturing Reborn

Right from the start of the Industrial Revolution, the way we make things has been subject to constant change – and our lives are shaped by the principles and practice of manufacturing in ways we barely even notice these days.

But what astonishing changes await us over the next couple of decades! 3D printing, nanotechnology, the 'maker movement', direct digital manufacturing, the wonders of graphene – these are just a few intriguing glimpses of what is now in the pipeline.

Above all, this new industrial revolution will need to be driven by extreme resource efficiency, dramatically reducing the amount of energy and raw materials we need to make things. And then we'll need to get smarter and smarter in the way we actually use materials.

There is a lot happening around the idea of a 'maker movement' – and it's for anyone who wants to be more than a consumer of what other people have made. You could join your nearest hackerspace, attend a Maker Faire or find out more about MakerBot Industries and its desktop 3D printers.

MakerBot
www.makerbot.com

The Great Recovery
www.greatrecovery.org.uk

Biomimicry for Creative Innovation (BCI)
www.businessinspiredbynature.com

Biomimicry 3.8
www.biomimicry.net

The Story of Stuff Project
www.storyofstuff.org

Shapeways
www.shapeways.com

'Make:' magazine
www.makezine.com

'Fast Company' magazine: Biomimicry
www.fastcompany.com/biomimicry

P216 → Slumdog Billionaires

For anyone who has spent any time at all in a big urban settlement in Africa, Asia or South America, the sheer scale of the problems needing to be addressed is utterly daunting. Realistically speaking, given the continuing momentum behind the process of urbanization, I can't envisage any scenario in which there aren't still billions of people living in less than ideal circumstances in 2050.

Even so, there's no reason why those lives shouldn't be a great deal better than they are today. And the most powerful 'force for good' that we have here is the extraordinary resilience and creativity of the people themselves – so often dismissively referred to as 'slum dwellers'. Sort out the energy supply, sort out the sanitation and sort out the water – and then see what happens!

Water and Sanitation for the Urban Poor (WSUP)
www.wsup.com

Practical Action
www.practicalaction.org

Shack/Slum Dwellers International
www.sdinet.org

International Institute for Environment and Development
www.iied.org

Grameen Foundation
www.grameenfoundation.org

Peepoople
www.peepoople.com

Practical Action
www.practicalaction.org

Majora Carter Group
www.majoracartergroup.com

Skoll Foundation
www.skollfoundation.org

The HUB
www.the-hub.net

Design with the Other 90%: Cities
www.designother90.org

Next Billion
www.nextbillion.net

Paul Polak, 'Out of Poverty: What Works when Traditional Approaches Fail' (Berrett-Koehler, 2009) www.blog.paulpolak.com

P222 → Taming Our Capital Markets

Governments need to find new and substantive sources of revenue – it's difficult to see how to squeeze much more out of the existing tax base. There are only two potential sources for new revenues: taxing carbon (see p.240) and taxing financial transactions.

The idea of a financial transaction tax (often referred to as a 'Tobin tax' after the guy who first came up with the idea) has been around for a long time. But its only in the last three or four years that some real momentum has built up behind the proposal, particularly in France. Unfortunately, both the UK and the USA remain implacably hostile.

But this tax would be a real win-win. We desperately need the revenues, and we urgently need to take the heat out of the riskiest, most speculative end of today's capital markets.

Move Your Money (US)
www.moveyourmoneyproject.org

Move Your Money (UK)
www.moveyourmoney.org.uk

Triodos Bank
www.triodos.co.uk

Co-operative Bank
www.co-operativebank.co.uk

Zopa
www.zopa.com

ShoreBank International
www.sbksbi.com

Robin Hood Tax campaign
www.robinhoodtax.org.uk

FairPensions
www.fairpensions.org.uk

New Resource Bank
www.newresourcebank.com

Tim Jackson, 'Prosperity Without Growth: Economics for a Finite Planet' (Routledge, 2011)

'Inside Job' (Charles Ferguson, 2010)
www.sonyclassics.com/insidejob

'97% Owned' (Michael Oswald, 2012)
www.youtube.com

P226 → The Law Steps Up

Many countries today have excellent legal protection for the natural environment – in theory! The tragedy is that those laws are rarely implemented, and even when sanctions are imposed, they are so inadequate that the deterrent effect is zero. China provides an all too depressing case study in that regard.

Properly enforced laws are the very minimum we need today. The campaign behind the ecocide proposal is designed to put things onto a very different footing, forcing us all to face up to the fact that some crimes against the environment threaten not only the natural world, but also the wellbeing of countless millions of people. Especially if today's criminal inaction on reducing emissions of greenhouse gases unleashes the full horror of irreversible climate change.

International Court for the Environment (ICE Coalition) www.icecoalition.com

ClientEarth
www.clientearth.org

Global Alliance for the Rights of Nature
www.therightsofnature.org

Stakeholder Forum
www.stakeholderforum.org

World Social Forum 2013
www.fsm2013.org

On the Commons
www.onthecommons.org

EnAct International
www.enact-international.com

International Court for the Environment
www.icecoalition.com

Eradicating Ecocide
www.eradicatingecocide.com

Law and Your Environment
www.environmentlaw.org.uk

Polly Higgins, 'Eradicating Ecocide' (Shepheard-Walwyn, 2010)

'Earth Day Special: Vandana Shiva and Maude Barlow on the Rights of Mother Earth' (2011)
www.democracynow.org/2011/4/22/earth_day_special_vandana_shiva_and

P229 → Older and Wiser

There are more and more people in the world (80 million more every year), and more of them are living longer – that's the backdrop to a lot of the environmental and social pressure points we're having to address.

This trend means there's clearly going to be some tension between the expectations of young people and those of older people – what I've referred to in this entry as the 'war of ages'. This is scary territory for politicians, who are understandably reluctant to confront their electorates with some of the basic truths about rising health budgets and social care costs. With octogenarians making up around a fifth of humankind by 2050 (globally, not just in today's rich world), we really need to be thinking a lot more about this today.

Alzheimer's Society
www.alzheimers.org.uk

AARP
www.aarp.org

National Council for Ageing (US)
www.ncoa.org

Age UK
www.ageuk.org.uk

Contact the Elderly
www.contact-the-elderly.org.uk

Create the Good
www.createthegood.org

NSF Socially Assistive Robots project
www.robotshelpingkids.org

WHO Age-friendly Environments Programme
www.who.int/ageing

The Natural Death Centre
www.naturaldeathcentre.org

Living well with dementia
www.livingwellwithdementia.com

IEEE Spectrum/Robotics
www.spectrum.ieee.org/robotics/medical-robots

Gransnet
www.gransnet.com

European Network of Green Seniors
www.greenseniors.eu

'100+', Sonia Arrison (Basic Books, 2011)

P234 → Travelling Differently

I've always subscribed to the view that being able to visit other places and countries provides incredible benefits – new experiences, access to different ideas and lifestyles, recreation, recuperation and so on. But with more than a billion people already enjoying those benefits, we simply have to get better at managing the massive environmental and social impact of so many people on the move all around the world.

No one wants to go back to the time when only the very rich could afford to travel, so 'rationing' access to special places by price alone just seems wrong. In effect, however, that's what's already happening in a number of cases.

The unknown here is technology – or rather, how long it will take before virtual travel and tourism provide a truly attractive alternative to the real thing. It's going to happen anyway – so get used it! In the meantime, travel slowly, responsibly and much more sustainably.

Tourism Concern
www.tourismconcern.org.uk

Sustainable Travel International
www.sustainabletravel.org

The International Ecotourism Society
www.ecotourism.org

3D Travel
www.3dtravel.com

Slow Travel
www.slowtrav.com

Holidays from Home
www.holidaysfromhome.co.uk/about-holidays-from-home

Airbnb
www.airbnb.co.uk

responsibletravel.com
www.responsibletravel.com

Tribewanted
www.tribewanted.com

Second Life
www.secondlife.com/destinations/real

Google Earth
www.google.com/earth

P239 → Climate Challenges

There are still a few scientists who continue to argue that the climate is not changing. And a few more who attribute any changes to natural causes rather than to the build-up of man-made greenhouse gases in the atmosphere.

But the overwhelming scientific consensus remains rock solid: the 500 billion tonnes of carbon we've put into the atmosphere since the start of the Industrial Revolution are already having a big impact, and if we want to avoid the horrendous prospect of runaway climate change, we should be doing everything in our power to limit future emissions to no more than another 500 billion tonnes in total.

A lot of scientists don't believe we'll be able to keep to that limit. This entry gives us a taste of what will need to be done over the next 30 years to prove them wrong!

But what's so frustrating is that we already have at our disposal everything we need to make that possible from a technological perspective. And once you start factoring in today's extraordinary innovation pipeline, then the prospects become more and more encouraging.

350.org
www.350.org

Climate Action Network
www.climatenetwork.org

Greenpeace (Stop Climate Change campaign)
www.greenpeace.org

Ashden Awards
www.ashden.org

The Climate Group
www.theclimategroup.org

Intergovernmental Panel on Climate Change
www.ipcc.ch

Tyndall Centre for Climate Change Research
www.tyndall.ac.uk

The Met Office UK
www.metoffice.gov.uk/climate-change

Scottish Renewables
www.scottishrenewables.com

'The Energy Report: 100% renewable energy by 2050', (WWF, 2011) www.wwf.org.uk

'Zero Carbon Britain 2030: A New Energy Strategy' (Centre for Alternative Technology, 2010)
www.zerocarbonbritain.com

P244 → Democracy By Demand

'The condition upon which God hath given liberty to Man is eternal vigilance' – surely as true today as in John Curran's original article in 1790.

And one thing you can absolutely guarantee is that we are going to have to be ever more vigilant over the next few decades. Some of the 'shocks to the system' that I've briefly touched on in different entries will put our democratic systems under massive pressure.

I suspect that this will prove to be the biggest challenge of all for sustainability campaigners. After all, there's no choice about us eventually learning to live sustainably on planet Earth: we either do it elegantly and intelligently, drawing on all our democratic freedoms to steer us through some very troubled territory; or we put things off for so long that the necessary changes come at a huge cost to our economies and our liberty.

People of my age really don't want to confront that reality. But I have a lot more faith in young people – who, I can't help but believe, will eventually rise up in one way or another to stop my generation further undermining their prospects. I hope that faith is not misjudged.

Avaaz
www.avaaz.org

Foundation for Democracy and Sustainable Development www.fdsd.org

Foundation for the Rights of Future Generations
www.intergenerationaljustice.org

Intergenerational Foundation
www.if.org.uk

Occupy Wall Street
www.occupywallst.org

Corporate Europe Observatory
www.corporateeurope.org

Reporters Without Borders
www.rsf.org

Global Voices
www.globalvoicesonline.org

Witness
www.witness.org

The Netizen Project
www.netizenproject.org

Alex Steffen, ed., 'Worldchanging: A User's Guide for the 21st Century' (Abrams Books, 2011)
www.worldchanging.com

P247 → Reefs: Back from the Brink

There are good reasons to be hopeful about the state of our coral reefs – and equally powerful reasons to be more than a little downcast.

On the hopeful front, a huge amount of work is already underway to put right the damage done over the last 30 or 40 years. I focused on the Apo Reef in this entry, where a massive campaign is underway, working with the local people, to restore basic productivity and biodiversity.

But, unfortunately, no number of brilliant local campaigns can address the two nightmares of rising ocean temperatures and increasing levels of acidification. These are global phenomena, arising from the build-up of greenhouse gases in the atmosphere.

That said, we simply have to focus on what can be done right now – especially if you are one of those lucky enough to have enjoyed any kind of diving experience or reef-based holiday. For anyone planning such a trip, my advice is to make sure you pick a tour operator that's approved by local or international conservation organizations.

International Coral Reef Initiative
www.icriforum.org

Coral Reef Alliance
www.coral.org

The Nature Conservancy (Coral reef initiative and Adopt a Coral Reef)
www.nature.org

Conservation International
www.conservation.org

WWF/Coral Triangle project
wwf.panda.org

Blue Legacy
www.alexandracousteau.org

Blue Marine Foundation
www.bluemarinefoundation.com

Reef Check
www.reefcheck.org

Reefs in the News
www.reefs.org

Ocean Conservancy
www.oceanconservancy.org

Nancy Knowlton, 'Citizens of the Sea: Wondrous Creatures from the Census of Marine Life' (National Geographic Society, 2010)

P255 → Shipping Cleans Up

Shipping is a huge industry that touches the lives of the vast majority of people today – but at such a distance that they are hardly aware of it. But as we've gradually woken up to the less benign impacts of the shipping industry (in terms of pollution, climate change and so on), it's now being held to account in much more telling ways.

The result is that good things are starting to happen – in terms of fuel efficiency, new technology and better designed ships. All that matters enormously, because of the critical role of shipping in world trade.

For me, a genuinely sustainable world is still a world where there's a lot of trade between countries, rather than where we all pull back to within our own national boundaries. But that will not be possible unless shipping becomes an exemplar industry on every single one of its sustainability challenges.

Sustainable Shipping Initiative
www.ssi2040.org

Shipping Efficiency/Carbon War Room
www.shippingefficiency.org

The Shipbreaking Platform
www.shipbreakingplatform.org

PlanetSolar
www.planetsolar.org

B9 Energy Group
www.b9energy.com

Maersk Group
www.maersk.com/SUSTAINABILITY

Wallenius Water
www.walleniuswater.se

SustainableShipping
www.sustainableshipping.com

P262 → Miracle Cures

Not a week goes by without some kind of announcement about the latest cutting-edge development in the world of high-tech medicine.

The journey between initial breakthrough and widespread adoption at the sharp end is often a long and painful one – for instance, it's more than 15 years since researchers started talking about the potential impact of stem cell therapy, and it's still a very long way from becoming commonplace.

Even so, the direction of travel is clear as more and more high-tech interventions open up extraordinary possibilities. The implications of all of this – from an economic, political and ethical perspective – are much less clear. Many believe that some kind of rationing system will be inevitable in the future, as the combination of increasing longevity, growing populations and the cost of high-tech interventions overwhelm the budgets that governments will have available for health services and care for the elderly.

You can see why politicians don't want to talk about it – but that just makes it harder to plan for the future.

The Global Fund to Fight AIDS, TB and Malaria
www.theglobalfund.org

TB Alliance
www.tballiance.org

Cellular Dynamics International
www.cellulardynamics.com

Dignity in Dying
www.dignityindying.org.uk

Exit International
www.exitinternational.net

Sonia Arrison, '100+' (Basic Books, 2011)

'Terry Pratchett: Choosing to Die'
(Charlie Russell, 2011)

P266 → The Great Turning

Imagine for a moment that it's technologically feasible to engineer a genuinely sustainable world for 8.6 billion people by 2050 – which I absolutely believe to be the case.

You then have to ask whether it's politically and economically feasible – and the answer that people give to that question usually depends on their view of human nature.

People who believe that we are driven primarily by self-interest and greed tend to answer 'no'; while those who believe that we prefer to live more cooperatively, looking out for others (given half a chance) as well as for ourselves, tend to answer 'yes'.

What has become clear to me, at the end of writing this book, is that it all comes down to our capacity for empathy: our ability to see and feel things through the eyes of other people. 'Planetary consciousness' may be a rather grand way of describing what's beginning to emerge, but once you start to look out for it...

The Evolution Institute
www.evolutioninstitute.org

Joanna Macy
www.joannamacy.net

David Sloan Wilson
evolution.binghamton.edu/dswilson

Paul Zak, 'The Moral Molecule' (Bantam Books, 2012)

Jeremy Rifkin, 'The Empathic Civilization' (Polity Press, 2010)

Richard Wilkinson and Kate Pickett, 'The Spirit Level: Why Equality is Better for Everyone' (Penguin, 2010)

Simon Baron-Cohen, 'Zero Degrees of Empathy' (Allen Lane, 2011)

'Overview' (Planetary Collective, 2012)
www.overviewthemovie.com
www.planetarycollective.com

Further Reading

Christopher Barnatt, '25 Things You Need to Know About the Future', Constable, 2012

Lester R. Brown, 'Plan B 4.0', W.W. Norton, 2009

Jamais Cascio, 'Hacking the Earth', 2009 (self-published)

Peter Diamandis & Steven Kotler, 'Abundance', Free Press, 2012

Mark Edwards & Lloyd Timberlake, 'Whole Earth? Aligning Human Systems and Natural Systems', Still Pictures Moving Words, 2012

John Elkington, 'The Zeronauts', Routledge, 2012

Thomas Friedman and Michael Mandelbaum, 'That Used to be Us', Little, Brown, 2011

Paul Gilding, 'The Great Disruption', Bloomsbury, 2011

Herbert Girardet & Miguel Mendonca, 'A Renewable World', Green Books, 2009

Al Gore, 'Our Choice: A Plan to Solve the Climate Crisis', Bloomsbury, 2009

Al Gore, 'The Future', W.H. Allen, 2013

Ray Hammond, 'The World in 2030', Editions Yago, 2007

David C. Korten, 'Agenda for a New Economy: From Phantom Wealth to Real Wealth', Berrett-Koehler, 2009

Satish Kumar & Freddie Whitefield eds., 'Visionaries: The 20th Century's 100 Most Important Inspirational Leaders', Chelsea Green, 2007

Kalle Lasn, 'Meme Wars', Penguin, 2012

Jeremy Leggett ed., 'The Solar Century', Profile Books, 2009

Amanda Little, 'Power Trip', HarperCollins, 2009

Bill McKibben, 'Eaarth: Making Life on a Tough New Planet', Henry Holt, 2010

Frances Moore Lappé, 'EcoMind', Nation Books, 2011

Amory Lovins, 'Reinventing Fire', Chelsea Green, 2011

Jorgen Randers, '2052: A Global Forecast for the Next Forty Years', Chelsea Green, 2012

Jeremy Rifkin, 'The Third Industrial Revolution', Palgrave Macmillan, 2011

Callum Roberts, 'Ocean of Life', Allen Lane, 2012

Johan Rockstrom & Mattias Klum, 'The Human Quest', Stockholm Text, 2012

Juliet B. Schor, 'Plenitude: The New Economics of True Wealth', Penguin, 2010

Laurence C. Smith, 'The World in 2050', Dutton, 2010

James Gustave Speth, 'America the Possible', Yale University Press, 2012

Alex Steffen ed., 'Worldchanging: A User's Guide for the 21st Century', Abrams, 2011

Mark Stevenson, 'An Optimist's Tour of the Future', Profile Books, 2011

Pavan Sukhdev, 'Corporation 2020', Island Press, 2012

Richard Watson, 'Future Files: A Brief History of the Next 50 Years', Nicholas Brealey, 2008

Richard Watson, 'Future Minds', Nicholas Brealey, 2010

Andrew S. Winston, 'Green Recovery', Harvard Business School Press, 2009

Paul J. Zak, 'The Moral Molecule', Bantam Press, 2012

'State of the World: Moving Towards Sustainable Prosperity', The Worldwatch Institute, 2012

Acknowledgements

I owe a particular debt of gratitude to colleagues at the Institute of Advanced Study at Durham University, where I had time as a Fellow back in 2011 to think through many of the concepts that eventually led to 'The World We Made'. And thanks too to Hartwell House, one of the National Trust's Historic House Hotels, for providing the most perfect writing retreat.

A special thanks to Alison Freeman and Julia Brown (both brilliant researchers!), and to Esther Maughan McLachlan for her wonderful marketing and coordinating skills.

This has been very much a Forum for the Future project, and I'm particularly grateful to Mel Trievnor, who has been involved right from the start, to Jude Lynn and Anne Paintin in my office, to Madeleine Lewis, Betsy Reed and Anna Simpson in Communications, and to the Futures team.

And a whole host of people have helped with information and encouragement:
David Agnew, Bryan Appleyard, Ramon Arratia, John Ashton, Peter Barnes, William Becker, Lynelle Cameron, Robert Care, Stephen Chapman, Ian Christie, Will Day, Michael Dixon, Niall Dunne, Mark Edwards, John Gardner, Cat Gazzoli, Diane Gilpin, Matt Gorman, Helen Goulden, Leonie Greene, John Guillebaud, Bill Hanway, Dorothy Harris, David Hillman, Isabel Hilton, Rupert Howes, Krishan Hundal, Oliver James, Jing Lu, Matt Kelly, Harriet Kitcat, Adam Koniuszewski, Dax Lovegrove, Joanna Macy, Tony Marmont, Roger Martin, Stephen Martin, Robin Maynard, Mike McCarthy, Jon Miller, Paul Monaghan, Alastair Morton, David Nussbaum, Alan Parker, Lucy Parker, Michael Pawlyn, David Pencheon, Sunand Prasad, Gavin Purchas, Nigel Ratcliffe, Kate Rawles, Richard Rogers, Sonia Roschnik, Lucy Sargisson, David Satterthwaite, John Sauven, Sarah Severn, Chris Shearlock, Rob Soutter, Jacob Sterling, Chris Sherwin, Andrew Simms, Soren Stig, Tristram Stuart, Cat Vinton, Andy Wales, Gage Williams, David Sloan Wilson, David Woollcombe.

Finally, a big thank you to everyone at Phaidon who worked for so long and so hard to bring all this together, especially Ellen Christie (the linchpin of the entire project!) and Victoria Clarke.

Jonathon Porritt

Glossary

3D PRINTING
→ Sometimes called additive manufacturing, 3D printing is a process of making three-dimensional objects from materials deposited (or 'printed') in successive layers, working from a digitally encoded template.

ADVANCED BIOFUELS
→ A general term that includes both second-generation biofuels (see below) and third-generation, algae-based biofuels.

AGRI-BUSINESS
→ In agriculture, a generic term for the various businesses involved in crop production, including farming, seed supply, agrichemicals, farm machinery, wholesale and distribution, processing, marketing and retail sales.

AGRICULTURAL RUN-OFF
→ A form of pollution that occurs when pesticides, fertilizers and other agricultural products dissolve in water flowing over the land and pollute surrounding rivers, lakes and oceans.

AGRO-ECOLOGY
→ The study and application of the ecological processes that influence agricultural production systems.

AGRO-FORESTRY
→ An integrated approach used by farmers and foresters, combining trees and shrubs with crops and livestock.

AGRONOMY
→ The science and technology of cultivating plants for food, fuel or fibre.

AIR-CAPTURE TECHNOLOGY
→ A variety of different technologies designed to draw carbon dioxide out of the atmosphere so that it can be put to use or safely stored away.

ALKANES
→ A series of saturated hydrocarbons, meaning that their molecules are made only of carbon and hydrogen atoms linked with single bonds. Alkanes occur widely as saturated oils and waxes, as well as petroleum.

ANAEROBIC DIGESTION SYSTEMS
→ Systems that use bacteria to break down organic matter in the absence of oxygen, producing methane.

AQUACULTURE
→ The farming of aquatic organisms such as fish, crustaceans and molluscs.

AQUAPONIC SCHEMES
→ Systems for more sustainable food production, combining traditional aquaculture with hydroponics (cultivating plants in water) to create a symbiotic growing environment.

ARTIFICIAL MEAT (IN VITRO MEAT)
→ A form of protein derived from animal cells and cultured in laboratory conditions.

ARTIFICIAL PHOTOSYNTHESIS
→ A chemical process that replicates the natural process of photosynthesis by capturing and storing the energy of sunlight in chemical bonds or fuels.

ARTIFICIAL REEFS
→ Human-made underwater structures, typically built to promote marine biodiversity and bring life back to damaged reefs.

B CORPORATIONS
→ 'Benefit corporations' – a new type of business that uses the power of enterprise to create benefits for the public as well as shareholders.

BALLAST WATER
→ Water stored in the ballast tank of a ship, when it does not have a cargo on board. It counterbalances the lateral forces experienced during sailing.

BIO-BUTANOL
→ Butanol is an alcohol which can also be used as a liquid fuel instead of petrol. Bio-butanol is derived from organic matter (crops or wastes).

BIOCHAR
→ A form of charcoal arising from pyrolysis (see below) which can be used as a soil additive, storing away carbon dioxide in the process.

BIODIESEL
→ The collective term for a range of types of diesel derived from crops (such as rape or jatropha), animal fats or recycled vegetable oils. It is typically made by reacting oils with an alcohol in a process known as transesterification.

BIODIVERSITY
→ The variety of life (animals, plants and other organisms) found on Earth and in particular habitats or ecosystems. Also known as biological diversity.

BIOECONOMY
→ The sum of many different commercial activities arising from research into and the development of biotechnology.

BIOFUEL
→ Liquid fuel derived from living matter (such as a crop or algae) or from organic waste.

BIOGAS
→ A source of renewable energy. The most common biogas is methane produced by the breakdown of organic matter in the absence of oxygen.

BIOMASS
→ Organic matter that is used as a fuel.

BIOMIMICRY
→ Looking at what works in nature, and copying or taking inspiration from particular forms, processes and systems in order to solve human problems.

BIO-PLASTICS
→ Plastics derived from renewable biomass sources (such as vegetable fats and oils from a variety of different crops) used increasingly in place of plastics made from hydrocarbons.

BIOSECURITY
→ Preventative measures designed to protect both humans and farmed animals against disease or other harmful biological agents.

BIOTECHNOLOGY
→ A growing area of research and development, using biological feedstocks of one kind or another to design and make novel products.

BRACKISH WATER
→ Also known as briny water, brackish water has more salinity than fresh water but not as much as seawater.

CAPTURE FISHERIES
→ Also known as wild fisheries, capture fisheries are made up of populations of different fish species that are exploited for commercial purposes.

CARBON CAPTURE AND STORAGE TECHNOLOGY (CCS)
→ The process of capturing carbon dioxide before it is emitted into the atmosphere from large sources such as fossil fuel power plants, and transporting it to an underground reservoir for long-term storage.

CIRCULAR ECONOMY
→ An industrial system which aims for the elimination of waste through the superior design of materials, products and systems. The desired goal is a 'restorative' economy that will help repair the environmental damage done since the start of the Industrial Revolution.

CITIZEN FINANCE
→ A movement made up of individuals and organizations intent on transforming the management of money through networks that encourage peer-to-peer lending, borrowing, investment and other financial services.

CLOSED-LOOP MANUFACTURING
→ Manufacturing systems where new products are made using recycled materials, component parts and already-used products that would otherwise end up as waste.

CLOUD COMPUTING
→ The provision of services which allow individuals or businesses to use a third party's servers and other computing services (both hardware and software) instead of taking up space on their own computers or mobile devices. Cloud-based applications are accessed through web browsers or mobile apps.

COLLABORATIVE CONSUMPTION
→ An economic model based on sharing, swapping, bartering, trading or renting access to products, rather than purchasing and owning them.

COMMODITY CHEMICALS
→ A group of basic chemicals that are manufactured on a large scale, relatively inexpensively. They include alcohols, amines, acids, waxes and oils.

COMPRESSED AIR ENERGY STORAGE
→ A way to store energy on a large scale. Off-peak electricity is used to compress air, which is then stored underground (for example, in a disused mine) and used to generate peak electricity as it decompresses.

CONCENTRATED SOLAR POWER (CSP)
→ A form of renewable energy that uses mirrors or lenses to concentrate a large amount of sunlight onto a small area. Electrical power is generated through converting the concentrated light into steam, which drives a turbine to produce electricity.

COOPERATIVE CAPITALISM
→ An economic system based on the market but motivated more by the principles of cooperation, collaboration and community than by the exclusive pursuit of profit.

CORAL BLEACHING
→ The whitening of corals due to loss of the symbiotic algae living in the coral skeleton, which provide the pigmentation. Coral bleaching is due to changes in the surrounding conditions, particularly sea temperature, acidity, light and nutrient balance.

CYANOBACTERIA
→ Also known as blue-green algae, cyanobacteria are a family of bacteria that obtain their energy through photosynthesis.

DEAD ZONES
→ A growing number of areas in the world's oceans and lakes where high levels of nutrient pollution remove the oxygen and kill off all marine life.

DESALINATION
→ Any of several processes that remove salt and other minerals from sea water (saline water), thus turning it into fresh water.

DIRECT AIR CAPTURE
→ See Air capture technology.

DISCARDS
→ The portion of a catch of fish which is not retained on board during commercial fishing operations and is returned, often dead or dying, to the sea (usually because it exceeds quota limits).

DRIP IRRIGATION
→ A process of watering crops by slowly dripping water directly onto the soil around the plants or their roots. The method saves water, reduces soil erosion and enhances the soil's ability to hold nutrients.

ETHANOL
→ A volatile alcohol which plays an increasingly important role in liquid fuels markets, notably in countries like Brazil and the United States, where it is produced from sugar cane and maize respectively.

FISHMEAL
→ A commercial product made from fish, including the bones and offal from processed fish.

FLYWHEEL
→ A heavy rotating wheel that acts as a mechanical device to store energy. The work exerted in making the wheel spin is stored as its kinetic energy (energy of motion).

FOSSIL WATER
→ Groundwater held within an underground aquifer for a long period of time.

FUSION POWER
→ The energy generated during a nuclear reaction in which the nuclei of materials with a low atomic number fuse together to form heavier nuclei, causing the release of large amounts of energy.

FRACKING
→ Also known as hydraulic fracturing, fracking is the process of drilling and injecting water and chemicals into the ground at high pressure in order to fracture shale rocks and release the natural gas trapped inside.

GEOENGINEERING
→ A general term used for a wide variety of large-scale interventions in the Earth's climate system, typically with the aim of moderating the build-up of greenhouse gases in the atmosphere.

GEOTHERMAL POWER
→ Energy derived from the heat in the interior of the earth. Steam from hot rocks is used either to drive a turbine to produce electricity or to provide heat directly for communities or businesses.

GREEN CHEMISTRY
→ A growing area of research and development that focuses on the use of novel processes and feedstocks to help reduce energy consumption, waste and toxicity.

GREY WATER
→ The wastewater from domestic activities such as laundry, dishwashing and bathing, but not toilet waste. It can be recycled for on-site uses such as irrigation and flushing toilets.

GRID PARITY
→ Grid parity occurs when renewable sources of energy can generate electricity at the same cost or more cheaply than by using coal, gas or nuclear power.

HIGH VOLTAGE DIRECT CURRENT TRANSMISSION (HVDC)
→ A system that uses direct current (rather than alternating current, where the voltage changes continuously between positive and negative) for the bulk transmission of electrical power.

HYDROPONIC FARMING
→ A method of growing food crops in soilless, mineral-rich water solutions.

HYDROPOWER
→ Electrical energy derived from the movement energy of falling water.

INTENSIVE AGRICULTURE (INTENSIVE FARMING)
→ A farming system characterized by extensive inputs of pesticides and chemical fertilizers to maximize yields of commodity-based crops such as wheat, rice and soya.

LIQUID FUELS
→ Fuels such as petrol, diesel or liquefied natural gas (LNG), which are combusted in engines and produce mechanical energy to power vehicles. First-generation biofuels already provide a growing percentage of the liquid fuels market.

MARINE RESERVE
→ An area of the sea or ocean which has legal protection from fishing or development.

MICRO-FINANCING
→ The provision of financial services to low-income individuals and small businesses without access to typical banking services.

MICRO-WIND
→ Domestic-scale wind turbines that generate small amounts of electricity to help power a household's lights and appliances.

MUNICIPAL BONDS
→ A bond issued by a local government or other local agencies, with a view to securing increased investments in local businesses, infrastructure or other wealth-creating opportunities.

MUTUALS (OR MUTUAL ORGANIZATIONS)
→ Organizations that are owned by and run for the benefit of their current and future members. Mutuals take many forms, including cooperatives, building societies, credit unions, housing associations and mutual insurers.

NANOFILTER
→ A high-tech variation of the standard membrane filter used for water purification. The extremely small pore size of a nanofilter means it can remove much smaller particles.

NANOTECHNOLOGY
→ A general term covering processes, applications and products resulting from the manipulation of matter at the atomic scale.

NEGAWATTS
→ An abstract concept used to emphasize that new energy supply options (measured in megawatts) can be avoided through investment in energy efficiency.

NITROGEN FIXING
→ The process by which nitrogen in the atmosphere is converted into nitrogen compounds. Nitrogen fixation is a natural process occurring in some micro-organisms, including rhizobia, which live in the roots of legume plants.

NO-CATCH ZONE
→ An area of the world's oceans, lakes or rivers where it is illegal to catch any fish.

NUCLEAR WASTE
→ A wide range of radioactive materials arising from nuclear power stations or the manufacture of nuclear weapons.

OCEAN FERTILIZATION
→ A type of geoengineering that introduces nutrients to the surface of the ocean. The idea is that these nutrients (such as iron) will increase the productivity of phytoplankton, which will in turn remove carbon dioxide from the atmosphere and ultimately reduce the effects of climate change.

PERSONAL GENOMICS
→ A branch of genetics concerned with sequencing an individual's genome.

PHOTOVOLTAICS (PV)
→ A method of generating electrical power from sunshine or light. Solar panels are made up of photovoltaic cells.

PYROLYSIS
→ The thermal decomposition of organic matter in the absence of oxygen.

RAINWATER HARVESTING
→ The gathering and storage of rainwater before it goes back into the ground. It is often collected from guttering for gardens, or used for livestock and irrigation.

RARE EARTH METALS
→ A particular category of minerals that are not actually that rare, but which are found in very dilute concentrations in rock formations. Rare earth metals play an important role in both electronics and renewable energy technologies.

REGENERATIVE MEDICINE
→ The process of replacing or regenerating human cells, tissues or organs to restore or establish normal function.

REINSURANCE
→ A form of insurance taken out by insurance companies, in which the insurance risks are shared in return for part of the associated premium.

RETROFITTING
→ Adding new elements that were not fitted during original manufacture. In relation to buildings, this refers to technologies that reduce the building's energy consumption.

SHALE GAS / SHALE OIL
→ Natural gas or oil formed and trapped within soft rock formations known as shale.

SECOND-GENERATION BIOFUELS
→ Biofuels derived from various types of plants, grasses, fast-growing trees and agricultural and forestry waste. They are distinct from first-generation biofuels, which are derived mainly from arable crops.

SHARIAH INVESTMENTS
→ Investments that comply with Islamic Shariah law. For instance, the charging of interest is not allowed under Shariah law, so that conventional interest-bearing investments are prohibited.

SKY SAILS
→ Rigid sails or kites used to help move large ships forward by wind power.

SOLAR RADIATION
→ Solar radiation is the radiant energy emitted by the sun. We experience it mostly as heat and light, but it also includes the total spectrum of electromagnetic radiation produced by the sun.

SOLAR THERMAL
→ A method of generating heat (thermal energy) from light (solar energy) to provide hot water.

STEM-CELL THERAPIES
→ Stem cells can be made to develop in vitro into any other type of body cell or tissue, which can then be used in a number of different therapies.

SUPERCAPACITOR
→ Also known as ultracapacitors, supercapacitors are devices that store large amounts of electrical energy as a static charge. They have longer lives than normal (electrochemical) batteries and can discharge the energy stored in them very rapidly, but they are much more expensive.

SYNTHETIC BIOLOGY
→ The design and creation of biological products and new organisms for a variety of different uses.

TAR SANDS
→ Also known as oil sands, tar sands are a mixture of sand, clay, water and bitumen. Extracting this oil involves steam-heating the sand to produce a petroleum slurry.

'THE LIMITS TO GROWTH'
→ The title of a book written in 1972, which used computer models to explore the impact of economic and population growth on finite resources and natural systems.

THERMOELECTRIC MATERIALS
→ Materials that show a strong thermoelectric effect, where a temperature difference across the material produces an electric current.

THORIUM
→ A mildly radioactive metal that is abundant in the Earth's crust. There is some interest in developing a thorium fuel cycle for nuclear power stations instead of the currently used uranium fuel cycle.

TIDAL STREAM TECHNOLOGY
→ Devices and turbines designed to harness the kinetic energy of fast-flowing water in tidal areas.

WAVE POWER
→ The kinetic movement of ocean surface waves as a source of energy. The energy can be captured by wave power technologies and used to generate electricity.

WEALTHCARE MANAGERS
→ Financial advisors who work to help wealthy clients manage their money.

ZERO TILLAGE
→ Also called no-till farming, zero tillage is a way of growing crops from year to year without disturbing the soil through tillage. This technique increases the amount of water and organic matter in the soil and reduces erosion.

Index

→ Figures underlined indicate images.

Picture Credits

Futuristic digital images by Charlotte Tyson
Illustrations by James Graham
Infographics by Catalogtree

Alamy/ArteSub: 252–253; Alamy/Michele Burgess: 190; Alamy/Nigel Cattlin: 86; Alamy/EPA/Francisco Guasco: 94; Alamy/Alan Gignoux: 113t; Alamy/Barry Lewis: 185; Alamy/Daniel Santos Megina: 123; Alamy/Matthew Oldfield Underwater Photography: 248; Alamy/Mirrorpix/Trinity Mirror: 32; Alamy/Prisma Bildagentur AG: 152; Alamy/Top Photo Corporation: 76; BIG/Glessner Group: 68–69; BrightSource Energy, Inc.: 20–21; Corbis/Alessandra Benedetti (Pope): 66; Corbis/CNP/Ron Sachs (convention): 53; Corbis/Demotix/Shameel Arafin: 189b; Corbis/EPA/Abedin Taherkenareh: 59; Corbis/EPA/Barbara Walton (treaty signing): 60; Corbis/Imaginechina: 134; Corbis/Liu Liqun: 117; Corbis/Minden Pictures/Norbert Wu: 251; Corbis/National Geographic Society/Tino Soriano: 55br; Corbis/National Geographic Society/Lynn Johnson: 89; Corbis/Ocean: 162–163; Corbis/Reuters/Mike Blake: 147; Corbis/Robert Harding Picture Library/Last Refuge: 241; Corbis/Splash News/Christian Mantuano: 144; Corbis/Visuals Unlimited/Paul & Paveena Mckenzie: 193; Corbis/XianPix: 246mr; Corbis/Xinhua Press/Wang Dingchang: 120; Corbis/Xinhua Press/Xia Chen: 246bl; Corbis/ZUMA Press/Koichi Kamoshida: 124; Marcel Croxson: 232–233; DESERTEC Foundation: 16 b; Dreamstime.com/Fiona Ayerst: 159; Dreamstime.com/S. Game: 102; Dreamstime.com/Karagis: 77; Dreamstime.com/Paul Radulescu: 264; Dreamstime.com/Olivier Steiner (cityscape): 48; The Earth Institute, Columbia University, New York/GRT, 2009: 140–141; Getty Images/AFP/Georges Gobet: 156b; Getty Images/Ian Gavan: 98; © Green Belt Movement: 167; iStockphoto.com/Adrian Beesley (landscape): 41; iStockphoto.com/Lorraine Boogich: 168; iStockphoto.com/Jacek Kadaj (landscape): 148; iStockphoto.com/J. Kendall (biorefinery): 41; iStockphoto.com/Elzbieta Sekowska: 23; iStockphoto.com/Simpy Creative Photography (biorefinery): 91; iStockphoto.com/Terraxplorer (Potala Palace): 65; iStockphoto.com/Tony Tremblay: 79; Institute for Science and International Security: 95; Jacques Descloitres, MODIS Rapid Response Team, NASA/GSFC: 154; John Innes Centre – Bioimaging/Andy Davis: 161; Julie Major: 142; KAVE (Keele Active Virtual Environment), Keele University: 174; Kjellgren Kaminsky Architecture: 38; Library of Congress, Washington, D.C.: 18; LIMPET Power Plant – image courtesy of Voith Hydro Wavegen Limited: 242; Marine Stewardship Council: 156t; McCamley UK Ltd (wind turbines) 148; Makerbot® Industries, LLC: 211; Masdar City: 130; MIT/Aurora Flight Sciences: 202–203; NASA/GSFC/METI/ERSDAC/JAROS, and U.S./Japan ASTER Science Team: 26tl; NASA/GSFC/METI/ERSDAC/JAROS, and U.S./Japan ASTER Science Team: 26tr; Copyright OMA: 199; P4P, The Energy, Water and Food security company™ (p4penergy.com), P4P Energy LLC 2013: 108–109; Panos Pictures/Petterik Wiggers: 85; Plantagon, Illustration: Sweco (urban greenhouse): 170–171, 172; Professor Marcelo Jacobs-Lorena, Malaria Research Institute, Johns Hopkins School of Public Health, Baltimore: 181; Rolf Disch Solar Architecture, Freiburg, Germany: 9, (housing) 10–11; SABMiller/Jason Alden/OneRedEye: 194; © Sahara Forest Project Foundation: 212–213; Science Photo Library/Carl Purcell: 186–187; Science Photo Library/Planetobserver: 183; SeymourPowell: 201, 236–237; Shutterstock.com/Robert Biedermann (map): 160; Shutterstock.com/Hywit Dimyadi (sugar cane): 91; Shutterstock.com/ExaMedia Photography: 126; Shutterstock.com/Kentoh: 42; Shutterstock.com/Koh Sze Kiat (religious leaders): 65; Shutterstock.com/Fedor Kondratenko: 31; Shutterstock.com/Inga Nielsen: 271; Shutterstock.com/Jeremy Richards (children): 180; Shutterstock.com/salajean (camera crew): 65; Shutterstock.com/Brandon Seidel (tricycle): 210; Shutterstock.com/Tony Moran (sea wind farm): 148; Shutterstock.com/Jeremy Richards (children): 180; Shutterstock.com/Tribalium (mosquito sign): 178, 180; Skanska (room): 12, 210; SolarSailor, Australia (solar sails): 260–261; Songdo International Business District: 127; Astrid Stavro Studio (digital artworking): 15, 29, 33, 48, 53 (logo), 66, 133, 160, 189t, 243, 244; Still Pictures/Mark Edwards: 113b, 226; Still Pictures/FFI/Juan Pablo Moreiras: 151l,151r; Still Pictures/Imagebroker/Ingo Schulz: 247; Still Pictures/Lineair/Ron Giling: 55bl; Still Pictures/Jorgen Schytte: 19, 221; Cat Vinton, catvphotography.co.uk: 234; United States Department of Energy/Jack W. Aeby: 97; Watercones.com: 107. With additional thanks to The Economist, Green Futures, The Guardian, Newsweek, and Time.

Phaidon Press Limited
Regent's Wharf
All Saints Street
London N1 9PA

Phaidon Press Inc.
180 Varick Street
New York, NY 10014

www.phaidon.com

A CIP record of this book is available from the British Library.

Editorial Manager: Victoria Clarke
Project Editor: Ellen Christie
Production Manager: Paul McGuinness
Picture Researcher: Louise Thomas

Designed by Astrid Stavro
Printed in the UK